Mastery and Slavery in Victorian Writing

Mastery and Slavery in Victorian Writing

Jonathan Taylor

Department of English and Drama
Loughborough University

First published 2003 by
PALGRAVE MACMILLAN
Houndmills, Basingstoke, Hampshire RG21 6XS and
175 Fifth Avenue, New York, N.Y. 10010
Companies and representatives throughout the world.

PALGRAVE MACMILLAN is the global academic imprint of the Palgrave
Macmillan division of St Martin's Press, LLC and of Palgrave Macmillan Ltd.
Macmillan® is a registered trademark in the United States, United Kingdom
and other countries. Palgrave is a registered trademark in the European
Union and other countries.

ISBN 0–333–99312–8

This book is printed on paper suitable for recycling and
made from fully managed and sustained forest sources.

A catalogue record for this book is available
from the British Library.

Library of Congress Cataloging-in-Publication Data

Taylor, Jonathan, 1973-
    Mastery and slavery in Victorian writing / by Jonathan Taylor.
        p. cm.
    Includes bibliographical references and index.
    ISBN 0–333–99312–8 (cloth)
    1. English fiction – 19th century – History and criticism. 2. Servants in
literature. 3. English prose literature – 19th century – History and criticism.
4. Power (Social sciences) in literature. 5. Master and servant in literature.
6. Domestics in literature. 7. Slavery in literature. I. Title.

PR878.S47 T39 2003
823'.809355–dc21

                                                                    2002029891

10 9 8 7 6 5 4 3 2 1
12 11 10 09 08 07 06 05 04 03

Printed and bound in Great Britain by
Antony Rowe Ltd, Chippenham and Eastbourne

This book is dedicated with love to my family –
my Mum, Marilla Taylor, Robin, Anna, Karen, Helen Taylor
and Maria Orthodoxou, and to the memory of my Dad,
John Taylor (1928–2001)

Contents

List of Figures

Acknowledgements

First, let me thank everyone at Palgrave Macmillan, including Becky Mashayekh, Emily Rosser, Eleanor Birne and the reader, for their advice and support. This book started life as a PhD thesis, the research for which was funded by a full scholarship from the Faculty of Social Sciences and Humanities and a bursary from the Department of English and Drama, Loughborough University. Many thanks are due to the academic and administrative staff concerned.

A great debt of gratitude is owed to Dr John Schad, my supervisor, without whose help and time none of this would have been possible, or even conceivable.

Many thanks to Professor Marion Shaw, my director of research, whose guidance was invaluable, and to Professor Bryan Cheyette, my external examiner, and Professor Clare Hanson, head of my department at Loughborough University. Thanks are also due to Dr Bill Overton, Dr Brian Jarvis and Rowland Cotterill for their assistance with various chapters of the book.

Thanks to Deborah Clarke, Sarah Cook, Pauline Higgs and everyone in the Department of English and Drama, Loughborough University, who offered me kindness over five years.

Thanks to Dr Richard McGrady whose original research on Joseph Emidy forms the starting and finishing point for everyone fascinated by this subject.

Thanks to Professor Jonathan Dollimore, Dr Catherine Burgass and all who attended the *Hierarchies* conference in July 2000. Thanks also to Simon King, Andrea Peterson, Caiwen Wang, James Holden, Andrew Cullingford and all the other postgraduate students in the Department of English and Drama.

All those many valued friends who helped me in so many different but invaluable ways during these five years – Laura Smith, Richard Lacquiere, Richard Steed, Gordon Millward, Jennifer Vereker, Lucie Sutherland, Robert and Hiroko Plant, Andrew Pye, Stuart Mulraney, Wendy Daniels, Steve Preston, Jay Millington, Katie Hope, Olwynne Goodrich, Sarah Dutton, Levon Ounanian, Ben Plant, Robert Robinson, Chris Dent, Francis Bowdery, Eric Leveridge and of course Helen Standard – are acknowledged with gratitude.

Thanks and love to all my family: my Grandpa, Albert Kelly; Christopher and his family; Edith and Ernest Jolley, as well as Susan, Raymond and Jill; Jo, Edgar and Christopher Snell, Roberta and Steven Dark; Reni, Steffi Schwarz-Birnbaum and family; and Linda and Asim Bardai and family.

The dedication to my family and Maria Orthodoxou is the best way I have of expressing my love and thanks for them.

Finally, heartfelt thanks for the memories of my Grandma, Margaret Kelly, and of my Aunt, Mildred Whitehead.

Introduction: Master–Slave Relations, Master–Slave Pacts

Masters, slaves and Hegel

> Of the two Self-Consciousnesses opposed to each other ... one
> enters into a condition of Slavery who prefers life to freedom.
>
> G.W.F. Hegel, The Philosophical Propaedeutic[1]

In the *Phenomenology of Spirit* (1807), Hegel sets out in detail his famous
and seminal paradigm of hierarchical relations, the so-called 'Master
and Slave Dialectic'. In a variety of ways, Hegel's dialectic has been
used as a theoretical starting-point or origin in my book, which is more
generally concerned with literary representations of master–slave and
master–servant relationships in works by Thomas Carlyle and others.
For this reason, it is necessary to begin with a short recapitulation and
examination of Hegel's archetypal model.

In the *Phenomenology of Spirit*, the master–slave relation constitutes a
very important stage of the process through which the subject, or Ego,
has to go in order to attain self-consciousness. The initial sections of the
Phenomenology describe various forms of simple consciousness, what
Hegel calls 'sense-certainty' – that is, a knowledge of the world provided
merely by the senses – and 'perception' and 'understanding'.[2] In order to
progress to *self*-consciousness, however, Hegel believes that engagement
with external objects and, ultimately, with another consciousness is necessary. In order to be conscious of self, it is necessary to be conscious of
what is *not*-self. Initially, this engagement with externality takes the form
of 'desire' and a manipulation of independent objects; as Hegel observes,

> self-consciousness is ... certain of itself only by superseding this
> other that presents itself to self-consciousness as an independent

1

life; self-consciousness is Desire. Certain of the nothingness of this other, it explicitly affirms that this nothingness is *for it* the truth of the other.[3]

Peter Singer notes,

> Self-consciousness ... cannot exist in isolation.... It requires an object from which to differentiate itself ... [but] although self-consciousness needs an object outside itself, this external object is also something foreign to it, and a form of opposition to it.... To desire something is to wish to possess it and ... to transform it into something that is yours, and thus to strip it of its foreignness.[4]

The violence inherent in this desire to supersede the object and 'strip it of its foreignness' subsequently informs the next encounter with externality – that between the self-consciousness and another self-consciousness. Since both subjects here try to supersede the other, a struggle emerges between them:

> Self-consciousness is faced by another self-consciousness.... It must proceed to supersede the other independent being in order thereby to become certain of itself as the essential being.... What is 'other' for it is an unessential, negatively characterised object. But the 'other' is also a self-consciousness.... Thus the relation of the two self-conscious individuals is such that they [have to] prove themselves and each other through a life-and-death struggle.[5]

The struggle, then, is an attempt to 'prove' self-consciousness, to gain the limited type of recognition from the other as that afforded by the objects manipulated by desire. It is an attempt to supersede the other in order to prove that the self is the essential self-conscious individual and the other a mere object. What these combatants do not realise, however, is that full recognition is possible only between two equally independent self-consciousnesses: only a free, self-conscious individual – as opposed to a mere object – can properly recognise another subject as a free, self-conscious individual. As Raymond Plant writes:

> desire and its satisfaction transform the objective world and as such contribute an advance in self-consciousness, but an even more significant advance is secured when the individual Ego can gain response not from merely inert reality, but from another free and developed consciousness.[6]

In Hegel's words, 'Self-consciousness exists in and for itself when, and by the fact that, it so exists for another; that is, it exists only in being acknowledged.... [The subjects] *recognise* themselves as *mutually recognising* one another.'[7] Such equal and mutual acknowledgement cannot, though, come about through a 'life-and-death struggle'. Evidently, if either subject dies during the struggle, the other loses the possibility of recognition at the very moment of his/her apparent victory.

> This trial by death ... does away with the truth which was supposed to issue from it, and so, too, with the certainty of self generally.... Death certainly shows that each staked his life and held it of no account ... but that is not for those who survived this struggle. They put an end to their consciousness in its alien setting of natural existence.[8]

According to Hegel, however, there is another possible – and more positive – outcome in which both subjects survive. This is the relation of master and slave, or lord and bondsman, and is instituted by the capitulation of one of the combatants in the struggle. As Plant notes, '[the] struggle for recognition ... reaches an impasse. One side involved in the struggle has to give way; he becomes the slave, the other the master.'[9]

In Hegel's formulation, 'one [subject] is the independent consciousness whose essential nature is to be for itself, the other is the dependent consciousness whose essential nature is simply to live or to be for another'. In other words, the slave's dependent consciousness acknowledges the master's independence and supremacy as a self-conscious individual: 'in this recognition,' Hegel notes, 'the unessential consciousness is for the lord the object, which constitutes the *truth* of his certainty of himself.'[10]

The problem with this relationship, however, is that it does not conform with the definition of reciprocal and equal recognition previously given. Perceived as a mere 'object', the slave's unessential consciousness cannot provide the kind of recognition the master really desires. As Singer writes, 'the master ... has the acknowledgement of the slave, to be sure, but in the eyes of the master the slave is merely a thing, not an independent consciousness at all. The master has, after all, failed to achieve the acknowledgement he requires.'[11] Or, in Hegel's words, 'the object in which the lord has achieved his lordship has in reality turned out to be ... not an independent consciousness but a dependent one. He is, therefore, not certain of *being-for-self* as the truth of himself.' For this reason, Hegel remarks, the lord's 'truth is in reality the unessential consciousness and its unessential action'.[12] That is, the lord's own 'truth' is defined by the servile recognition she or he receives – the lord is really the 'unessential consciousness'.

The slave's or bondsman's truth is also the reverse of what it first appears. As J.N. Findlay suggests, 'the recognition the serf accords to his lord, and the work he does for him, will raise him to a far higher consciousness of active universality than the lord can ever enjoy'.[13] The slave's position is initially defined by his/her fear of death – expressed most obviously by surrender during the struggle – and by his/her subsequently being set to work by the master. But it is precisely by virtue of these two experiences of fear and work that, over time, the slave gains self-certainty and 'a far higher consciousness of active universality'. Through fear of death, Hegel writes, the slave unconsciously realises

> its own essential nature ... [whilst] through work ... the bondsman becomes conscious of what he truly is.... The bondsman realises that it is precisely in his work wherein he seemed to have only an alienated existence that he acquires a mind of his own.[14]

By experiencing the fear of death, the slave realises the significance of life; through work, as Richard Norman makes clear, 'the slave ... realises himself and objectifies himself.... In shaping and forming the natural world, he can find in the product of his work an objective and lasting expression of his own identity.'[15] The slave, that is, finds in the product of his/her work an external and objective expression of self-consciousness and identity. In this way, the dialectical relation of master and slave is eventually overturned, the master being subsumed into the position of slave, the slave working towards mastery and freedom.

Masters, slaves and history

> While the ante-historical is that which precedes political life, it also lies beyond self-cognizant life.
>
> (Hegel, *The Philosophy of History*)[16]

What the *Phenomenology of Spirit* never makes explicit is any historical, political or contextual application for the 'Master–Slave Dialectic'. Nevertheless, even its placing in the work as a whole carries with it certain implications. Whilst the sections of the *Phenomenology* up to and including the 'Master–Slave Dialectic' seem rather abstract and ahistorical, the subsequent section moves on to a discussion of a specifically historical movement: 'Stoicism', As Singer notes,

> the section on master and slave is followed by a discussion of Stoicism, a philosophical school that became important under the Roman Empire and included among its leading writers both Marcus Aurelius the Emperor, and Epictetus, a slave. Stoicism therefore bridges the gulf between master and slave. In Stoicism the ... slave ... can find a type of freedom; for Stoicism teaches withdrawal from the external world – in which the slave remains a slave – and retreat into one's own consciousness.[17]

Whilst not representing an entirely successful form of freedom for the slave, Stoicism is portrayed as one of the end-points of mastery and slavery because, through the experiences afforded by slavery, it has become possible for the slave to withdraw into his/her own consciousness. Previously, this has not been possible precisely because such consciousness has not been fully formed. In short, for Hegel, the master–slave relationship represents a formative moment of transition in which self-consciousness comes into being.

If, in the *Phenomenology*, the implication is that this moment occurs at a point anterior to the philosophical self-consciousness and self-absorption of the Stoics, many of Hegel's other works locate the master–slave relationship in different historical contexts. In *The Philosophy of History* (1831), for example, Hegel attempts to systematise a geographical view of history, according to which the master–slave relation is associated, in different ways, with Africa and certain Asian states. Since, according to Hegel, Africa as a whole is 'no historical part of the World' and has never progressed beyond what he calls the '"Natural condition"', enslavement for the Africans themselves has been 'the occasion of the increase of human feeling.... Slavery is a phase of advance from [their] ... merely isolated sensual existence – a phase of education – a mode of becoming participant in a higher morality and the culture connected with it'. As the beginning of self-consciousness, slavery is, for Africa, the beginning of history, morality and human development. Otherwise, Africa in general has 'no movement or development to exhibit'.[18]

In contrast, parts of Asia, or 'the East', have as a whole progressed into the initial stages of history, political life and self-consciousness, whereby entire states are founded on a system of mastery and slavery. As Hegel writes, 'with China and the Mongols – the realm of theocratic despotism – History begins.... In China the Monarch is Chief as Patriarch.... All that we call subjectivity is concentrated in the supreme head of that State.'[19] Similarly, in the *Lectures on the History of Philosophy* (1840), Hegel asserts that 'finitude of the will characterises the orientals, because with them the will has not yet grasped itself as universal, for thought is not yet free for itself. Hence there can but be the relation of lord and slave.'[20]

For Hegel, 'the orientals' are stuck in what should be merely a first, transitional stage of historical development. Surpassing this stage is, apparently, the prerogative of the Western world; as Hegel insists in the *History of Philosophy*, 'the blessedness of the West is thus so determined that ... [the] people ... know themselves as free.... We [in the West] ... know our real Being in so far as personal freedom is its first condition, and hence we never can be slaves.'[21] None the less, elsewhere Hegel contradicts this extreme claim. In *The Philosophy of History*, for instance, he argues that 'every intermediate grade between [the "Natural condition"] ... and the realisation of a rational State retains ... elements and aspects of injustice; therefore we find slavery even in the Greek and Roman States, as we do serfdom down to the latest times.'[22] Despite his claim in the *History of Philosophy*, Hegel acknowledges here that versions of the master–slave relation exist even in contemporary Western society.

Indeed, what underlies Hegel's view of this relation is the anxiety that, perhaps, it cannot be superseded, but rather is to be found everywhere and traced 'down to the latest times'. When Jean-Paul Sartre remarks of Hegel's dialectic that 'slavery is not a historical result, capable of being surmounted ... [but] the permanent structure of my being-for-others',[23] he is pointing out something that is latent in Hegel's own texts. In the *Elements of the Philosophy of Right* (1821), Hegel writes that 'slavery occurs in the transitional phase between natural human existence and the truly ethical condition' attainable only in the state which is 'in and for itself ... [an] ethical whole, the actualisation of freedom'.[24] It is clear, though, that Hegel is talking here of his ideal 'rational State' and that, in the nineteenth century, this ideal has yet to be realised; so the nineteenth century is still in the 'transitional phase' in which various forms of the master–slave relation are perpetuated *even* in the Western world. After all, just as serfdom was not abolished in Russia until 1863, the slave-trade was conducted legally through British ports until 1808, and slavery itself was not abolished in the British colonies until 1833 and in the United States until 1863. Furthermore, in the *Elements of the Philosophy of Right*, Hegel makes what is, for this book, a vitally important comparison between slavery and modern servitude; he attempts to draw a

> distinction ... between a slave and a modern servant.... The Athenian slave perhaps had easier tasks and more intellectual work to perform than our servants normally do, but he was nevertheless a slave, because the entire scope of his activity had been alienated to his master.[25]

Merely by making this distinction, Hegel is simultaneously comparing and equating modern servitude and Athenian slavery, but it is clear that the distinction breaks down anyway, in that nineteenth-century depictions of servitude often seem to imply that 'the entire scope' of a servant's activity, like a slave's, is 'alienated to his master'. For many servants of the time, according to Wilkie Collins, 'life means dirty work, small wages, hard words, no holidays, no social station, no future'.[26]

It is self-evident that various forms of slavery existed in the nineteenth century, and that domestic servitude often bore traces of slavery. What is important to note here, though, is the applicability of Hegel's view of mastery and slavery not only to some pre-historical moment but also to the modern world and the modern state. What Hegel implies in his many different conceptualisations and recontextualisations of the master–slave relation is that it is somehow 'the permanent structure of ... being-for-others'.

Chapter 1 ('Capitalists, Castrators and Criminals') is an investigation of Hegel's implication and Sartre's claim in this regard. As I argue there, in highlighting this implication, I am not wholly agreeing with it and taking Hegel to be correct for all times and all places. Rather, I use the 'Master–Slave Dialectic' as a theoretical point of departure to discuss how and why certain nineteenth-century literary portrayals of hierarchical relations seem at once both to appropriate *and* complicate Hegel's discourse. In other words, I am concerned with points of intersection and, perhaps even more importantly, points of divergence between literary texts, historical moments and Hegel's dialectic.

Indeed, what I find throughout my study is that Hegel's dialectic is a particularly useful means of analysing discourses which at once assimilate the Hegelian notion of a one-to-one, violent hierarchy, but which also diverge from, and even undermine, this model. Accordingly, the study focuses on liminal historical and literary moments, which show that the kind of individualised, 'life-and-death' relationship Hegel describes is in the process of being transformed into something different. In short, as a 'transitional phase', Hegel's 'Master–Slave Dialectic' lends itself to the investigation of other transitional phases.

Chapter 2 ('"Servants' Logic" and Analytical Chemistry'), for instance, explores some of the ways in which a feudal, one-to-one, master–servant relationship is gradually subsumed during the nineteenth century into a more generalised, inter-class relation.

Chapter 3 ('Slaveholders and Democrats') illustrates how a Hegelian myth of mastery and slavery is at once appropriated and complicated in antebellum America during the liminal period between the abolition of the slave-trade and the abolition of slavery as a whole.

Likewise, Chapter 4 ('Heroes, Hero-Worshippers and Jews') investigates the ways in which the Romantic myth of the master-musician as revolutionary hero was gradually modified by the post-revolutionary, bourgeois era of the later nineteenth century.

In designating these moments as 'transitional phases', I am not arguing that what comes after supersedes or wholly overcomes the master–slave relation. Rather, the chapters pinpoint and analyse a number of turning-points in the history of slavery and servitude for which the myth of an individualised, 'life-and-death' master–slave relation was still vital, but which also marked an attempt to move away from this model into other, emergent discourses of domination. These very various discourses are formed, or framed, by all sorts of nineteenth-century developments, among them bourgeois democracy, the collectivisation of labour, *laissez-faire* economics, middle-class hegemony, racial supremacism and so-called 'free-trade' imperialism. In this way, the study is concerned not only with the historical turning-points in themselves, but also with the before and after which are competing within those moments.

Just as my argument takes as its starting point Hegel's dialectic and, indeed, the early nineteenth-century context in which Hegel's dialectic was produced, it is also critically concerned with what, during the later nineteenth century, seems to come *after* Hegelian modes of mastery and slavery. Chapter 4, for instance, moves from an exposition of the mythical and *pseudo*-Hegelian origins of music mastery as posited by various nineteenth-century writers, to a discussion of the ambivalent position of the emergent class of professional musicians in Victorian England, to a speculative and metaphorical analysis of the ways in which the 'mastery' wielded by late nineteenth-century musicians becomes increasingly identified with capitalist, bourgeois democracy. Similarly, Chapter 3 combines an analysis of the trans-Atlantic slave-trade, the actual Southern slave system and the white supremacy of post-Civil War America – and this is almost inevitable, given the fact that many of the works under consideration do the same. Chapters 3 and 4 end with a discussion of how democratic forms of power relate to Hegelian concepts of mastery and slavery. In this way, the study attempts to show that, for various contemporary writers, bourgeois nineteenth-century democracy did not represent merely the end-point or antithesis of the master–slave relation, despite many such claims. Indeed, though many of the discourses of domination cited above – democracy, free-trade imperialism, *laissez-faire* economics and politics – are frequently defined in opposition to the master–slave relation, my study investigates the ways in which these 'end-points' are also transitional phases, still haunted by Hegelian modes of mastery and slavery. It hardly needs pointing out that post-1833 colonialism, whilst appearing to many contemporaries to represent a break with the master–slave relation, perpetuated that relation in other guises. As Patrick Brantlinger remarks, 'paradoxically, abolitionism contained the seeds of empire'.[27] This failed, or fake, conclusion to the master–slave relation is discussed further in the 'Afterword'.

In its secondary discussion of *supposed* end-points to mastery and slavery, the main emphasis of this study is on the rise of democracy in the nineteenth century. This can be justified in various ways. Whilst much recent and invaluable work has investigated the modes of racial slavery perpetuated by imperialism and colonialism, this study seeks to (re-)cover new ground by analysing the ways in which certain kinds of mastery and slavery were seen to be perpetuated or eroded by the movement towards democracy. This movement, after all, constitutes one of the great themes of theorists as diverse as diverse as Hegel, Thomas Carlyle, J.S. Mill, Richard Wagner, Alexis de Tocqueville and Leo Tolstoy.

Furthermore, the emphasis on images of democracy is justified by the Hegelian context of the book as a whole; as a means of purportedly superseding the master–slave relation, democracy is peculiarly open to comparisons with the solution to mastery and slavery proposed by Hegel himself – that is, mutual recognition. Generally speaking, Hegel denies the connection between recognition and modern democracy, but the link, whether intended or not, between an egalitarian state where all subjects '*recognise* themselves as *mutually recognising*' one another' and the ideal of democracy is an obvious one, as is shown in the recent (if problematic) work of Francis Fukayama. He argues that, 'for Hegel ... liberal society is a reciprocal and equal agreement among citizens to mutually recognise each other.... Life in a liberal democracy ... shows us the way to the ... end of recognition of our freedom.'[28] As one of the 'end-points' of this study, Chapter 5 investigates this vision of democracy-as-mutual-recognition, and how it is appropriated in portrayals of populist mastery and majoritarian rule by Carlyle and Dickens.

Arguing in these ways for (and against) the general applicability of Hegel's philosophical models makes it necessary to acknowledge that many possible subjects of discussion will be sidelined; in selecting certain aspects of post-Hegelian mastery and slavery, I necessarily must sideline others. Issues of race, class, nationhood and imperialism are raised without being the main focus of the book. Similarly, though Chapter 1 explores some of the possible connections between notions of masculinity, femininity and Hegel's dialectic, the subjects of gender and, indeed, the Victorian patriarchal family do not receive extensive treatment. My hope is that, by demonstrating the applicability of Hegel's paradigms to certain specific literary and historical contexts, my book will gesture towards other possible contexts and connections which might, indeed, be the basis for future thought and work.

Masters, slaves and pacts

> In the end, the loser must not perish if he is to become a slave. In other words, the pact [between master and slave] is everywhere anterior to the violence before perpetuating it.
>
> (Jacques Lacan, *Écrits*)[29]

This study is not only an argument *for* the general flexibility and applicability of Hegel's 'Master–Slave Dialectic', it is also an argument *with* Hegel's abstract schematisation. In *Écrits*, Lacan points out what he calls Hegel's 'error in the *Phenomenology*',[30] an error that seems to originate in Hegel's conflation of death and surrender. For Hegel, 'victory' in the life-and-death struggle means *either* the death of the other, or the other's enslavement: mastery over the slave seems to be the same as mastery over death. What Lacan suggests, however, is that these two types of mastery are fundamentally different, since it is obvious that 'the loser must not perish if he is to become a slave'.

Hegel's attempt to equate death-mastery with slave-mastery is untenable even according to his own logic. He describes slave-mastery as 'that ... which supersedes in such a way as to preserve and maintain what is superseded, and consequently survives its own supersession'. Here, the slave, though superseded, *does* survive; but this survival is irreconcilable with Hegel's description of the life-and-death struggle, which constitutes the moment of supersession and enslavement. In a life-and-death struggle, according to Hegel, it is necessary that, 'just as each stakes his own life, so each must seek the other's death'.[31] On this definition, however, mastery and slavery are impossible, since any kind of capitulation implies an unwillingness on the part of the slave to stake his/her life wholly, just as any acceptance of that surrender implies that the master was never wholly seeking the slave's death. Conversely, the slave is not seeking the master's death by submitting, and, by accepting that submission, the master shows that he was never staking his own life. Surrender necessarily exposes the absence of a genuine struggle of life-and-death; or, to put this another way, mastery and slavery ironically depend on the *non*-existence of a total life-and-death struggle. The only possible result of a real life-and-death struggle is the death of the other, an eventuality that, as we have seen, renders mastery, slavery and even consciousness inconceivable. Lacan's comment that 'one may ask oneself whether murder is the absolute Master'[32] points up the irony of Hegel's position. According to Hegel's scheme, the death of the other is presupposed by a life-and-death struggle, but such mastery becomes, at the moment of its achievement, obsolete and nonsensical. Rather, the master–slave hierarchy is structured as a mutual agreement on the part of the opposing parties to avoid the death of either. This is why, as Lacan notes, 'the pact [between master and slave] is everywhere anterior to the violence', which Hegel sees as its origin. As Lacan points out, this is a false origin, for a pact must always already be in place. The establishment of the master–slave hierarchy necessarily involves the deferment, perhaps indefinitely, of the life-and-death struggle.

This is not to underestimate the terrible violence possible *within* the master–slave hierarchy. By emphasising the master–slave *pact*, instead of its origin, Lacan refers to a different kind of violence–a contingent, rather than absolute, violence which the pact 'perpetuates'. Mastery and slavery are mediated by types of violence that are *un*-Hegelian, that do not necessarily depend on either party self-consciously staking his/her life or seeking the death of the other–types of violence that are often designed to reinforce the pact and prevent the slave from bringing forward a life-and-death struggle.

It is with these types of violence, these techniques of an *un*-Hegelian mastery, that this book is partly concerned. Chapter 1 discusses how, in Wilkie Collins' *The Woman in White* (1859–60), Count Fosco maintains his position of power by continually threatening a life-and-death struggle which he does not and perhaps cannot realise, the violence of Fosco's power being specifically psychological. Chapter 3 refers to various literary representations of slavery in nineteenth-century America, and shows how the perpetuation of such slavery is dependent on the deferral of a Hegelian confrontation. William Lloyd Garrison implies this kind of deferral in his 'Preface' to Frederick Douglass's *Narrative* (1845), when he notes that 'whips, chains, thumb-screws, paddles, bloodhounds, overseers, drivers, patrols [are] ... all indispensable to keep the slaves down, and to give protection to their ruthless oppressors!'[33] Keeping slaves down with the violence of control is a way of avoiding confrontation rather than seeking it; this kind of un-Hegelian violence is used precisely as a means of avoiding the murderous – and perhaps *revolutionary* – violence of a master–slave or inter-class life-and-death struggle.

Here, there is an important connection to be made with Marxian notions of revolution. Though the life-and-death struggle seems to vanish as the originary past of mastery and slavery, Marx posits a version of it as the future, or end, of all hierarchical relationships. In this, he is echoing in socio-materialist terms the *end* of Hegel's dialectic. As he writes in *The Communist Manifesto* (1848):

> the history of all hitherto existing society is the history of class struggles. Freeman and slave, patrician and plebeian, lord and serf, guild-master and journeyman, in a word, oppressor and oppressed, stood in constant opposition to one another, carried on [a] ... now hidden, now open fight, a fight that *each time ended ... in a revolutionary reconstitution of society*.[34]

For Marx, mastery is always heading *towards* its own overthrow in the life-and-death struggle of revolution. So, for example, the mastery of the nineteenth-century bourgeoisie must necessarily be moving towards destruction by the proletariat. Marx envisages the inevitable victory on the part of the proletariat in terms of the non-mastery of Communism:

> All the preceding classes that got the upper hand sought to fortify their ... status by subjecting society at large to their conditions of appropriation. The proletarians cannot become masters ... except by abolishing ... every other previous mode of appropriation.[35]

As with Hegel's model, though, there is another problem here, which is betrayed by Marx's association of Communism with proletarian *mastery*. If the proletarians are to 'become masters', their mastery will depend on the end of revolutionary struggle and the re-establishment of a form of class hegemony, albeit rule by 'the immense majority'.[36] The future rule of the proletariat cannot be absolute mastery for the same reason that renders all mastery contingent, temporary and relative. In Lacan's terms, any form of mastery must be seen as a pact that at once ends and belies the struggle which brought it into being. Put another way, Marx's teleological view of the history of hierarchies is only an adaptation of Hegel's originary model.

To posit an end is, of course, also to posit an origin; though each class opposition ends in an 'open fight', this fight also marks the 'reconstitution of society' and hence the re-establishment of a pact between a different set of oppressors and oppressed. This reconstitution of mastery after revolution retrospectively renders the revolution itself meaningless: the revolution was not a life-and-death struggle after all, because mastery is still possible after it, and thus that post-revolutionary mastery itself cannot be absolute in a Hegelian sense. Only at the moment of revolution can that revolution rightly be considered a genuine life-and-death struggle.

In the twentieth century, this problem with Marx's scheme can be understood as the theoretical difference between Trotsky and Stalin. Trotsky attempts to avoid the problem of origins and ends by appealing to 'permanent revolution ... which makes no compromise with any form of class rule ... which goes over to socialist measures and to war against the reaction from without ... which [involves] the complete liquidation of all class society'.[37] Stalinism, on the other hand, is defined by C. Wright Mills in terms of a 'consolidation',[38] which involves the mastery of the proletariat over the bourgeoisie, not the 'liquidation of all class society'. As Stalin writes, 'The dictatorship of the proletariat [is] ... the domination of the proletariat over the bourgeoisie [and is] ... based on violence against the bourgeoisie.'[39]

Nineteenth-century forms of mastery can be seen as a similar post-revolutionary 'consolidation' or pact. Just as Stalinism seems to render the Bolshevik Revolution meaningless, Napoleon Bonaparte's imperial coronation can be seen as a refutation of the French Revolution he had represented. In his book *Heroes and Hero-Worship* (1840), Carlyle distinguishes between Napoleon as revolutionary hero and Napoleon as 'charlatan':

> Through [Napoleon's] ... brilliant Italian Campaigns ... one would say, his inspiration is: 'Triumph to the French Revolution'.... Through Wagrams, Austerlitzes; triumph after triumph, – he triumphed so far.... He rose naturally to be the King ... [and to] Chief-consulship, Emperorship, [achieving] victory over Europe.... But at this point, I think, the fatal charlatan-element got the upper hand. He ... strove to connect himself with Austrian Dynasties, Popedoms, with the old false Feudalities ... [and] considered that *he* would found 'his Dynasty' and so forth; that the enormous French Revolution meant only that! ... His ceremonial Coronations, consecrations by the old Italian chimera ... 'wanting nothing to complete the pomp of it,' as Augereau said, '... but the half-million of men who had died to put an end to all that!'

Napoleonism is, in retrospect, 'a flash as of gunpowder wide-spread.... For an hour the whole Universe seems wrapt in smoke and flame; but only for an hour. [Eventually] it goes out.'[40] For Carlyle and many of his contemporaries, Napoleon is an emblematic figure for all subsequent forms of mastery in the nineteenth century. As a hero who achieved 'victory over Europe', he is repeatedly appropriated as a reference point for and by subsequent *pseudo*-masters. In *The Woman in White*, for instance, Fosco attempts to establish his mastery by declaring, '"I personally resemble Napoleon the Great."'[41] At the same time, Napoleon is paradigmatic in another sense: his assumption of 'Emperorship' in 1804 exemplifies and prefigures the bourgeoisie's retreat from revolutionary forms of power throughout the nineteenth century. For Carlyle, Napoleon is emblematic of the nineteenth century as *both* a revolutionary hero *and* as a post-revolutionary charlatan. After each revolution, the bourgeoisie retreated from a revolutionary identity and a revolutionary alliance with the proletariat, seeking instead to re-establish and *consolidate* a class hegemony of their own.

During its struggle with the old feudal order, the bourgeoisie had 'played a most revolutionary part' in which, according to Marx, it was 'compelled to set the whole proletariat in motion ... [to] fight ... the remnants of absolute monarchy'.[42] Following victory, however, this revolutionary identity was discarded; as Bruce Robbins remarks, after 'the bourgeoisie ... achieved hegemony [it] ... began to fear the militant masses beneath it'.[43] There are many historical moments which, like 1804, can be seen to mark this retreat, including 1815, the year of the Congress of Vienna; 1832, the year of the first Reform Act; 1834, the year the 'Tolpuddle Martyrs' were convicted; 1848, the year the Chartist Movement collapsed; 1849, following the European revolutions of 1848; 1852, the year Louis Napoleon was made Emperor of France; and so on.

The difficulty of isolating one particular date must necessarily bring into question Carlyle's, Marx's and Hegel's respective attempts to differentiate between revolution and post-revolutionary consolidation. According to Lacan, mastery is always already involved in a post-revolutionary pact. This is true for both Victorian England and nineteenth-century France. Victorian England had to look back as far as 1648 for a revolutionary origin, an origin that was negated by the Restoration in 1660; nineteenth-century France only had to look back to 1789, but Napoleon's subsequent enthronement as Emperor seemed, to many writers, to undermine and bring into question the transcendental meaning of the Revolution and the Revolutionary Terror which had preceded it.

Such suspicion is encoded even within Carlyle's assessment of Napoleon as 'our last Great Man'. That is, Carlyle suspects that the later Napoleon's charlatanism retrospectively invalidates the earlier Napoleon's revolutionary and heroic identity: 'He was a great *ébauche*,' writes Carlyle, 'a rude-draught never completed; as indeed what great man is other? Left in *too* rude a state, alas!'[44] In other words, Carlyle's description of Napoleon's 'Coronation' implies – perhaps unwittingly – a common nineteenth-century fear that any kind of revolutionary overturning is *just* an overturning, and merely involves the re-establishment of charlatanism and sham-mastery. In *Latter-Day Pamphlets* (1850), Carlyle writes of the aftermath of the 1848 revolutions:

> Some remounting – very temporary remounting, – of the old machine, under new colours and altered forms, will probably ensue soon in most countries: the old histrionic Kings will be admitted back under conditions, under 'Constitutions,' with national Parliaments ... and everywhere the old daily life will try to begin again. But there is now no hope that such arrangements ... can be other than poor temporary makeshifts.[45]

Carlyle outlines here a framework within which various kinds of nine-teenth-century mastery can be understood. Though new, many forms of mastery in the nineteenth century appeal for legitimation to *past* hierarchies, despite the fact that these past hierarchies have supposedly been discredited.

As we shall see in Chapter 2, Dickens' *Our Mutual Friend* (1865) pro-vides an example of this in the Veneerings' 'temporary' financial mastery, which represents both an overturning of the old order – in so far as they are socially aspiring, *nouveaux-riches* members of the bour-geoisie – *and* an appropriation of those older forms of mastery. Though 'bran-new people in a bran-new house', the Veneerings use the trap-pings of feudal mastery in an attempt to legitimise their own status. As Dickens writes, 'All their furniture was new, all their friends were new, all their servants were new, their plate was new, their carriage was new, their harness was new, their horses were new, their pictures were new.'[46] Such mastery is deconstructed by its impossibly paradoxical nature: though the very existence of bourgeois mastery depends on the overthrow of the old order, this new mastery also becomes dependent on reference to past forms in order to legitimise itself. It is in this sense that all mastery must render meaningless the revolutions which brought them into being, just as those revolutions render all preceding and subsequent forms of mastery meaningless.

Carlyle's heroes are often caught in similar paradoxes. Though Carlyle *seems* to be attempting to distinguish between Napoleon's revolutionary heroics and subsequent reconstitution of feudal mastery post-1804, he does not maintain this opposition consistently. Napoleon blatantly did not rise *through* 'Wagrams and Austerlitzes … to be the King', since these battles (in 1805 and 1809 respectively) followed his coronation as Emperor. Likewise, even during what Carlyle calls 'his first period', Napoleon is both a revolutionary hero *and* an embodiment of past heroes: in the soldier Napoleon, Carlyle claims, 'the old ages are brought back to us'.[47] Carlyle undermines Napoleon's revolutionary signification at the very moment of establishing it; Napoleon can be a hero or master only as long as he is not a hero or master. Like the Veneerings, Napoleon is always already both 'bran-new' *and* a reconstruction of past mastery. For Carlyle, Napoleon is a hero in so far as 'his inspiration is: "Triumph to the French Revolution; [and] assertion of it against these [feudal and imperial] Austrian Simulacra"', but he is also a re-embodiment of the mastery he is trying to destroy even whilst destroying it. Carlyle asserts that 'hero-worship exists for ever, and everywhere',[48] thus attempting to *de*historicise heroism and mastery. But this dehistoricisation is inconsistent with his claim that Napoleon is 'our last Great Man'. In this sense, all reference to heroism and hero-worship *must* be a reference to the past, so a revolutionary hero is an impossibility, a contradiction in terms. All the eternal truths of heroism are also references to a past, but this past has been discredited by these revolutionary heroes. Carlyle acknowledges that 'many of our late Heroes have worked ... as revolutionary men',[49] but this means that many (if not all) of Carlyle's heroes are impossible paradoxes like Napoleon. What underlies Carlyle's work is an anxiety that all of his heroes might just be impossibilities – that every single one of them might actually just be what he calls a 'sham-master' or 'Sham-Hero'.[50] If Carlyle is constantly comparing the sham-master with the genuine hero, what underlies such a comparison is the anxiety that 'in *all* of us [a] ... charlatan-element exists'.[51] In a revolutionary hero like Napoleon, the charlatan-element consists precisely in his reference to the past; he is a *sham*-master because he is a *past* master.

Carlyle's system can accommodate the notion of the sham-master precisely because he acknowledges the element of the 'pact' that Lacan finds in the master–slave relationship, but which Hegel generally omits. Carlyle had certainly come across Hegel's work and was heavily influenced by German Idealism and Romanticism in general, if not by Hegel in particular, but his writings also modify these early nineteenth-century writers' models and point towards later, *post*-Romantic, *post*-Idealist theories of mastery, slavery and history.[52] Whereas, in the *System of Ethical Life* (1802-3) Hegel asserts that 'there is no contract [possible] with the slave',[53] Carlyle admits in *Chartism* (1839) that 'conquest ... never yet went by brute force and compulsion [alone].... Conquest, along with power of compulsion, must bring benefit along with it, or men ... will fling it out.'[54] For Carlyle, the potentially subversive gap between absolute mastery and slave-mastery in Hegel's scheme is ideally filled by a (pseudo-) Christian notion of right: true mastery is based on a pact of 'might and right'. He declares that 'might and right, so frightfully discrepant at first, are ever in the long-run one and the same'.[55] It is this element of 'right' in mastery which induces the slave to accept the master–slave pact. Indeed, for Carlyle, it is right which ideally constitutes this pact and represents the 'benefit' brought to those conquered by the conqueror. It is in this way that the master can be said to be the people's 'servant,' as Carlyle repeatedly emphasises in *Past and Present* (1843).[56]

Evidently, such a formulation has overt Christian resonances: for the Victorians, Jesus Christ would be the most obvious example of a 'servant-master' in this sense. Christ may, though, lack 'might' for

Carlyle, so it is to Oliver Cromwell that he looks for an ideal combination of heroic might and Christian right. Cromwell's life-and-death
struggle is seen as a religious, philosophical and revolutionary fight:
'He stood bare,' writes Carlyle, '[and] grappled like a giant, face to face,
heart to heart, with the naked truth of things!' Carlyle's Cromwell is a
felicitous combination of 'Virtue, *Vir-tus*, manhood, *hero*-hood ...
Courage and the Faculty to *do*.'[57]

In this way, Carlyle's creed of hero-worship represents a moment of
mediation between Hegel's belief in absolute mastery and Lacan's
absolute scepticism. He seeks to make transcendental the 'great men'
by Christianising the pact Lacan detects in all master–slave relations.
Cromwell is a hero because he not only unleashes revolutionary force,
but uses that force to impose Christian order on England:

> He ... fought and strove, like a strong, true giant of a man, through
> cannon-tumult and all else.... *He* stood there as the strongest soul of
> England, the undisputed Hero of all England, – what of this? It was
> possible that the Law of Christ's Gospel could now establish itself in
> the world! The Theocracy which John Knox in his pulpit might
> dream of ... this practical man ... dared to consider as capable of
> being *realised*.[58]

The difficulty for Carlyle is that this kind of 'theocracy' so easily slips
into sham-mastery. Once Hegel's absolute mastery is modified by a
master–slave 'pact', mastery becomes dependent on absolute notions of
right. Without absolute force, mastery can avoid being a 'sham' only
by reference to another absolute code. This is the unacknowledged
problem with Carlyle's reference to 'might and right'. If Carlylean
mastery is not to be merely relative and contingent, it must refer to a
Romantic notion of 'Nature' in order to legitimise transcendental
forms of mastery – and, at the same time, to damn sham-mastery:

> The Noble in the high place, the Ignoble in the low; that is, in all
> times and in all countries, the Almighty Maker's Law. To raise the
> Sham-Noblest ... this ... is, in all times and countries, a practical
> blasphemy, and Nature will in no wise forget it.[59]

Indeed, it would seem that any kind of 'Monarchy' or 'Hierarchy'
always needs to base its discourses on some form of transcendentalised
code or 'Almighty Maker's Law' in order to maintain itself, and it is
with these discourses that this book is concerned. Chapter 2, for
example, discusses George Eliot's middle-class servant-mastery in terms

of her transcendentalisation of 'reason'. Chapter 3 discusses how American slavery was often justified by reference to a transcendental and progressive Hegelian history; and Chapter 5 describes how many forms of nineteenth-century industrial mastery depended on a perception of democracy as an end in itself.

The problem with these transcendentalised discourses, these Victorian dreams of an absolutely rightful mastery, is the problem with *any* notions of absolute right in a post-revolutionary, post-feudal, post-Romantic, post-Christian England. At times, Carlyle seems acutely aware of this problem; for instance, it is not surprising, in this context, that he spends most of the section on Cromwell in *Heroes and Hero-Worship* defending his hero against accusations of 'Falsity and Fatuity ... "hypocrisy," "ambition," [and] "cant".' '"Detect Quacks?"' he asks, 'Yes do, for Heaven's sake; but know withal the men that are to be trusted!'[60] The opposition, though, between 'quack' and 'the men ... to be trusted' is remarkably insecure, as the example of Cromwell illustrates. Carlylean heroes are, like Cromwell, always unstable compromises of might and right, dependent as they are on a transcendental, divine order. Indeed, the instability becomes even more obvious when, later in his career, Carlyle finds himself writing not only in a post-revolutionary, post-feudal, post-Romantic, post-Christian England, but, furthermore, in a *post-Darwinian* England. For a writer whose views of mastery depend on a divinely ordered and hierarchical Nature, Darwinian Nature is obviously a peculiarly subversive concept, as Carlyle himself seems to recognise in a posthumously-published essay entitled 'Last Words of Thomas Carlyle: On Trades-Unions, Promoterism and the Signs of the Times' (1882). Attacking that ultra-capitalist sham-master, the 'Promoter', Carlyle writes:

Who knows? If Atheism be the real religion and Last gospel of Mankind; if right and wrong be mere association of Ideas; and the true Beginning of us a kind of Blubber, or Protoplasm (which the Nettles also have in common); if we all were at one time Apes and even Oysters, and animalcules, who (chiefly by judicious choice in marriage it appears) rose to this stupendous pitch of humanhood and civilisation, – may not, to a poor necessitous Promoter, this peculiar Life-theory of his, with the like Life-praxis superadded, be truly the natural one?[61]

In a post-Darwinian world, it is the 'Life-theory' of sham-mastery that is 'the natural one'. It is sham-mastery that is sanctioned by Darwinian nature, not genuine mastery.

This admission, though, is a rare one for Carlyle, who usually tries to repress what Lacan and others suggest – the fear that *all* masters and heroes are in some way shams, that *all* heroism and mastery are necessarily based on 'cunning tricks (*ruses*)'.[62] Eric Bentley asserts that 'Carlyle's hero wears a halo, but his name is Machiavelli'.[63] What underlies Carlyle's deification or sanctification of the hero is the anxiety that the element of 'right' *might* be just another ruse to maintain hierarchical structures. Just as Cromwell *might* just be a 'premeditative ever-calculating hypocrite, acting a play before the world', so Napoleon 'believed too much in the *Dupeability* of men'.[64] All the other nineteenth-century discourses of mastery can be seen as mere ruses, which seek to 'dupe' the other into a master–slave pact. Though Carlyle argues that 'Universal History ... is at bottom the History of the Great Men who have worked here',[65] Carlylean history can also be read as the history of sham-masters who have duped others. What is so significant about Carlyle's notion of sham-mastery is its implications for a Hegelian view of history, implications which, again, Lacan points out. If power is only ever contingent, never absolute, if revolution is merely overturning, and thus continuation of sham-mastery in another form, the Hegelian and Marxian dialectical view of historical progress becomes inconceivable. For Hegel, the master–slave relationship represents an originary dialectic from which the vast historical dialectics he describes develop. As Norman observes, 'the relationship of master and slave is seen as a first step from the state of nature to social life'.[66] What Carlyle, perhaps unwittingly, gestures towards, however, is a different, static history which merely staggers from one, mediated and contingent sham-mastery to another. Time and again, Carlyle foreshadows the twentieth and twenty-first centuries in which dialectical histories and the progress they imply have become viewed with increasing scepticism.

1
Capitalists, Castrators and Criminals: Violent Masters and Slaves in Wilkie Collins' *The Woman in White*

> The fight for recognition, in its extreme form, can only occur in the natural state, where men exist as single, separate individuals; but it is absent in civil society and the State because here the recognition for which the combatants fought already exists.
>
> (G.W.F. Hegel, *Philosophy of Mind*)[1]

> Slavery is not a historical result, capable of being surmounted.... [It is] the permanent structure of my being-for-others.
>
> (Jean-Paul Sartre, *Being and Nothingness*)[2]

In his 'Master and Slave Dialectic' (1807), Hegel argues that the slave becomes a slave after capitulating in a 'life-and-death struggle'[3] with the master; mastery and slavery, for Hegel, are constituted by, and as, absolute violence. In the *Philosophy of Mind* (1830), Hegel locates this kind of mastery and slavery in the ancient past, positing the life-and-death struggle as an originary moment of history; here, he argues that violent forms of mastery and slavery are absent from the modern state, which has surpassed them. As Richard Norman writes, 'the relationship of master and slave is seen as a first step from the state of nature to social life, typifying the societies of the ancient world, but subsequently giving way to a form of society in which all men are recognised as free.' In *Being and Nothingness* (1943), however, Sartre rejects Hegel's historicisation of the 'Master and Slave Dialectic' and detects its presence in *all* human relations. As Norman notes:

> Sartre's discussion is of great value in so far as it shows how the master–slave relation can be given a much wider application. In this

sense it can ... plausibly be maintained that the attempt by each self to enslave the other is the permanent and necessary structure of self-consciousness.[4]

In Wilkie Collins' *The Woman in White* (1859–60), however, Hegelian mastery and slavery are shown to be both present *and* absent from the Victorian state and its hierarchies: though the forms of power within the novel move ever closer to absolute violence, Hegel's life-and-death struggle is never made wholly present. This is not, though, to claim that violence is absent from the hierarchies within Collins' novel; rather, it is to suggest that the novel exposes the *other* kinds of violence which underlie all hierarchies, modes of violence which at once gesture towards *and* elide Hegel's life-and-death struggle.

Violence would *seem* to be wholly absent from the novel's most recognisably modern form of mastery – Frederick Fairlie's hiring of Walter Hartright as a 'drawing-master'.[5] The relationship between Fairlie and Hartright is based on a bourgeois, nineteenth-century code of liberal capitalism, whereby the '"pecuniary arrangements ... are ... most satisfactory"' and 'the terms ... surprisingly liberal' (41, 16). Fairlie's mastery is repeatedly couched in the language of modern, progressive liberalism: he espouses a 'liberal social theory' and says to his drawing-master, '"You will find your position here, Mr. Hartright, properly recognised"' (41). The introductory contract, or 'memorandum of terms', offers the opportunity of knowing '"distinguished people ... on ... gratifying terms of equality"' (14, 16); Fairlie's mastery apparently consists only in the abdication of that mastery and the assertion of equality.

Fairlie also, however, repeatedly undercuts any sense of equality by asking Hartright to perform various menial tasks: he asks Hartright, for example, '"Do you mind putting this tray of coins back in the cabinet, and giving me the next one to it?"' Of this, Hartright remarks, 'as a practical commentary on the liberal social theory which he had just favoured me by illustrating, Mr. Fairlie's cool request rather amused me' (41). The 'request' reaffirms Hartright's servile position and implies that the language of liberalism is merely a disguise for illiberal mastery. Hartright is not so much a drawing-*master* as a servant. Language itself – as 'a memorandum of *terms*' – here stands in for the violence of the life-and-death struggle. It is the 'surprisingly liberal ... terms' of employment which induce Hartright to become a drawing-master, but these terms merely mask the subordinate nature of the position.

Language, then, works for Fairlie's mastery as a trick or *ruse*; as Jacques Lacan remarks, 'the master–slave relationship ... is pregnant with ... cunning tricks (*ruses*).'[6] The trick or *ruse* in this case consists in the fact that the modern language of liberalism disguises traces of older and more violent forms of mastery and subordination, which haunt the relationship between Fairlie and Hartright. Superficially, Fairlie's liberal social theory is based on an absolute disavowal of past mastery – as he remarks, '"[T]here is none of the horrid English *barbarity* of feeling about the social position of an artist in this house.... I wish I could say the same of the gentry ... in the neighbourhood. They are sad *Goths* in Art, Mr. Hartright"' (41: my emphasis). Fairlie asserts that his mastery has nothing whatever to do with the barbarism of the Goths and the aristocratic mastery of the local gentry, and, in this sense, bourgeois, liberal mastery posits itself as a total break with the past. At the same time, the relationship between Fairlie and Hartright gestures *towards* these other, more extreme hierarchies. Despite his protestations, Fairlie is, after all, a '"distinguished person"' and member of the gentry himself, and his liberal, capitalist relationship with Hartright is implicitly compared to his *feudal* relationship with the valet Louis – Louis being, of course, the very name of French aristocracy. Indeed, this comparison emphasises the differences between aristocratic and bourgeois power structures and the slippage of one into the other. As an aristocratic privilege, Fairlie can even deny Louis's masculinity and humanity to his face; in conversation with the lawyer, Gilmore, he exclaims,

'You provoking old Gilmore, what can you possibly mean by calling him [Louis] a man? He's nothing of the sort. He might have been a man half an hour ago, before I wanted my etchings, and he may be a man half an hour hence, when I don't want them any longer. At present he is simply a portfolio stand.' (159)

In contrast, when speaking to Gilmore and Hartright, Fairlie's speech assumes an air of 'familiarity and impudent politeness' (45). He still obtains, though, almost all the same privileges from their service as he does from Louis's. Hartright, for instance, is asked to perform various menial tasks during his first meeting with Fairlie, and finally volunteers to stand in for Louis entirely when Fairlie asks him, '"Do you mind ringing for Louis to carry the portfolio to your room?"' to which Hartright replies, '"I will carry it there, myself, Mr. Fairlie"' (44). Disguised as it is by the language of liberalism, Hartright's status as employee is both a break with *and* a continuation of older forms of servitude.

At the same time, Hartright's and Louis's roles in the text function as metaphors for the violence of other *contemporary* modes of *capitalist* servitude. Though the role of valet is certainly a feudal institution, Louis is presumably paid for his services – and Louis, as well as being the name of French aristocracy, was also one of the names of French capital: the *louis* was once the name of the currency in France.

As a '"portfolio stand"', Louis is a sign of both Fairlie's aristocratic power *and* of his capitalist mastery – Fairlie's denial of his valet's humanity is certainly an exhibition of a more absolute form of mastery than that which he wields over Hartright and Gilmore, but Marx finds such denial of humanity within *bourgeois* rule. In *Capital* (1867), Marx argues that capitalism necessarily involves 'the personification of things and the reification of persons'.[7] If this reification is overt in the relationship between Fairlie and Louis, it is also at work between Fairlie and Hartright, for the relationship between Fairlie and Louis represents the repressed truth, or the unconscious, of Fairlie's and Hartright's capitalist bond. Under Fairlie's mastery, Louis's status as a valet is undermined and he is transformed into any *thing* his master desires him to be. Similarly, Hartright's position as drawing-master slips into generalised servitude and menial labour in which he has to put coins in cabinets, carry portfolios, check the children and ring bells. Hartright's specific 'identity' as an artist is subsumed into a non-specific servitude in which his employer can ask him to do or be anything. Indeed, under Fairlie, even his work as an artist is described as 'only of the humble manual kind' (45), in which he is merely restoring the etchings of *Old Masters* – manual work, that is, which only reinforces his subjection to Fairlie and those Old Masters. As Marx observes in *The Communist Manifesto* (1848), 'the bourgeoisie … has stripped of its halo every occupation hitherto honoured and looked up to with reverent awe. It has converted the physician, the lawyer, the priest, the poet, the man of science, into its paid wage-labourers.'[8] To this list can be added the artist. Indeed, Fairlie himself makes clear that it is modern masters who are 'sad Goths in Art', not the feudal masters of the Middle Ages, when he remarks that '"the gentry in the neighbourhood … would have opened their eyes in astonishment, if they had seen Charles the Fifth pick up Titian's brush for him"' (41). With respect to the artist, contemporary mastery is *more* violent, *more* barbaric than previous hierarchies because of its failure to recognise him/her as anything but a paid wage-labourer. Marx explains this failure when he writes,

> the bourgeoisie … has put an end to all feudal, patriarchal, idyllic relations. It has pitilessly torn asunder the motley feudal ties that

bound man to his 'natural superiors,' and has left remaining no other nexus between man and man than ... callous 'cash payment'.... It has resolved personal worth into exchange value.[9]

It is the bourgeois master's total reliance on cash payment which homogenises those occupations 'hitherto honoured' and reduces feudalism's various patriarchal relations to a simple class relation between employer and generalised wage-labourer; under capitalist rule, there is no other form of recognition than cash payment. The (non-) relationship between Hartright and Fairlie embodies this 'cash nexus'. Following Hartright's first visit, cash payment represents almost the only connection between the two men. As Hartright notes, 'throughout the whole of the period [of employment], Mr. Fairlie ... had never been well enough to see me for a second time' (110).

For Marx, hierarchies have been traditionally constituted by feudal and patriarchal ties, which provided at least some sort of 'personal worth', some sort of individualised recognition between the master and servant. In *The Woman in White*, however, the portrayal of the *modern* master–servant relationship is emptied of such recognition, and comes to signify its apparent opposite – to encode a whole critique of the nineteenth-century (dis-)connection between industrial master and employees, none of whom is known personally or individualised by the relationship. This is not, of course, to argue that Hartright himself suffers an appalling mode of industrial, capitalist servitude, but rather that his (ludicrously) comfortable mode of servitude bears traces of its apparent opposite – of the various modes of exploitative wage-labour existing beyond the text.

What Kathleen Tillotson calls 'the lighter reading of the eighteen-sixties'[10] seems to define itself in opposition to the industrial and socially-aware novels of the 1840s. This, though, does not mean that the violence of modern capitalist hierarchies is simply absent from such novels as *The Woman in White*. Bruce Robbins argues that, in the realist tradition, 'the literary servant might serve as [the] representative of the people ... in the absence of any realistic depiction',[11] and adds that, 'by the most frequent definitions, the servant not only "occupied himself with the personal needs of an employer" but did so "in such a way that this occupation established a relationship of personal dependence on the employer"'.[12]

Hartright's servitude departs noticeably from these usual models, however: the emphasis in *The Woman in White* is on the *lack* of such interdependence between servant and master. In this sense, the

Hartright/Fairlie relationship is very close to *laissez-faire* capitalism. As Thomas Carlyle notes in *Chartism* (1839), 'self-cancelling Donothingism and *Laissez-faire* ... have got so ingrained into our Practice, [that it] is the source of all ... [our] miseries.' Like Marx, Carlyle finds *laissez-faire* mastery everywhere in modern capitalism; and, again like Marx, he compares such mastery unfavourably with feudal institutions: 'Yet we do say,' he asserts, 'that the old Aristocracy were the governors of the Lower Classes, the guides of the Lower Classes.... For, in one word, *Cash payment* had not then grown to be the universal sole nexus of man to man.'[13] Here, cash payment functions as a middle-term, undoing feudal and patriarchal relations and making unnecessary any kind of recognition or mutuality. This is clearly the case in *The Woman in White*, where the 'pecuniary arrangements' between Fairlie and Hartright render irrelevant any other kind of mastery on the part of Fairlie. Indeed, cash payment here mediates a *laissez-faire* pact, a mutual agreement by both master and servant to avoid feudal *or* Hegelian confrontation, so that the lack of contact between Fairlie and Hartright is described as a 'satisfactory arrangement [for] ... both sides' (110). Cash payment mediates the dialectical and confrontational nature of the Hegelian life-and-death struggle and thereby excludes the recognition Hegel finds in and after that struggle. Through the life-and-death struggle, both 'individuals ... prove themselves and each other',[14] according to Hegel, but there is no life-and-death struggle between Fairlie and Hartright, and, consequently, no true recognition. The violence of the capitalist relationship between Hartright and Fairlie consists, ironically, in the lack of a life-and-death struggle.

In the *Philosophy of Mind*, Hegel argues that 'the fight for recognition, in its extreme form ... is absent in civil society and the State because here the recognition for which the combatants fought already exists', but this optimistic and progressive view of the modern state is utterly contradicted by later writers like Collins, Carlyle and Marx. For these writers, the state is almost an absence itself, and is certainly unable to provide recognition for its subjects. Hartright and Louis gain little or no recognition from the forms of servitude legitimised by the capitalist state, just as, later, state law fails to restore Laura Fairlie's true identity. As Hartright remarks, 'the justice that sits in tribunals is powerless' (454). For Carlyle, a state in which 'cash payment [is] ... the universal sole nexus of man to man' is merely 'an insane scramble ... [in which] whoever in the press is trodden down, has only to lie there and be trampled broad'.[15] This is because the modern state is based on the principle that 'men are to be guided only by their self-interests [and] ... government is [merely] a good balancing of these'.[16] In this sense, government is almost non-existent for Carlyle, and the state is almost *no* state. Britain, in fact, is still in what Hegel calls 'the natural state, where men exist as single, separate individuals'.

The relation between the Victorian state and the primitive struggle for recognition is fundamental to *The Woman in White*. The Italian agent Pesca is evidently convinced by Hegel's analysis of civil society when he remarks that 'you Englishmen ... have conquered your freedom so long ago, that you have conveniently forgotten what blood you shed ... in the conquering' (589), but the whole novel testifies to the ways in which such 'primitive' blood-letting is ingrained in the Victorian world. Later in the novel, for instance, Hartright repeatedly uses stratagems 'first learnt ... in the wilds of Central America ... in the heart of civilised London!' (464).

In *My Miscellanies* (1875), Collins writes in similar terms of a maid-servant, whom he calls 'Number Two':

Life means dirty work, small wages, hard words, no holidays, no social station, no future.... No state of society which composedly accepts this, in the cases of thousands, as one of the necessary conditions of its selfish comfort, can pass itself off as civilised.... How shocked we should all be, if we opened a book about a savage country, and saw a portrait of Number Two in the frontispiece.[17]

The master–servant relationship here flatly contradicts Hegel's faith in civilisation and civil society; power relations in Victorian England have failed to progress from a state of 'savagery'. As Sartre notes, 'slavery is not a historical result, capable of being surmounted'.

Indeed, capitalist hierarchies, as portrayed by Collins, have not even arrived at the life-and-death struggle, let alone surmounted it, so the kind of recognition Hegel envisages is inconceivable. For Hartright and Fairlie, it is the *termination*, not the inception, of the master–servant connection which is described as '"a case of life and death"' (110). A revolutionary struggle is envisaged here as the end, not the origin, of capitalist mastery and servitude, as it is, of course, for Marx. The relationship between Hartright and Fairlie functions as a pact, as a mutual agreement to avoid confrontation. As Lacan writes, 'the pact [between master and slave] is everywhere anterior to the violence before perpetuating it'.[18] The modern state cannot accord its subjects recognition because that state has not yet reached the struggle Hegel posits as the origin of human consciousness. That is to say, the anarchy Carlyle finds in modern human relations is an historical throwback, not because it represents a return to a primal life-and-death struggle, but

because it represents a return to a state of 'savagery' *before* that struggle
– a state in which, Hegel writes, 'self-consciousness is, to begin with,
simple being-for-self.... [so] what is "other" for it is an unessential,
negatively characterised object'.[19] This self-centred objectification of
the other pre-exists the life-and-death struggle and the master–slave
relationship for Hegel; for Collins, in contrast, it is fundamental *to* the
master–servant relationship. Hartright is to Fairlie no more than each
'batch of drawings' (110) he restores and sends to his master, and
Fairlie is to Hartright no more than a few notes and the 'pecuniary
arrangements' between them. This mutual objectification is the anarchic, primitive and almost *pre*-Hegelian 'violence' *within* the modern
master–servant relationship.

This is not life-and-death violence, however: Collins' master–servant
relationship is based on forms of violence that are *un*-Hegelian. One of
these is the peculiarly non-confrontational and non-face-to-face violence, which is 'sodomy'. Tamar Heller writes that 'to be "possessed" as
a servant at Limmeridge means to be economically sodomized'.[20]
Indeed, the text seems to imply actual sodomy as well, since it is
evident from his description of Fairlie that Hartright feels sexually
threatened by his master. He notes that Fairlie's 'feet were effeminately
small, and were clad in ... little womanish bronze-leather slippers....
He had a languidly-fretful, over-refined look [which had] something
singularly and unpleasantly delicate in its association with a man' (39).
The 'unpleasant' association or threat this description encodes is that
of homosexuality. According to D.A. Miller, this impression is
confirmed by Fairlie's speech. Miller suggests that 'what subtends
Mr. Fairlie's malicious greeting ("So glad to possess you at Limmeridge,
Mr. Hartright" [40]) ... is virtual rape'.[21] In fact, virtual rape and
sodomy seem to be inscribed in the very notion of servitude, since, for
Fairlie, 'servants are ... asses' (42) and are presumably to be used as
such. Paid servitude necessarily seems to bear traces of prostitution; in
a sense, Hartright is Fairlie's mistress.

It is the cash payment he receives as a servant that feminises
Hartright and turns him into a kind of mistress. His relation with
Fairlie is thus analogous to that between Mrs Catherick and Sir Percival
Glyde. Mrs Catherick, like Hartright, is a mistress who is not a mistress.
The supposition that she has or had a sexual liaison with Sir Percival is
shown to be false, but, by her own admission, she is kept *like* a mistress: 'I had a better income, a better house over my head, better
carpets on my floors, than half the women who turned up the whites
of their eyes at the sight of me. The dress of Virtue, in our parts, was

cotton print. I had silk' (546). Percival pays Mrs Catherick to *appear* to be his mistress. As Hartright observes, 'it was Sir Percival's interest to keep her at Welmingham [to encourage] ... the suspicion that he was Anne's father' (482). Mrs Catherick is procured as a sign of Pericval's masculine identity as adulterer and father. Percival's masculine and masterful signification depends, that is, on its opposition to the femininity and passivity of Mrs Catherick.

Hélène Cixous argues that *all* hierarchies are based on such an opposition between masculinity and femininity: 'Organisation by hierarchy,' she notes, 'makes all conceptual organisations subject to man. Male privilege [is] shown in the opposition between activity and passivity, which he uses to sustain himself.'[22] For Cixous, all hierarchies are inherently patriarchal: the master term in any hierarchy must always posit itself as masculine, whilst the slave is always constituted as feminine. This is evident in a great deal of nineteenth-century thought on mastery and slavery. All the heroes described by Carlyle in *Heroes and Hero-Worship* (1840) are male, and all exhibit a 'manhood [that] is ... first of all, what the Germans well name it, *Tugend* (*Taugend*, *dow*-ing or *Dough*-tiness), Courage and the Faculty to *do*.'[23] Carlyle thus suggests that the opposite of heroism is a passive femininity – the kind of passive femininity, in fact, that is exhibited by Mrs Catherick. The cash payment she receives from Percival turns her into his mistress precisely by ensuring her passivity. As she says, 'Percival ... was ... willing ... to make me a handsome yearly allowance ... on two conditions. First, I was to hold my tongue.... Secondly, I was not to stir away from Welmingham' (545-6). It is cash payment which symbolically castrates both Hartright and Mrs Catherick, rendering them passive and feminised subjects; by the end of his servitude to Fairlie, Hartright declares that he 'had done with [his] ... poor man's touchy pride' (109) and, presumably, his manhood in general. There is certainly a connection to be made between capitulation into slavery during Hegel's 'life-and-death struggle' and castration. The link is betrayed by a slippage of translation in A.V. Miller's edition of the *Phenomenology of Spirit*. Hegel writes of the slave's failure in the life-and-death struggle: '*Es ist darin innerlich aufgelöst worden, hat durchaus in sich selbst erzittert und alles fixe hat ihm gebebt*'[24] – a passage Miller translates as 'in that experience [the slave] ... has been quite unmanned, has trembled in every fibre of its being, and everything solid and stable has been shaken to its foundations'.[25] The word 'unmanned' – *unbemannt* in German – is not in the original, but its appearance in the translation betrays the castration trauma that forms the Freudian unconscious of Hegel's life-and-death struggle.

Indeed, what Hegel calls the slave's 'first experience'[26] is surely analogous to Freud's 'primal scene'. A castration trauma, Freud argues, typically results from a child's first experience of the mother's possession by the father. The moment in *The Woman in White* when Marian reveals to Hartright Laura's previous engagement can be read as a kind of primal scene, and Hartright's subsequent capitulation to Marian's wishes seen as a metaphoric castration. As Cyndy Hendershot writes, 'Marian thwarts Hartright and Laura's romance as a father might.'[27] Marian stands in for Laura's real father, who 'sanctioned ... on his death-bed' (72) Laura's and Percival's engagement. Hartright consequently witnesses prior connections between Laura and her father, Laura and Percival, and – perhaps most significantly – Laura and Marian. After all, Marian later calls herself a 'woman rival in ... [Percival's] wife's affections' (188). This is the lesbian and Freudian subtext of the early part of the novel: Hartright is unmanned when he witnesses Laura's apparent possession by Marian.

What so unmans Hartright is his attribution of masculine power to Marian. From their very first meeting, Hartright repeatedly emphasises Marian's 'masculine form and masculine look', pointing out 'the dark down on her upper lip [which] was almost a moustache' (32). Miller argues that Hartright's description of Marian's 'head' when he first meets her

> virtually proves her a man in drag .... [It is] unsurprising ... that an obsessively phallocentric system of sexual difference, always and everywhere on the lookout for its founding attribute (if only in the case of women to make sure it isn't there), should sometimes ... find this attribute even in its absence.[28]

It is this *apparent* masculinity that informs Marian's symbolic 'mastery' over Hartright early on in the novel. As Hendershot notes, 'a woman in a traditional position of power is merely the reverse of phallocentrism: she represents the same tyranny turned upside down', so Marian functions as a 'phallic woman'.[29] In other words, the relationship between Marian and Hartright is, oddly enough, based on the same man/woman opposition which Cixous finds in all hierarchies: Marian assumes the conventionally masterful role of man, whilst Hartright is subsumed into the conventionally servile role of woman. Hartright is subjected to a hierarchical opposition in which Marian's masculine power renders him servile and feminine. Their entire relationship is based on a phallocentric *ruse*, whereby Marian possesses the masculine, phallic mastery Hartright lacks.

In this case, Hartright's feminisation is not (merely) effected by cash payment, since Marian is not directly Hartright's employer in this way. Marian at once invokes and disavows the '"social inequalities"' (71) between her and Hartright, but the power imbalance between them *can* be interpreted in terms of a symbolic or metaphoric master–servant relationship. Indeed, lacking as it does the mediation provided by cash payment, their relationship is closer to Hegel's model than the novel's literal master–servant relationships; since Marian cannot depend on cash payment to mediate her 'mastery', she is compelled to use other means of domination. Certainly, her mastery implies more violent forms of power, such as castration, but this does not mean her mastery is unmediated. In fact, just as Marian's phallic mastery is really a *ruse*, so Hartright's 'castration' and disempowerment is effected by another trick. This consists primarily in Marian's insistent appeals to Hartright's sense of masculinity, in a *ruse* meant to conceal from him the reality of his own emasculation: of his love for Laura, she declares that he should '"tear [it] ... out [and] trample [it] under foot *like a man*"'. Hartright accepts her definition of manhood unreservedly:

> The ... strength which her will ... communicated to mine, steadied me. We ... waited for a minute.... At the end of that time, I had justified her generous faith in my manhood; I had, outwardly at least, recovered my self-control. (71)

The problem is that such 'self-control' is not a sign of manhood here, whatever Marian would have Hartright believe. The self-control and self-mastery she enjoins of him is defined by its passivity, by the willingness to retreat from Limmeridge and leave Laura. This passivity is what Marian paradoxically calls Hartright's 'self-sacrificing courage' (72). According to Carlyle's definition, courage is 'the Faculty to *do*', but Hartright does nothing except 'act ... in the strictest accordance with [Marian's] ... wishes' (73). Such courage is not of the heroic, masculine and masterful kind Carlyle describes, but is merely slavish, self-sacrificial and therefore 'feminine'. Self-denial is designated elsewhere in the novel a feminine, not masculine, characteristic. As Heller writes – of Marian, ironically – 'it is evident that ... self-denial is one of her feminine (rather than masculine) traits'.[30]

Marian's appeal to Hartright's 'self-sacrificing courage' is a peculiarly cunning *ruse* in that it shifts responsibility for the operation of power onto Hartright – from, that is, the master to the slave. Marian manages to dupe Hartright into struggling with himself rather than with her, as in Hegel's scheme. He gains control of himself, so she does not need to; he notes that 'the look she fixed on me, and ... the hold on my arm ... steadied me ... [and] ... I ... recovered my self-control' (71). Under her disciplinary gaze, Hartright internalises Marian's authority and self-consciously disempowers himself. In Hegel's words, the slave 'sets aside its own being-for-self, and in so doing itself does what the first [the master] does to it'.[31]

Self-sacrifice, self-control and self-mastery are also forms of self-slavery. As Michel Foucault writes:

> A real subjection is born ... from a fictitious relation. It is not neces-sary to use force to constrain the convict to good behaviour, the madman to calm, the worker to work.... He who is subjected to a field of visibility, and who knows it, assumes responsibility for the constraints of power; ... he inscribes in himself the power relation to which he simultaneously plays both roles.[32]

Hartright inscribes in himself and his 'narrative' the fictitious rela-tion of Hegelian mastery and slavery. His total subjection to Marian's wishes is inscribed *and* constituted by the life-and-death terms of his reaction to her revelation that '"Laura Fairlie is engaged to be married"': 'the last word,' he comments, 'went like a bullet to my heart' (71). It is Hartright who posits Marian's mastery in life-and-death terms; it is Hartright who inscribes in himself an absolute failure, which goes far beyond Marian's own words, when he says that his 'mad hopes were dead leaves, too, whirled away by the wind like the rest' (71); it is Hartright who inscribes in his subjec-tion an absolute, Hegelian violence that is really present only as a threat. Certainly, Marian's 'hold on [Hartright's] ... arm' seems, metonymically, to *threaten* castration – her grip is such that Hartright's 'arm lost all sensation'. Indeed, this hold is used repeat-edly as a sign of Marian's mastery: 'her will,' he remarks, '[was] concentrated in ... the hold on my arm' (71). It is, however, Hartright who actualises this threat and symbolically carries out the castration on himself. Self-denial and self-sacrifice are displaced forms of self-castration.

In his polemic *On the Genealogy of Morals* (1887), Friedrich Nietzsche makes the connection between self-castration and self-sacrifice – a self-castration he terms the 'self-deception of impotence'. Marian's *ruse* and

Hartright's passive acceptance of her power foreshadow Nietzsche when he writes:

> Out of the ... cunning of impotence, the oppressed, downtrodden, and violated tell themselves.... 'The good man is the one who ... harms no one, who attacks no one'.... But ... this cleverness of the lowest rank, which even insects possess (insects which, in situations of ... danger, probably play dead in order not to do 'too much'), has, thanks to the ... self-deception of impotence, clothed itself in the magnificence of self-abnegating calm ... exactly as if the weakness of the weak man ... were ... something willed, chosen a *deed*, a *merit*.[33]

Marian' s cunning *ruse* consists precisely in this *moral* affirmation of 'self-abnegating calm', or 'self-sacrificing courage', and Hartright's 'self-deception' consists precisely in his servile acceptance of this morality. Hartright really does believe, as he says, that she 'appealed ... to my heart, my honour, and my courage' (70). Demanding his '"absence"', Marian says to Hartright, '"if I had less belief in your honour, and your courage, and your sense, I should not trust to them as I am trusting now.... It is something to know that you will ... be ... honest ... manly [and] ... considerate towards [your] ... pupil"' (72). Marian uses Hartright's own morality – his own 'honour ... courage, and ... sense' – *against* him in what is really an *a*moral and egocentric power struggle. Indeed, what connects Collins and Nietzsche are *pseudo*-Darwinian theories of 'Survival of the Fittest' and the universal 'Struggle for Existence'. After all, Collins' novel and Darwin's *Origin of Species* (1859) are contemporaneous, and Nietzsche's social-Darwinian subtext is betrayed by his biological analogy between the 'cleverness of the lowest rank' and insects. For both Collins and Nietzsche, a biological 'Struggle for Existence' is also inherent in *human* history and the modern state, notwithstanding Hegel's insistence on the absence of violence in 'civil society'. For Collins and Nietzsche, it would seem that 'men [still] exist as single, separate individuals', who have to fight for their own, individual recognition. For Nietzsche, a pseudo-Darwinian evolution seems to legitimise a violent, potent, masculine and egocentric mastery. As he writes,

> There is no mistaking the predator beneath the surface of all ... noble races, the magnificent *blond beast* roaming lecherously in search of booty and victory.... Let me be granted a glimpse, just *one* glimpse of something complete, wholly successful, happy, powerful,

triumphant, something still capable of inspiring fear! A glimpse of a man who justifies *mankind*![34]

No such glimpse, however, is afforded by *The Woman in White*, where none of the characters is violent in the predatory or confrontational way Nietzsche envisages. On the contrary, Collins seems to emphasise the amorality of *all* mastery and struggle in a Darwinian world; *all* forms of mastery in *The Woman in White* are based on what Nietzsche calls the 'ingenuity ... [and] intelligence introduced by the power-less'.[35] For Collins, egocentricity is neither good nor evil – it is merely an amoral and necessary fact of Darwinian evolution. In *The Woman in White*, there are no 'blond beasts': Marian's apparently masterful reference to a morality of self-abnegation is as much defined by the 'cunning of impotence' as is Hartright's servile acceptance of that morality.

Marian's mastery is, then, both impotent and amoral – in her speech, she herself undermines the very moral imperative on which that mastery is based. Hartright '"must leave"', she says, '"because Laura ... is engaged to be married"'. But, when she comes to describe the engagement, she fails to make clear the moral necessity of the marriage, her emphasis being on the lack of any real connection between Percival and Laura:

'Till you came here [Laura] ... was in the position of hundreds of other women, who marry men without being greatly attracted to them or greatly repelled by them, and who learn to love them (when they don't learn to hate!) after marriage, instead of before.' (72)

Marian is not extolling Laura's and Percival's marriage prospects here, and what becomes increasingly clear is that her apparently moral action in revealing Laura's previous engagement is really an act of selfishness. Morality is merely a disguise, a masterful *ruse* for Marian at this point. Marian does not take Laura from Hartright for Percival's sake; she takes Laura from Hartright for herself. This is revealed retro-spectively when she describes herself as Percival's 'woman rival in his [future] wife's affections', as well as by her distress when Laura's and Percival's marriage is approaching:

Putting myself and my own feelings entirely out of the question (which it is my duty to do, and which I have done), I ... have no doubt ... [that] a separation between Laura and me is inevitable....

Before another month is over ... she will be *his* Laura instead of mine!' (187–8)

By putting herself out of the question, Marian loses Laura to Percival in the same way that Hartright previously surrendered Laura to her in a sacrifice of himself. As Miller notes, Marian is herself converted 'into the castrated, heterosexualised "good angel" [(643)] of the Victorian household at the end'[36] of the novel. By putting herself out of the question, Marian surrenders not only Laura, but also her masculine, egocentric mastery.

In fact, much of *The Woman in White* revolves around an amoral struggle for possession of Laura and Laura's identity, possession of Laura being also possession of mastery. Hartright remarks that the 'key to [Laura's] ... whole character [is a] ... generous trust in others' (52), but it is precisely this selfless trust which renders her prone to appropriation as a kind of slave by Hartright, Marian and Percival – she gives everyone the 'key' to herself. Indeed, if the key is a kind of phallus, Laura is always willing to surrender that phallus to others. When, for instance, she confesses her love for Hartright to Sir Percival, she adds:

'It is the truth, Sir Percival, ... which I think my promised husband has a claim to hear, at any sacrifice of my own feelings. I trust to his generosity to pardon me, and to his honour to keep my secret.'
'Both those trusts are sacred to me,' he said, 'and both shall be sacredly kept.' (172)

Of course, neither of these trusts is sacredly kept: after they are married, whenever Percival '"is angry with [Laura] ... he refers to what [she] ... acknowledged to him ... with a sneer or a threat"' (233). Laura's willingness to sacrifice herself and her own feelings merely gives Percival a means of control over her within the marriage. Indeed, it is clear throughout *The Woman in White* that the institution of marriage – so fundamental to Hegel's view of the ideal state – is itself perceived in terms of violence, of struggle, of a master–slave relation. As Marian exclaims, '"No man under heaven deserves these sacrifices from us women. Men! .... they take us body and soul to themselves, and fasten our helpless lives to theirs as they chain up a dog to his kennel"' (183). Once again, women are defined in terms of self-sacrifice, and it is her self-sacrificial 'nature' that makes Laura so attractive to Percival and other masters in the novel. After she confesses her love for Hartright and avows a '"truth which ... [a] promised husband has a claim to hear"', Percival comes to value Laura as '"the noblest of her sex'" (173) because he has thus gained a means of control over her. Similarly, it is her earlier deference to Hartright as a real drawing-*master* – as a real authority – that first attracts Hartright. As he says, '"the ... questions that she put to me ... with such an earnest desire to learn all that I could teach ... attracted ... my attention"' (53). Laura is attractive to others because, through her self-abnegation and self-effacement, she functions as a sign of their mastery.

Laura is, specifically, a sign of masculine authority: she personifies everything that masculinity is not. Everything about Laura suggests phallic lack: it is phallic lack which is surely the 'something wanting' (50) Hartright detects in Laura's expression and, indeed, the nature of her 'whiteness'. Hartright's initial description of her repeatedly emphasises her feminine passivity: her eyes, for example, '[are] large and tender and quietly thoughtful' (49). In marked contrast, Marian's 'expression ... appeared ... to be altogether wanting in those feminine attractions of gentleness and pliability, without which the beauty of the handsomest woman alive is beauty incomplete' (32). Marian's active masculinity is constituted by her difference to Laura's and other handsome women's gentleness and pliability. What is important to note is that, in 'an obsessively phallocentric system of sexual difference', the presence implied by Marian's 'moustache' can signify only in relation to its absent opposite. Since, as Cixous argues, all hierarchies are based on an opposition between man and woman, the secondary and servile term is vital to the first and actually constitutes the first. Marian can signify as a masterful 'man' only by defining herself in opposition to Laura, that epitome of feminine lack. This is why Marian demands Hartright's '"absence"' (72): his presence disrupts the binary opposition between them. In a sense, then, symbolic castration in the text consists in Laura being taken away or possessed by another. This is the nature of Hartright's emasculation by Marian and the nature of the '"absence"' she demands of him.

The relationship between Marian and Hartright thus brings to consciousness a fundamental problem with the phallocentric mastery of all those who gain power in the novel. Marian's mastery depends on a male/female opposition that is, of course, only ever metaphorical – her 'moustache' is merely a sign of a masculinity that cannot wholly be made present. If the relation between Hartright and Marian is flawed in this way, such phallocentric, master/servant oppositions break down throughout the novel. The masculine, sexual potency signed by mastery is never made wholly present, just as the castration of slavery is never fully realised: neither presence nor absence are ever absolute. Though Percival seems to keep Mrs Catherick as a mistress, this relation is only apparent; in fact, she gains a hold over him in what is *mutual* blackmail. She is not wholly sexualised and castrated within this relationship, but still possesses traces of masculinity, symbolised by the rather masculine gift she receives from Percival – the 'gold watch and chain' (544). Similarly, Count Fosco rules his wife with a 'rod of iron ... which ... never appears in company – it is a private rod, and is always kept up-stairs' (225). Just as the rod never appears in company, so the phallus – as Lacan would predict – is never made present. Instead, Marian suggests that Madame Fosco still possesses a 'tigerish jealousy' and that 'her present state of suppression may have sealed up something dangerous in her nature' (219) – Madame Fosco's own masculine power is suppressed and sealed up, but not entirely absent. The sexual mastery implied by marriage is again undercut in the relationship between Percival and Laura, where even Laura does not function as absolute feminine absence. Just as Hartright reads Marian's face as a sign of masculinity, so Percival reads his wife's face as a sign of another man's presence; as he says to her, '"I have wanted to find out the man [you loved], and I have found him in your face to-night"' (265). Finally, though Laura's and Hartright's marriage at the end of the novel may seem to reconstitute a patriarchal, phallocentric mastery, in which Hartright's sexual potency is evidenced by his fathering a child, this resolution is undercut when Marian *asks* Hartright about his own child: '"Do you know who this is, Walter?"' (643). Even fatherhood is no absolute guarantee of phallocentric mastery.

What *The Woman in White* exposes is the failure of masculine, masterful presence to signify outside its fictional systems of opposition. Marian's initial status as a 'phallic woman' is constituted by Hartright's attribution of masculinity to her; it does not exist independently of their relationship, whatever he believes. Later, Hartright's fatherhood cannot recognise itself, but instead depends on Marian's acceptance of it. Again, Fosco's 'iron rod' is never seen – its existence is merely assumed by Marian – and Percival's sexual mastery depends on a certain reading of his relationship with Mrs Catherick. As Hartright remarks, 'appearances ... pointed one way, while the truth lay, all the while, unsuspected, in another direction.... Sir Percival courted the suspicion that was wrong, for the sake of diverting from himself some other suspicion that was right' (482). Mastery depends on a certain (mis)reading of its signs; in the case of Percival, his masculine and masterful status as adulterer and father of Anne depends on a certain reading of the 'lace handkerchiefs ... two fine rings ... new gold watch and chain [and other] ... gifts' (478) he gives Mrs Catherick.

This dependence on (mis)reading is never more obvious than when Marian tries to interpret the text that is Count Fosco and the many signs by which he is constructed – his fatness, his singing, his 'cockatoo ... canary-birds, and ... white mice' (222). She comes to the conclusion that all these signs signify a hidden power – an iron rod he keeps upstairs. 'He *looks*,' she writes, 'like a man who could tame anything' (219: my emphasis). She accepts and passively repeats Fosco's own reading of himself as '"a bad man"' (239), as '"a man who snaps his big fingers at the laws and conventions of society"' (561), as '"an Influence that is felt, a Man who sits supreme!"' (584). Marian's reading of Fosco thus becomes a kind of repetition-compulsion in which 'she can only repeat' (226) his masterful status. She exclaims, 'how much I seem to have written about Count Fosco! And what does it all amount to?' (226) As Freud might predict, the castration trauma of servitude results in a repetition automatism; mastery is sustained and made present by the servant's acceptance and repetition of appearances. Anne Catherick, for instance, 'merely repeated, like a parrot' (550) the existence of Percival's secret – and thus becomes herself a sign of that secret, part of the 'text' that is his secret. Similarly, after his submission to Marian, Hartright finds himself subject to a form of 'monomania' in which he is continually 'tracing back everything strange that happened, everything unexpected that was said, always to the same hidden source' (80). Again, Mrs Catherick does not expose Percival's secret to Hartright, but only repeats Percival's masterful status: '"Yes," she repeated, in tones of the bitterest, steadiest contempt. "A baronet – the possessor of a fine estate – the descendant of a great family"' (500). For Marian, such repetition is endless: her writing can never fully encompass or interpret Fosco. By the end of her journal, she finds herself caught up in 'ceaseless writing, faster and faster, hotter and hotter, driving [her] on more and more' (342). The Freudian repetition-compulsion here is analogous to the work that the Hegelian slave must undertake; as Hegel writes, 'the thing is independent *vis-à-vis* the bondsman, whose negating of it, therefore, cannot go the length of being altogether done with it to the point of annihilation'.[37] In his later narrative, Hartright's initial mode of detection also becomes stuck in a servile acceptance and self-perpetuating repetition of Percival's and Fosco's mastery. Hartright seeks long and hard for a transcendental signifier which will legally convict his enemies of being *master*-criminals; specifically, he searches for '"the simplest and surest of all proofs [which is] the proof by comparison of dates"' (453). In the same way, the solution or transcendental signifier that Hartright looks for in his detection of Percival's secret would confirm Percival as the masterful, aristocratic adulterer that his 'gifts' to Mrs Catherick would suggest him to be. Hartright, though, eventually comes to understand the arbitrariness of signs. He eventually comes to understand that the relation between signifier and signified is wholly arbitrary. As Saussure puts it, 'the link between signal and signification is arbitrary ... [and] the linguistic sign is arbitrary'.[38] In Collins' words, Hartright comes to realise that 'appearances had pointed one way, while the truth lay ... in another direction'. Instead of discovering a masterful presence, a transcendental signifier, Hartright discovers in the church register 'a blank space [which] ... told the whole story!' (520). By unveiling Percival's illegitimacy, Hartright unveils a signifying absence, an absence that itself tells a story and disrupts and belies *all* binary oppositions between masterful presence and servile absence in the novel. The space is at once absence and presence, thus signifying the impossibility of any mastery based on an opposition between absolute presence and absolute absence. All of the forms of mastery Percival embodies as an aristocrat, an adulterer, a father, a husband and a man are exposed as *illegitimate*. Indeed, with the fire that subsequently consumes Percival and the church, the novel goes further and destroys all forms of absolute and transcendental mastery, including that of God. Like the space in the register, the fire is at once both presence and absence, for, though it is 'nothing', it is also 'a sheet of living fire'. Similarly, the '"dust and ashes"' (530), which Percival and the church become in the fire, are at once sign and signified, servant and master, absence and presence – and, therefore, none of these things entirely. Clearly, Percival no longer signifies as father, husband, aristocrat or adulterer; but he is, at the same time, '"beyond mortal reach"' (563), so he cannot *serve* as a sign of Hartright's detective mastery – he cannot *sign* a confession of the conspiracy.

Fosco, in contrast, does make '"a full confession of the conspiracy, written and *signed* in [Hartright's] ... *presence"'* (605: my emphasis). In the climactic confrontation between Hartright and Fosco, it would seem that Hartright finally makes mastery wholly present whilst turning Fosco into a mere sign of that presence. Hartright seems, that is, to reconstitute an absolute mastery based on a binary opposition between presence and absence. Indeed, his masterful presence is defined in Hegelian terms: when he declares that 'one of us must be master of the situation – one of us must inevitably be at the mercy of the other' (593), he is evidently appealing to a dialectical model of mastery; and when he tells Fosco that his errand is '"a matter of life and death"' (600), the Hegelian implications of the scene become apparent. Hartright finally gains mastery over Fosco in a life-and-death struggle – or so it would appear.

The problem is, of course, that the struggle between Hartright and Fosco does not fulfil Hegel's criteria. Hegel writes of the life-and-death struggle that 'just as each stakes his own life, so each must seek the other's death'.[39] Though both Hartright and Fosco continually gesture towards such absolute violence, neither is entirely risking his life or seeking the death of the other. Hartright is not really staking his life: as he says before his meeting with Fosco, 'I [had] ... to do all that lay in my power to lessen the risk.' This entails sending a letter to Pesca which Hartright calls a 'mine under [Fosco's] ... feet' (594), and a mine, of course, represents a form of violence which implies the absence, not presence, of the aggressor. In fact, a mine represents exactly the kind of violence – and violent *ruse* – of which Hegel seems profoundly unaware, a kind of violence in which the aggressor avoids staking his/her life. And that is precisely what Fosco is also trying to avoid – hence his willingness to '"come to ... terms"' (603) with Hartright. Like Hartright, Fosco is concerned to lessen the risk to himself; as he declares to Hartright, '"the risk of shooting you on the place where you stand, is less to *me*, than the risk of letting you out of this house, except on conditions that I dictate and approve"' (603).

If neither Fosco nor Hartright stakes their life, nor do they seek the other's death: Fosco does not run the risk of shooting Hartright on the spot, and Hartright's victory depends on Fosco remaining alive so he can write and sign the confession. Even in the novel's most extreme confrontation, masculine mastery is present only as a threat: Hartright does not possess on or in himself the means to kill Fosco, and Fosco's gun is never seen, or even named in the text. Rather, this deadly weapon is 'kept hidden in the drawer' (601), just as his 'iron rod' was previously kept out of sight upstairs. Mastery, then, is *still* based on a pact, in which the antagonistic individuals agree not to make present a deadly violence. Just as the apparently benign relationship between Hartright and Fairlie was constituted by a 'memorandum of terms', so the apparently dialectical relationship between Hartright and Fosco is based on its own contractual '"terms"' (604). Once again, 'the pact is everywhere anterior to the violence' of a life-and-death struggle; once again, the life-and-death struggle is only present as a future and a threat when Fosco says to Hartright, '"You [will] give me the satisfaction of a gentleman.... The time and place ... to be fixed in a letter from my hand.... We meet as mortal enemies hereafter"' (605–6).

The threatened duel does not take place, and what becomes increasingly apparent is Fosco's inability to make present such masterful violence. Hartright's mastery of Fosco consists in his realisation of the latter's weakness in this respect, not in a dialectical struggle between them. Hartright comes to recognise that Fosco's mastery merely involves '"attempting to frighten [others] by threatening what he cannot really do"' (561). Fosco's inability to realise a life-and-death struggle is finally exposed when he sees Pesca and, as a result, 'a mortal dread ... *mastered* him, body and soul' (585: my emphasis). Hartright witnesses both this mortal dread and Fosco's subsequent 'extraordinary anxiety to escape Pesca' (586), and it is in this way that Hartright discovers Fosco's unwillingness to stake his own life and seek the other's death. What Hartright realises is that, despite his claims, Fosco is *not* a master-criminal or master-murderer. Rather, Fosco's mastery consists of a 'mountebank bravado' (606), which is peculiarly reminiscent of Carlyle's notion of the 'Sham-Hero'. Indeed, Collins may well have drawn on Carlyle in his portrayal of Fosco; as Carlyle writes,

> Examine the man ... who goes about ... struggling to force everybody, as it were begging everybody for God's sake, to acknowledge him a great man, and set him over the heads of men! ... A *great* man? ... It is the *emptiness* of the man, not his greatness. Because there is nothing in himself, he hungers and thirsts that you would find something in him.[40]

Of course, almost all the characters in the novel do acknowledge Fosco's claims to greatness, do find something in him, and most commentators have followed suit. Marian goes so far as to compare him with one of Carlyle's heroes, Napoleon Bonaparte:

'He is a most remarkable likeness ... of the Great Napoleon.... This striking resemblance certainly impressed me, to begin with; but there is something in him besides the resemblance, which has impressed me more. I think the influence I am now trying to find, is in his eyes.... They have at times a cold, clear, beautiful, irresistible glitter in them, which forces me to look at him.' (221)

Fosco's mesmeric power here is, however, more reminiscent of Napoleon Bonaparte's nephew, Louis Napoleon, than of Napoleon himself; in *The Eighteenth Brumaire of Louis Bonaparte* (1852), Marx describes Louis Napoleon as 'a conjuror [who is] under the necessity of keeping the public gaze fixed on himself'.[41]

Moreover, just as Fosco is always threatening a life-and-death struggle but never realises it, so Louis Napoleon was always threatening a *coup d'état* – a kind of life-and-death struggle – but also continually postponing it. As Marx writes, 'The *coup d'état* was ever the fixed idea of Bonaparte.... He was so obsessed by it that he continually ... blurted it out. He was so weak that, just as continually, he gave it up again.'[42] The main action of *The Woman in White* is set between 1849 and 1851, just at the time when Louis Napoleon's threats were most obvious yet still unrealised. Whereas, according to Carlyle, Napoleon Bonaparte rose 'through Wagrams, Austerlitzes; triumph after triumph [and] ... victory over Europe',[43] Fosco and Louis Napoleon gain power by merely *threatening* such life-and-death violence. Fosco and Louis Napoleon only *resemble* the Great Napoleon – they are Sham-Napoleons whose mastery at once refers to and elides the kind of heroism he represents. As Carlyle asserts, 'Napoleon ... was ... our last Great Man', so the post-heroic world of the mid-nineteenth century is, it seems, necessarily a 'Valet-World ... governed by the Sham-Hero'.[44] All heroes and masters in this context can only be poor copies of previous heroes, unable to signify in-themselves and for-themselves. As Marx writes of such heroes, 'they anxiously conjure up the spirits of the past to their service and borrow from them names, battle-cries, and costumes'.[45] For Marx, it would appear that all heroism is a parody of previous heroism, which is, in turn, a parody of previous heroism, and so on. Indeed, Carlyle implies as much of Napoleon Bonaparte himself – in Napoleon, he writes, 'the old ages are brought back to us'. For Carlyle, Napoleon is a poor copy of Cromwell: 'Napoleon does by no means seem to me so great a man as Cromwell.... What Napoleon *did* will in the long run amount to what he did *justly*.... The rest was all smoke and waste.'[46] Carlyle dare not pursue this argument to its logical conclusion – that all mastery and heroism are 'smoke and waste' and a poor copy of previous poor copies.

Mastery, it appears, is not constituted as a Nietzschean, individualistic will-to-power, but rather always depends on reference to a previous hero's mastery. What is clear, however, is that the reference to, and copying of, a heroic past was particularly obvious in the post-Napoleonic, post-revolutionary Europe of the 1850s and 1860s. Such Sham-Heroism was particularly obvious in Louis Napoleon, whose Imperial mastery was legitimised only by his being descended from a past, dead hero. Marx characterises Louis Napoleon as the 'adventurer who hides his commonplace repulsive features under the iron death mask of Napoleon',[47] and much the same could be said of Fosco.

When Fosco dies, however, he becomes that death mask. In the Paris Morgue, his corpse assumes both the absence *and* presence of a mask. As Maurice Blanchot notes, 'the cadaver is its own image.... And if the cadaver is so similar, it is because it is ... similarity par excellence: altogether similarity, and also nothing more.'[48] All that is left of Fosco after death is his masterful mask or pose – this is the nature of 'the *sublime* re*pose* of death' (640: my emphasis). Fosco had previously defined his resemblance to Napoleon the Great in terms of his '"power of commanding sleep at will"' (610), and, in death, his corpse *is* that resemblance and nothing else: he does not become Napoleon in death; he becomes his resemblance to Napoleon. All that is left of Fosco is his masterful disguise. To be more precise, in death he has become both master *and* slave. On the one hand, he has met his 'dreadful end' and become the subject of 'the flippant curiosity of a French mob'; on the other, his corpse is 'sublime'. As Hartright comments, 'the broad, firm, massive face and head fronted us so grandly, that the chattering Frenchwomen about me lifted their hands in admiration, and cried in shrill chorus, "Ah, what a handsome man!"' (640). Fosco's masculine mastery is reconstituted by the necrophilic desire of the Frenchwomen in the crowd; as a corpse, his masculine mastery is, ironically, both absent *and* present. Like Percival's dust and ashes, Fosco's corpse disrupts a signifying chain based on binary oppositions between absence and presence. This is why his corpse cannot confirm Hartright's mastery at the end of the novel; as Hegel makes clear, the dead cannot afford 'the required significance of recognition ... for those who survive'.[49] Confronted by Fosco's corpse, it is Hartright who retreats. This is surely also the intended effect of Napoleon's tomb at *Les Invalides* and of the embalmed corpses of Lenin and other Communist leaders in the twentieth century. The dead become signs of their own heroism and mastery when alive, a heroism and mastery that may or may not have existed. Indeed, whilst alive, 'Fosco discovered, among other wonderful inventions, a means of petrifying the body after death, so as to preserve it, as hard as marble, to the end of time' (223), so, as with Lenin's corpse, this sign of Fosco's mastery can be perpetuated *ad infinitum*.

2
'Servants' Logic' and Analytical Chemistry: Intellectual Masters and Servants in George Eliot and Charles Dickens

Masters, servants and logic

> In reasoning with servants, we are likely to be thwarted by discovering that our axioms are not theirs.... [For them] any two or more circumstances which can be mentioned will account for a given fact, and ... nothing is impossible, except that they can have been in the wrong.
>
> (George Eliot, 'Servants' Logic')[1]

In her essay 'Servants' Logic' (1865), George Eliot complains that servants' 'standard measures are of a private kind', such as 'a good lump [or] ... a handful' (SL, 392). As far as she is concerned, this is a prime example of what she calls 'servants' logic'. According to Eliot, servants are incapable of comprehending any unit of measurement that does not have reference to something as private as their own bodies. Clearly, she assumes that her own imperial measurements are, by contrast, both public and non-arbitrary – and British law supports her in this assumption. The power of the master over the servant in Victorian society would *seem* to be legitimised by a hierarchy of discourses, whereby the middle class have recourse to an accepted and universal system of measurement, whilst the servant class have reference only to their personal measurements. There is, though, no real difference between 'a handful' and the imperial unit of, for instance, 'a foot' – both measurements, in fact, derive from the private context of the body. Rather, Eliot's essay can be seen as part of a Victorian, middle-class strategy to try to restrict servants' discourse to the domestic sphere, whilst portraying 'masters' logic' as a wider 'truth' (SL, 391).

45

Eliot's *public* measurements are just perceived as such by her implied, middle-class readers. These measurements are public only in so far as they are private to her class. Since they are not shared by servants, we are left to infer that the servants' *'standard'* measurements are private only in so far as they are public to the servant class. If Eliot's humour is to be shared by her readers, it is necessary that those readers' servants must also use such measurements as 'a good lump' and 'a handful'. The hierarchy Eliot attempts to establish of public measurements over private measurements is just the opposition between two, equally private, *class* discourses – between, that is, two equally 'context-bound' discourses, to use Basil Bernstein's term.[2] Every opposition Eliot attempts to set up within her essay conforms to this pattern; every opposition is constituted not by the difference between public and private assumptions, or by the difference between the 'carefully drawn conclusion' and the 'bold fallacy' (SL, 391), but by the conflict between the class-bound discourses of masters and servants. As Eliot writes, 'servants are little disposed to think that the opinions of gentlefolks can have any ... value for them', and this divergence of opinion is defined not by an opposition between public and private, right and wrong, but simply by masters' and servants' differing economic status. 'Our remedies ... methods ... [and] explanations,' she writes, 'are like the drapery and tailoring we pay so much for; they correspond to the supposed scale of our income' (SL, 395). The rich bourgeois masters of the nineteenth century have *bought* different remedies, methods and explanations.

They have failed, however, to buy the public acceptance of these codes on the part of other classes, such as servants. The problem, as Eliot declares, is that 'the majority of minds are no more to be controlled by strong reasons than plum-pudding is to be grasped by sharp pincers.... [and] unfortunately, our keenest experience of this sort has reference to our own domestic affairs' (SL, 391). Ironically, Eliot's own language is marked by the domestic – for her, 'control' over other minds is analogous to an attempt to grasp 'plum-pudding' with 'sharp pincers'. The analogy unwittingly deconstructs the very opposition it is meant to establish, between the reasoning master or mistress and the unreasoning servant who cannot think beyond the specificities of the kitchen. The culinary incompetence of Eliot's servants is mirrored by her metaphorical attempt to grasp 'plum-pudding ... by sharp pincers'. The culinary incompetence of her servants, that is, is mirrored by the incompetence of the reasoning masters' attempts at mind control.

Eliot gives two examples of the reasoning master – the 'dyspeptic physiologist' and the 'genius' (SL, 393). Both are male, though the latter uses his wife as a mediator between himself and his cook. Eliot addresses him directly, writing: 'You ask your wife with ... unusual emphasis on "My dear," to inquire into the making of the soup. Your wife ... is rather frightened at the cook' (SL, 393). As mediator, the genius's wife, Mrs Queasy, belongs to neither the drawing-room nor the kitchen – she is neither a reasoning master nor an unreasoning servant. Not only is she excluded from Mr Queasy's 'genius', but, as E.S. Turner observes of the Victorian mistress in general, the servants can also '"blind her with [their kind of] science"'.[3] Significantly, Eliot leaves unmentioned the most obviously problematic confrontation – that between mistress and male servant. If 'reason' belongs to the bourgeois male, then the locus of reason within the relationship between mistress and male servant is doubly ambivalent. The issue of gender remains the unspoken concern of Eliot's essay.[4]

Though Eliot speaks of the 'triumph of ... ideas' (SL, 392), the real subject of the essay is the triumph of the master's power within the home. Eliot seems to imply this when she declares that 'we may look to the next century for the triumph of our ideas, but it is impossible to look there for our dinners.... [Here] the immediateness of the success is everything' (SL, 392). Eliot here *claims* that intellectual mastery is not her present interest, and that she is more immediately concerned with her dinner. The fact is, though, that a satisfactory dinner *does* entail the triumph of her bourgeois ideas, since the domestic power of the bourgeois master or mistress – symbolised by a good dinner – seems to depend on intellectual superiority.

This was increasingly true as brute force gradually disappeared from the master–servant relationship during the eighteenth and nineteenth centuries. During the eighteenth century, Dorothy Marshall claims, 'physical punishment ... [of servants] tended to become less frequent ... [particularly] because a master or mistress with a bad reputation found difficulty in securing good servants'.[5] By the nineteenth century, 'punitive practices [generally] ... no longer touched the body', according to Michel Foucault. Punishments, he argues, became 'deprived of their physical display'.[6] Without such display, however, the Victorian master or mistress must *seem* to possess less power. Eliot's Mrs Queasy needs only to complain too much for Sally, the cook, to 'give warning'. Subsequently, the mistress can only retreat 'upstairs again' (SL, 394). Sally cannot be *physically* forced to make soup without fat, because she will leave her mistress's employment if the means of compulsion become unacceptable. N.N. Feltes cites one woman who, in the same year as Eliot's essay was published, writes to the *Daily Telegraph* about 'a cook who, at the slightest reproach threatens to leave: "What is this" [she asks] "but a species of tyranny that servants, as a class, try at in a variety of ways?"'[7] Feltes argues that, by the 1860s, 'domestic servants ... have learned, in E.J. Hobsbawm's phrase, "the rules of the game"'; that is, they have 'clearly learned the use, *intra moenia*, of a free labour market'.[8] Indeed, as Marshall observes, the nineteenth century gradually made 'things ... easier' for servants to find employment: 'there [were] ... reliable registry offices to be found [and] ... the use of advertisements for servants became common'.[9] When Mrs Queasy's cook 'give[s] warning', she is exchanging the 'private' discourse of the kitchen for the very public discourse of a 'free labour market'.

By contrast, Eliot seeks to escape from that public discourse, exchanging it for the private one of a feudal, authoritarian relation to domestic servants. She seeks to mystify a master–servant bond based merely on cash payment and free labour by an appeal to 'authority and tradition [as] ... the chief, almost the only safe guides of the uninstructed' (SL, 395). 'Tradition' can refer only to the feudal past the Victorian bourgeoisie so often sought to appropriate in order to legitimise their mastery. By buying mastery with a cash payment, they also sought to buy into a tradition of mastery. 'Authority', however, is not only engendered but also eroded by a cash payment: without force or even the threat of force, servitude loses its context-bound specificity, and so Sally *can* look 'out of the window' (SL, 394) for alternative employment. For a servant in the 1860s, there is usually a job elsewhere, so she/he is not bound to one private context. Simple, physical coercion no longer binds the servant to his/her master. As cash payment replaces all other ties under capitalism, it becomes apparent that a master is *anyone* with money.

For Eliot, however, the master also has reason, and this acts as a substitute for the legalised violence of feudal mastery. The exchange between Sally and the dyspeptic physiologist ends with a dismissal of what Eliot calls Sally's '*nonsense*' (SL, 393). Eliot thus tries to uphold a hierarchical division of sense and nonsense, and, in so doing, she demonstrates the way that, as Robbins writes,

the master's authority [is able] ... to close off speech, to frame all confrontation. Within such a frame, there can be no 'Servants'

Logic,' no ultimate purposefulness that would bestow rational meaning on ... [the servants'] actions in their own right.

Robbins, however, also notes 'just how near Eliot's dialogues come to suggesting the existence of such a logic',[10] and Eliot herself admits that, in a direct confrontation, 'carefully-drawn conclusions are quite powerless by the side of a *good* bold fallacy' (SL, 391: my emphasis). Though she claims that servants' logic is necessarily fallacious, she nevertheless manages to suggest the power of such logic. In each of the exemplary conversations between masters and servants, the masters are defeated by reasoning servants whose minds refuse to be 'controlled'. Even the physiologist's dismissal of his cook's speech as 'nonsense' is a form of retreat: '"Say no more, I'm in a hurry"' (SL, 393).

Despite herself, Eliot constructs dialogues that stage a struggle not so much between sense and non-sense, but between middle-class rationalism and working-class empiricism, an empiricism in which 'conclusions are determined ... by vague, habitual impressions and by chance associations ... and any two or more circumstances which can be mentioned will account for a given fact' (SL, 391–2). As Eliot knew well, Immanuel Kant had divided knowledge into two types in the *Critique of Pure Reason* (1781–7), one form 'altogether independent of experience, and even of all sense impressions ... called *a priori*' and the other 'empirical knowledge, which has its sources *a posteriori*, that is, in experience'.[11] Wendell Harris argues that 'the fundamental metaphysical opposition of the nineteenth century', which divides almost all writers of the time, is 'the very old one of whether all understanding of the world ... depend[s] on the application of logic to careful observations, or on faculties superior to logic and observation'.[12] Harris uses the terms 'empiricist' and 'transcendentalist' to differentiate between the two positions. Eliot's rationalism, however, undermines such categorisation by being at once empiricist *and* transcendentalist. In her essay 'The Future of German Philosophy' (1855), she is evidently in accord with the philosopher Otto Gruppe whose work she is reviewing. Gruppe, she says, 'renounces the attempt to climb to heaven by the rainbow bridge of "the high *priori*" road', though she does assert that 'the uphill *a posteriori* path ... will lead ... to an eminence whence we may see very bright and blessed things on earth'.[13] In 'Servants' Logic', the path to this 'eminence' would seem to legitimate a certain authoritarianism: servants must be guided by 'a mild yet firm authority ... without urging motives or entering into explanations' (SL, 395). This is precisely the kind of authoritarianism that Harris identifies as typical of the nineteenth-century transcendentalist, for whom 'seers of special insight are required ... to lead ... [whilst] others ... follow. Thus, there are times at which dissent ought not to be tolerated.'[14] What legitimates such authoritarianism for Eliot is her 'reflection that the life of collective mankind is slowly swayed by the *force* of truth' (SL, 391: my emphasis). Universal truths, in contradistinction to 'nonsense' and 'twaddle' (SL, 391), do exist for the Eliot of 'Servants' Logic'. For instance, her amusement at the servants' belief that 'an effect may exist without a cause' (SL, 392) assumes that the law of causality is universal and absolute. For Eliot, such laws and truths possess a force that will eventually sway mankind and bring about 'blessed things on earth'. Eliot elevates reason to an almost divine status, in a sense transferring absolute authority from God to those who reason – the philosophers.

This move may derive from Plato's (in)famous demand for 'communities [to] have philosophers as kings',[15] but, more immediately, Eliot seems to be continuing the project of the Enlightenment and, in particular, Kant's *Religion within the Limits of Reason Alone* (1792–3). Of this work, Sylviane Agacinski writes:

> For Kant ... only the law of Reason can impose absolute and universal obligations on *humanity*, and nothing else could be truly sublime.... Reason – as the faculty for knowledge of the unconditioned absolute – was the only true master.

For Kant, however, reason perpetuates itself only as an *externalised* master in so far as it seeks its own effacement. According to Agacinski, Kant believes that the 'moral law ... [is] turned inwards' through 'genuine education'[16] – through education, we internalise the mastery of reason and morality. As Agacinski suggests, 'we need no longer bow down before anything external, but only before the [universal] moral law *within*'.[17] Kant calls himself 'the teacher of pure reason',[18] but this apparently masterful role consists in passing on to others the mastery of reason and morality, and hence in making others reasoning and ethical masters. By contrast, Eliot asserts that 'wise masters and mistresses ... will *not* give [their servants] ... reasons' (SL, 395). Eliot's reasoning masters are clearly *not* teachers in the Kantian sense. Rather, Eliot seems to want to perpetuate a fixed and externalised relationship between reasoning master and unreasoning servant.

What Eliot's servant-mastery and Kant's educative-mastery have in common, though, is a belief in the universal truth of reason. As Agacinski notes, for Kant,

> anything that could not be said unequivocally by the voice of reason belonged to empirical singularity, to the private sphere, and

had nothing to do with genuine education.... [Such] philosophy
reassures us by identifying the true with the universal.[19]

If, however, Kant is wrong in 'identifying the true with the universal' –
if he is wrong in attributing an absolute and universal mastery to reason
– then his system of education is as much an arbitrary exercise of power
as Eliot's servant-mastery. Both systems of mastery depend for their
legitimacy entirely on the existence of a universal reason, of universal
truths. In 'The Future of German Philosophy', Eliot seems to equivocate
over the possibility of discovering absolute and universal laws when she
states that 'the language of all peoples soon attains to the expressions
all, universal, necessary, but these expressions have their origin purely in
the observations of the senses [and] ... experience'.[20] For Eliot, human
knowledge would seem to be contingent on observation, despite the use
of expressions 'all, universal, [and] necessary'. If, though, the principle
of causality, for example, were to have its origin 'purely in the observations of the senses', it seems peculiar that Eliot should not allow servants, who have based their opinions empirically on 'two or more
circumstances' (SL, 392), to question the principle. Since servants' logic
is seen to be derived from 'private' contexts and 'circumstances', Eliot's
dismissal of it is ironic, particularly given the wish she expresses elsewhere to derive 'the abstract ... from the concrete'.[21] The definition of
the 'boundary of ... [human] knowledge' seems to be that which
excludes all knowledge of servants. In this sense, principles that are
empirically contingent for masters become absolute and universal laws
for their servants, and servants are merely talking nonsense when they
question these universal laws. Eliot's inconsistency arises from her
attempt to keep her empirical philosophy separate from her analysis of
domestic affairs. The discourse she employs in 'Servants' Logic' belongs
to a *private*, domestic context, which she attempts to isolate from the
apparently public discourse of her philosophical essays. The servants in
'Servants' Logic', however, highlight her inconsistency by exhibiting
the empiricism she elsewhere declares as her own.

If the servants parody her empirical philosophy, Eliot and her fellow
mistresses and masters come closer to Kant. He seems to stand behind
Eliot when she claims authority over the servant who believes that 'an
effect may exist without a cause' (SL, 392). Kant himself asserts that the
fact 'that in the sphere of human knowledge we have judgements
which are ... in the strictest sense universal ... [is] an easy matter to
show.... The proposition, "Every change must have a cause," will
amply serve our purpose.'[22] If, as Kant and Eliot assume, this law is

universal and true, the servant is simply in the wrong. Nevertheless, given Eliot's disavowal of *a priori* knowledge, her assumption of the universality of causality is at least as 'nonsensical' in Kantian terms as the servants' provisional avowal that 'an effect *may* exist without a cause'. Even Kant acknowledges that, without universal *a priori* laws, 'the very notion of a cause would entirely disappear'.[23] The servants' questioning of causality is subversive only in Eliot's *a posteriori* system.

What makes it so *politically* subversive is that the relationship between cause and effect is hierarchical, thereby constituting a philosophical analogy for the master–servant relationship, in which the cause is the master and the effect is the servant. Indeed, the notion that the master should represent the 'cause' of the servant's servitude and work is implicit in Hegel's 'Master–Slave Dialectic' (1807). For Hegel, the master unequivocally causes the other's slavery by overpowering that other during a 'life-and-death struggle' – causation is here constituted by brute force. Indeed, the point is made explicit in Hegel's earlier work, the *System of Ethical Life* (1802–3), where he remarks that, in the master–slave relation, 'one is might or power over the other.... So the former is related to the latter as cause.'[24] As masters, the physiologist and the genius in Eliot's essay want to be Hegelian in that they expect that their 'orders' should be sufficient cause for their cooks to squeeze the spinach thoroughly and to 'send up ... soup free from fat' (SL, 394). Unlike Hegel's master, however, Eliot's masters and mistresses do not possess sufficient power over their servants, either physically or philosophically, to enforce this rigid form of causality. For Eliot's servants to claim that 'an effect may exist without a cause' or that 'like causes will constantly produce unlike effects' (SL, 392) is, then, to question the very authority of the master over the servant and what the servant produces.

In this respect, Eliot's servants function as physicists, peculiar as that may seem. Like physicists, their strange ideas about causality come from the fact that they 'see ... deeply into the causes of things' (SL, 394). According to A.D. Lindsay, Kant relies too heavily on 'the finality of Newtonian physics',[25] and the same criticism could be levelled at Eliot. In contrast, the servants' questioning of causality seems to foreshadow some of the most important trends of twentieth-century physics – namely, quantum and chaos theories. As Oliver Lodge argues, the 'basis of ... the doctrines of Relativity and Quantum' can be traced back to Clerk Maxwell's work in the 1860s, and, in particular, to what Lodge calls 'the extraordinary Memoir'[26] published by Maxwell in the same year as Eliot's essay, 1865. As Robin Gilmour writes:

> Maxwell argued that the laws of matter at the molecular level could have only a statistical validity, not mechanical certainty.... [Maxwell] ... said [that] ... 'molecular science teaches us that ... no law deduced from [our experiments] ... can pretend to absolute precision.'[27]

Lodge argues that such contingency may even foreshadow Werner Heisenberg's 'doctrine of uncertainty' (1925), according to which 'all events are made up of immense numbers of ... minutiae'.[28] Heisenberg observed that it was impossible to measure both the speed and location of an electron as it orbited the atom without altering one or the other. The implications of this hypothesis are, as was recognised early on, potentially vast. In retrospect, it seems to render nonsensical Eliot's optimistic faith that empirical science will lead to absolute, universal knowledge and 'bright and blessed things on earth'. According to Heisenberg, it is simply impossible to know everything. As Lodge explains, Heisenberg's doctrine can be used

> to seek ... physical justification for the admission of an element of contingency amid physical phenomena.... [For example,] it is held that ... the law of causation may have gaps in it, when we come to deal with the smallest particles.... The discovery of the quantum is supposed to affect the deterministic philosophy in a revolutionary manner.[29]

Strangely, servants such as Eliot's cook Sally seem to question deterministic philosophy in much the same way – they come to deconstruct the strict causal sequence of Newtonian logic by their preoccupation with 'immense numbers of ... minutiae'. Sally suggests that her servitude is not simply caused by the power of her present mistress or master; rather, she has reference to immense numbers of other causes and factors which at once constitute and complicate her relationship with her master. She talks, for instance, of other masters, such as '"Mr. Tooley"' (SL, 394), and is sufficiently her own mistress to threaten resignation. She suggests, that is, the multiplicity of causes and effects modifying any hierarchical relation. Though Eliot and Mrs Queasy would have us believe otherwise, her oblique references to Tooley, resignation, Mr Queasy's '"constitution"' and '"the cat eating the white sauce"' (SL, 394) are certainly not nonsensical irrelevancies to the effect of the soup, but are all minor causes in themselves. When, as Eliot writes, servants 'presuppose ... that like causes will constantly produce unlike effects' (SL, 392), they are justified in retrospect by twentieth-century physics. Ironically, it is not Eliot but her 'physicist'-servants who, in a sense, 'may look to the next century for the triumph of ... [their] ideas' (SL, 392).

Masters, servants and chemistry

> Thought without Reverence is barren, perhaps poisonous; at best, dies like cookery with the day that called it forth.
>
> (Thomas Carlyle, *Sartor Resartus*)[30]

Mr Queasy, who is 'a genius', complains about the soup because the dyspepsia – or 'the interesting facts in animal chemistry' (SL, 393) to use Eliot's phrase – comes between him and his work. A long-established hierarchy here is reversed: as Eliot remarks, rather than being able to 'evolve' a 'momentous theory', Mr Queasy is himself the subject of a process of 'evolution of fatty acids' (SL, 393). Rather than science being mastered and shaped by Mr Queasy and his theory, the 'facts' of science are mastering him. Just six years before Eliot's essay, the genius who *did* evolve a momentous theory of evolution, Charles Darwin, had demonstrated that mankind was a product of nature, so never again could science or the scientist truly believe themselves to be the absolute masters of nature. In failing to locate absolute mastery in the reasoning bourgeois male, Darwinian nature becomes as poisonous to Mr Queasy's form of scientific mastery as is Sally's soup. What poisons mastery is that the scientific *facts* of nature, like Sally's soup, are independent from any kind of hierarchical control, simple causal sequence, or master–servant relation. Empirical scientific facts come to subvert Mr Queasy's theory and his mastery because of this independence.

The independence of Sally's soup and other foods from the stringent demands of consumers was, in fact, increasingly a subject of public concern during the nineteenth century. In 1820, an analytical (rather than animal) chemist called Friedrich Accum had pointed out that food might *always* be a kind of poison. As Michael Cotsell writes, Accum's

> *Treatise on Adulterations of Food and Culinary Poisons* ... first drew public attention to the facts of food adulteration.... [Accum]

believed that 'In reference to the deterioration of ... the necessaries and comforts of existence ... *in the midst of life we are in death.*'[31]

Victorian servants involved in the preparation or the serving of food might, therefore, always already be poisoning their masters, whether they know it or not. In this sense, it does not matter whether Sally is *consciously* 'putting arsenic in food' (SL, 393) or not.

Cotsell cites Accum as the principal model for the butler in Charles Dickens' *Our Mutual Friend* (1864–5), a novel exactly contemporaneous with Eliot's essay. The 'Analytical Chemist', as the butler is known, presides over the Veneerings' dinner parties and announces that '"dinner is on the table"' as if to say '"Come down and be poisoned"'.[32] Through the work of people like Accum, the middle class had become more aware of food adulteration, and more fearful of the control its servants had over both food and wine. The Analytical Chemist thus embodies those anxieties, as does Sally in Eliot's essay. Indeed, a few years earlier, in 1857, Louis Pasteur had demonstrated that the fermentation process is engendered by living micro-organisms; so the Analytical Chemist embodies the awareness, on the part of his masters, that the very micro-organisms which are fermented into wine might just poison – that the distinction between wine and poison is, in a sense, non-existent. Significantly enough, the Analytical Chemist 'always seem[s] ... to say, after "Chablis, sir?" – "You wouldn't if you knew what it's made of"' (OMF, 52).

The threat of poison is certainly as constant at the Veneerings' as it is at the Queasys'. As Deborah Thomas observes, 'the ... people who dine repeatedly with the Veneerings seem resigned to habitual dyspepsia',[33] so Twemlow is 'susceptible to east wind' and 'Lady Tippins lives ... in a chronic state of inflammation arising from the dinners' (OMF, 52, 683). Yet if, as Thomas suggests, 'the mercenary feast ... is ... provided to enrich, aggrandize, or otherwise promote ... self-interests',[34] then, by extension, the more one is able to eat – and thus the more one is able to overcome digestion – the greater one's aggrandisement. Whilst Twemlow is eventually forced to take 'two pills' as a '"precautionary measure in connection with the pleasures of the table"', Lady Tippins seems to assert her pre-eminence over the other guests by making 'a series of experiments on her digestive functions [which are] ... extremely complicated and daring' (OMF, 684, 53). It seems that, unlike Eliot's Mr Queasy, Lady Tippins is not mastered by facts of animal chemistry; rather, she *attempts* to prove her mastery over the facts of dyspepsia in her own scientific 'experiments'. In contrast, the

Lammles' disgrace and disempowerment are consummated by the Veneerings' eating 'on' (*OMF*, 683) them, in a near-cannibalistic gesture of mastery. This is not, however, merely a competition between guests at the table; it is also a way of validating mastery over the non-guests – namely, the cooks who produce the food and the retainers who serve it up. If the words '"Come down and be poisoned"' are a challenge to mastery from these servants, Lady Tippins is willing to meet such a challenge like a 'hardy battle cruiser' (*OMF*, 53).

Despite such violent imagery, however, digestive mastery at the Veneerings' is both subverted *and* perpetuated as an uneasy stand-off. In order to avoid a full-scale confrontation, the servants refuse to take responsibility for the poison in the food. Sally, Eliot's cook, 'fires up' (*SL*, 393) with indignation at the merest mention of arsenic, whilst the Analytical Chemist can safely acknowledge the fact of poison without taking responsibility for the cooking. Likewise, their masters – Queasy and the Veneerings respectively – avoid confrontation and thus assertion of their power by the very way they seek to *prove* that power: that is, by consuming everything their servants provide them to eat or drink. Dining well is a sign of mastery because of the contrast with those who do *not* dine so well – and, indeed, with those who are starving. The 'circumstance that some half-dozen people had lately died in the streets of starvation' (*OMF*, 186–7) is separated from the world of the Podsnaps and Veneerings by its utter *other*-ness. Giving 'a dinner on ... whatever befalls' (*OMF*, 683) is a way of overcoming the poor precisely by ignoring them.

This is *laissez-faire* mastery, depending as it does not on intervention but distance. Podsnap, for instance, seeks to prove his mastery by 'putting ... behind him' (*OMF*, 187) such things as the poor; as he declares, '"I do not admit these things.... If they do occur (not that I admit it) ... it is not for *me* ... to impugn the workings of Providence"' (*OMF*, 188). These 'things' – the Victorian 'facts [of] ... starvation' (*OMF*, 187) – will not, however, go away. As Thomas Carlyle writes in *Chartism* (1839), it is 'vain ... to think that the misery of one class ... can be isolated'. Like Dickens whom he greatly influenced, Carlyle is concerned with the '*facts*' which Podsnap's kind of mastery attempts to ignore. As he warns the Victorian masters of *laissez-faire*: 'The haggard naked fact speaks to us ... Are these millions guided? ... Fact searches for his third-rate potato, not in the meekest humour ... and does not find it.' The 'naked fact', it seems, *still* speaks, despite the ruling classes seeking ways and spaces in which, like Podsnap, they can make labourers and 'misery ... go out of sight', as Carlyle puts it. Significantly, Carlyle adds that, 'a ... briefer method' of achieving this disappearance 'is that of arsenic'.[35]

Poisoning between classes is mutual, it seems; in Victorian society, *our mutual 'friend'* is actually poison. In a sense, mutual poisoning stands as a metaphor for *laissez-faire* class relations as a whole; whilst Hegel's master–slave relationship is constituted by face-to-face combat, poisoning represents a means of struggle which can make the other 'disappear' whilst the poisoner is also absent. Poisoning, that is, represents violence by very covert, indirect and distant means, and these are the very hallmarks of *laissez-faire* government.

Distance is certainly fundamental to the world of *Our Mutual Friend*, where the ruling class and the lower classes are separated from each other both geographically and structurally – different classes generally belong to different locations and different chapters. Geographically speaking, the Veneerings are separated from the river by '"a goodish stretch"' and Lizzie Hexam is '"removed"' from Eugene Wrayburn by being a '"working girl"' in the Paper-Mill (*OMF*, 60, 761). The eminently Victorian institution of the factory expresses mastery by segregation – and, during the nineteenth century, it is into such institutions that the intense and highly individualised feudal relationship between master and servant gradually vanishes, into a generalised (non-) relation between classes.

Indeed, the actual master–servant relation itself underwent an analogous change at this time, gradually becoming expressive of a peculiarly domestic version of industrial *laissez-faire*. In a chapter entitled 'The Widening Gulf', Turner argues that it was particularly during the early part of the nineteenth century that 'the "lower classes" ... [became] literally the lower classes [as] they were relegated to basements.... To this submerged plane the self-respecting mistress did not dream of descending.' Furthermore, by being 'liberated from household chores', the mistress tried to 'deepen the chasm between [herself] ... and her ... servants'. Idleness becomes a sign of power, separating the Victorian mistress from her servants' domestic context and space: 'since she would not have known how to instruct the denizens [of the kitchen] in their duties,' Turner observes, 'it was better to make a virtue of aloofness'.[36] In the nineteenth century, the bourgeois master and mistress sought to establish authority by a mode of retreat.

This rule-by-distance, however, was undermined by upper servants, such as the butler, with whom the master and mistress had at least to come into some contact. When waiting on the Veneerings, the Analytical Chemist represents the collision of one social space with another. In this sense, the novel's most dangerous character is not part of the proletariat, but occupies a liminal position *between* proletariat and bourgeoisie. The danger lies in the fact that the servant might, by working, throw into relief the idleness of his masters. This, in part, explains why the duties of the Victorian butler were relatively light in front of guests. The Analytical Chemist appears merely to announce dinner, serve the wine and deliver messages. As Turner writes, 'the butler [was] ... as often as not ... kept for ostentation';[37] indeed, at the Veneerings', the 'four pigeon-breasted retainers in plain clothes [simply] stand in line in the hall' (*OMF*, 49). The position of such immobile retainers is paradoxical in the extreme: though they must not appear too much like their hardworking fellow servants, nor must they appear too much like their idle masters. The retainer is, on the one hand, the *mutual* friend of both masters and servants and, on the other, the friend of neither.

Indeed, throughout the nineteenth century, the distance between the servant and his/her master only increases. As Robbins writes, after 'the symbolic *volte-face* of 1848, the bourgeoisie backed away from its identification with the servant figure as it achieved hegemony and began to fear the militant masses beneath it'.[38] This fear is at work when Frances Power Cobbe argues, in 1868, for the replacement of 'the whole patriarchal idea of service ... with ... a contract'.[39] What Cobbe is advocating is precisely the kind of non-relationship that exists between the Analytical and his masters. When he speaks, it is to announce dinner to *everyone*, so individual contact is avoided; personal communication is necessitated only by the written messages (*OMF*, 59, 693) he passes on to Mortimer and Eugene. In this respect, the Analytical Chemist points up, in effect, the specifically *written* aspect of Cobbe's contractual account of service – in a sense, the 'document' which 'the Analytical is, in a ghostly manner, offering' (59) to Mortimer and Eugene is a contract. For Cobbe, the master–servant contract represents an escape from patriarchal service; for Dickens, however, such writing momentarily brings master and servant together: on receiving his message, Eugene and the Analytical speak 'in responsive confidence' (*OMF*, 693). *Pace* Derrida, writing here constitutes a moment of intimate closeness – a closeness that is obviously disruptive of bourgeois rule-by-distance. Moreover, the messages function as literal invitations to a world outside the domestic hierarchy, invitations to the masters to risk their power in an empirical engagement with the world of the poor and starving – Mortimer's story of the 'Man from Somewhere' (*OMF*, 48) gains empirical specificity only when he receives his message and leaves the Veneerings'. The messages, like the wine, are a kind of poison to generalised *laissez-faire* mastery.

Otherwise, the outside world *and* the Analytical himself are subject to the generalised mastery of the Veneerings and the diners. The Analytical too is subjected to a *laissez-faire* mastery based not on individual contact, but on a generalised, impersonal class relation. The Analytical, in fact, is wholly invisible to his masters on a personal basis, and can only ever be seen and heard by everyone at once. When he attempts to attract Mortimer's personal attention, Mortimer 'remains unconscious' of him 'in spite of all the arts of the chemist' (*OMF*, 59) – 'everybody looks at him' (*OMF*, 58), except Mortimer. The Analytical fascinates the guests *collectively* – and does so both despite *and* because of their wish to ignore him. As Dickens puts it, 'everybody looks at him [but] ... not because anybody wants to see him' (*OMF*, 58). He is so fascinating because he appears so meaningless: he possesses what Timothy Clark calls 'the nightmare fascination of a world without interiority'.[40] No one, not even Dickens, has access to his interior meanings – he is only ever '*seeming* to say ... "You wouldn't if you knew what it's made of"'; and he is only '*like* a gloomy Analytical Chemist' (*OMF*, 52: my emphasis). *Like* one of Maurice Blanchot's corpses, he is 'altogether similarity and also nothing more'.[41]

Eliot, like so many others, criticises Dickens for merely 'rendering the external traits'[42] of his characters. This is never truer than with the Analytical Chemist. The point, though, is that the servant – and particularly the visible, upper-servant – is *denied* any internal traits by such employers as the Veneerings. His meaninglessness is imposed on him because of the Veneerings' avoidance of any kind of individualised, paternalistic or quasi-feudal master–servant relationship: to his employers, he is less than human. Indeed, because of the lack of any humanising recognition, he becomes, in a sense, a machine. For the Victorian bourgeoisie, servants could ideally be machines, just as machines could be servants – the two terms shade into each other. At its most popular in the 1860s, the 'dumb-waiter' is a machine which is also a servant. Conversely, the 'Analytical Chemist' is a servant who is also an 'Analytical Machine' or 'Analytical Engine' – the name Charles Babbage gave, in 1834, to a projected 'general purpose programmable computing machine'.[43] The machine could be programmed with punched cards – so, like the Analytical Chemist, it was programmed wholly by its masters' orders. Like the Analytical Chemist, the Analytical Engine was wholly constituted by its masters and their instructions. Both Analytical Chemist and Analytical Engine are denied self-consciousness and self-motivation by their masters.

It is, however, this very absence of interiority that so fascinates the masters – and, in this sense, both the servant and the machine also come to be programmed by their masters' anxieties. It is evident that any sign of consciousness or independence on the part of either machine or servant will be deeply troubling; but, even if there are no such signs, the masters will still neurotically detect them. The Analytical Chemist's internal meaning seems to be necessarily 'diabolical' to his masters, and it is inevitable that he must 'object as a matter of principle to everything that occurs on the [Veneerings'] premises' (*OMF*, 305, 159). Likewise, in *The Difference Engine* (1991) – a recent fictional account of Babbage's Engines by William Gibson and Bruce Sterling – Babbage's co-inventor, Ada Byron, argues that the Analytical Engine might eventually gain a self-consciousness independent of its inventors. She makes explicit this fascination with that which lacks or borders on consciousness when she writes, 'an Engine [could be said to] *live* ... and could indeed *prove* its own life, should it develop the capacity to look on itself. The Lens for such a self-examination is of a nature not yet known to us; yet we know that it exists, for we ourselves possess it.'[44] A whole sub-genre of science fiction has been based on this premise – on, that is, the fear that a machine will gain an interiority, a 'Lens for ... self-examination'. Sussman points out that the fictional Ada Byron's words 'echo the actual words of [the historical] Ada Byron Lovelace in her published *Notes* on the Babbage Engine'.[45] In 1843, she wrote that the proposed Analytical Engine established

> a uniting link ... between the operations of matter and abstract mental processes.... We are not aware of ... anything partaking of the nature of what is so well designated the *Analytical* Engine has been hitherto proposed ... as a practical possibility, any more than the idea of a thinking or of a reasoning machine.[46]

The possibility of a *reasoning* machine is deeply subversive to the industrialised world of the Victorians, based as it is on a simple opposition between bourgeois, reasoning master and unreasoning industrial machine. The subversive possibility, in an industrial setting, of a reasoning machine is analogous to the subversive possibility of a reasoning servant in a domestic space. After all, it is just such servants who upset Eliot's opposition between reasoning master and un-reasoning servant in 'Servants' Logic'.

By relying on this opposition, however, bourgeois mastery steadily erodes the status of the servant during the nineteenth century. Since the opposition reduces the servant to the level of an unskilled, unreasoning machine, it also reduces him or her to the status of the workman, who is, in Marx's words, 'an appendage of the machine'.[47] The servant gradually becomes indistinguishable from the industrial labourer. Indeed, by becoming increasingly machine-like and proletarian, the servant becomes increasingly 'other' to the masters and mastery. As Turner puts it,

> In the nineteenth century the servant's status steadily slumped. Lord Chesterfield had viewed menial servants as his 'equals in Nature … inferiors only by the difference of our positions'; but the employers of the nineteenth century would have none of this.[48]

Servants are gradually subsumed into a proletariat to which they themselves do not feel they belong. The erosion of the distinction between paid labour and domestic servitude is reflected by an increasing slippage between the two terms on the part of the ruling class: as Feltes points out, 'the [parliamentary] Act of 1867 was … the last to be entitled a "master and servant act"', after which 'employer' and 'employee'[49] became the usual terms.

Needless to say, the Analytical Chemist does not seem to consider himself a proletarian. On the contrary, he is willing to defend his higher status in an assertive manner, in complete contrast with his employers' *laissez-faire*. This is apparent in the duel he has with the truly proletarian 'Coachman' who enters with a message during one of the dinners:

> The Analytical is beheld in collision with the Coachman; the Coachman manifesting a purpose of coming at the company with a silver salver … the Analytical cutting him off at the sideboard. The superior stateliness … of the Analytical prevails over [the Coachman, who] … retires defeated. (*OMF*, 693)

The Analytical here occupies a peculiar role whereby he is not only his masters' sole poisoner but also their sole defender against a potentially insurgent proletariat. As Pamela Horn notes, '[upper-servants] … served … [a] valuable purpose in "*protecting*" their employers from … callers'.[50]

The Analytical is willing to protect his employers and his own position because he has a greater claim to a feudal tradition and aristocratic pre-history than do his masters. As Marshall points out, during feudal times, 'the great [domestic] officials such as the steward [and] the comptroller [were] ... in many cases ... drawn from the nearer kinsmen of aristocratic householders', and she goes on to connect the duties of such officials with those of the 'modern butler'.[51] Although distant, the Analytical can lay claim to exactly the kind of inheritance the Veneerings cannot.

In an essay entitled 'Old and New Servants' (1867), Dickens calls male retainers 'Wonderful aristocrats! .... Their manner and air, if imported into the classes above, would be the perfection of refined hauteur and accomplished languor.' In these servants, Dickens argues, it is possible to 'distinguish regular traces of circles above them'.[52] In the case of the Analytical, these aristocratic traces take the form of the 'Analytical solemnities' that the 'bran-new' (*OMF*, 258, 48) Veneerings so desire for themselves. On coming into power, the bourgeoisie sought to naturalise itself by assuming the trappings of the feudal aristocracy it had deposed. All the 'new' things the Veneerings have bought, such as 'their plate ... their carriage ... [their] coat-of-arms' (*OMF*, 48) and the Analytical Chemist himself, are signifiers of an aristocratic lineage. As G.K. Chesterton remarks of the Analytical, 'the truth about servants ... is simply this: that the secret of aristocracy is hidden even from aristocrats. Servants, butlers, footmen, are the high priests who have the real dispensation.'[53]

The Analytical does indeed function like a 'priest'. When he 'concedes' the 'chalice' (*OMF*, 56, 53) to those at the table, he seems to be officiating at a secular Eucharist. After all, Christ and his priests *are* servants: at the Last Supper, Christ washed the feet of his disciples. Indeed, like the modern Analytical Chemist, Christ was also an empiricist – Agacinski notes the 'absolute risk which inheres in the belief that God was *this particular man*, an empirical and historical reality'. Significantly enough, it is Kant whom Agacinski accuses of ignoring the empirical nature of the incarnation in his *Religion Within the Limits of Reason Alone*: 'he abstracted,' writes Agacinski, 'from love for the God-become-man who gave the infinite such a specific face.' Kant's religion cannot comprehend empirical singularity, but is concerned only with an absolute 'law of Reason'.[54] It is these absolute laws, however, which Christ's empiricism puts at 'absolute risk'. The empiricism of Christ and the Analytical Chemist puts in jeopardy the transcendental and absolute laws on which all mastery bases itself, whether that mastery is the educative-mastery enjoined by Kant or the bourgeois mastery of the Veneerings.

This is despite the fact that these forms of mastery also *depend on* Christ and the Analytical, respectively. The Christ who is God *seems* to support Kant's rational religion, just as, in his secular Eucharist, the

Analytical *seems* to 'concede' or 'proffer' (*OMF*, 54) not only wine but also power to the Veneerings. What the Analytical really dispenses, though, is an *illusory* power: the wine is only Champagne and Chablis and nothing more. In a century of scientific discovery, the transubstantiation of wine into Christ's blood would have seemed like 'nonsense' to an Analytical Chemist, so, in that sense, the wine has no transcendental meaning. Nor can the Champagne and Chablis function any longer as the indicators of aristocratic status they have been for centuries, since the Analytical Chemist is subversively aware that Chablis is merely a compound of other substances. The cup-bearer himself does not believe in the transcendental nature of the wine, but is quite aware what the Chablis is 'made of'. Since, as Thomas Thomson writes, chemical 'analysis [is] the art of determining the constituents of which every compound is composed',[55] it is clear that, by definition, analysis is deconstructive. As Miss Cornelia Blimber declares, in Dickens' *Dombey and Son* (1846–8), '"the word analysis, as opposed to synthesis, is thus defined by Walker: 'The resolution of an object ... into its first elements.' As opposed to synthesis, you observe."'[56] The Veneerings' power depends on the synthesis of elements that is Chablis or Champagne, as well as on the assumed synthesis of the signifiers 'Chablis' or 'Champagne' with the supposed signified – transcendental or aristocratic power. The Analytical Chemist opposes such synthesis.

It is, of course, the subversive knowledge of what the Chablis is 'made of' which makes the butler seem 'like a gloomy Analytical Chemist' (*OMF*, 52). Historically speaking, it was quite conceivable that such knowledge would be within the Victorian butler's reach. 'From time to time,' writes Turner, 'the butler withdrew to the cellars in order to perform rites of rectification and purification.' Some butlers, indeed, were even called on to 'brew beer' themselves.[57] As Horn notes, 'the skilful butler in the large household was ... expected to know how to fine or clear wines and brew beer ... [and] could ... detect [any] ... adulterations'.[58] Nevertheless, it is rather strange that this vestigial aristocrat and priest should be associated with the very modern science of analytical chemistry. The Analytical, though, haunts the Veneering dinners as a Banquo-like ghost – a ghost, that is, of extinct aristocratic and priestly hierarchies – and this is the nature of his 'ghostly manner' (*OMF*, 59). He is thus witness to the precariousness of any class of masters *and* a reminder to the new masters of how they deposed previous hegemonies, philosophically and scientifically speaking. Since, as Robbins notes, the bourgeoisie abandons its 'revolutionary self-image' at the moment of its 'arriving in power',[59] it becomes afraid of the revolutionary 'progress' of history it has in part unleashed. When the Analytical Chemist first seems to say, '"Come down and be poisoned, ye unhappy children of men"' (*OMF*, 51), it is as if he is announcing the Last Judgement to his bourgeois masters. If, as Cotsell writes, '"children of men"' is the biblical phrase for all those destroyed by the Deluge,[60] the Analytical seems to be announcing a second Deluge – a second revolution. Mme de Pompadour[61] is said to have prophesied the French Revolution of 1789 with the words 'Après moi, le Deluge' and the Analytical Chemist echoes these words.

George Eliot, though, seems not to hear this echo. Her declaration that 'we may look to the next century for the triumph of our ideas' is, for all its flippancy, part of a bourgeois philosophical agenda which attempted to appropriate a potentially revolutionary future in the name of the bourgeoisie – and crucial to this attempt was science. Ironically, the new masters of the nineteenth century often saw science as *their* weapon. As Gilmour observes, the Victorians' faith in science was largely based on the 'hero-worship' of certain scientists: 'the ambition ... behind ... the writings of Huxley and Tyndall,' he asserts, 'was to challenge the *de facto* priesthood for cultural leadership.'[62] The bourgeoisie attempted to construct what Galton called a 'scientific priesthood',[63] a priesthood of which Dickens' Analytical Chemist is surely a *parodic* member. This secular priesthood was to replace its Christian predecessor; as Beatrice Webb writes, at this time 'the men of science ... were routing the theologians [and] confounding the mystics'.[64]

There is, though, an inherent contradiction within the Victorian bourgeoisie's perception of science, for whilst they seemed ready to accept the necessity of scientific empiricism, they were unwilling to lose sight of a transcendental purpose and a spiritual authority in science. Even if chemistry was no longer engaged on 'the never-ending search for the philosopher's stone and the elixir of life',[65] as Charles-Albert Reichen puts it, scientists were themselves *believed in* as never before. By the mid-nineteenth century, science was believed to have the potential, as Gilmour writes, 'to solve the problems of life'[66] – a more generalised, though equally transcendental, purpose as that of searching for the philosopher's stone. The kind of utopian and positivist stance Eliot displays in 'The Future of German Philosophy' masks transcendentalism with an apparent acceptance of the empirical methods of science. It is transcendentalism which lies behind Eliot's assertion that 'the uphill *a posteriori* path ... will lead ... to an eminence whence we may see very bright and blessed things on earth'.

Here, Eliot attempts to combine the *a posteriori* or empirical methods of science with a transcendentalist and bourgeois notion of progress.

The combination of science and bourgeois hegemony was, though, always threatened by empiricism. Demanding the kind of positivist 'Philosophy of Science' first proposed by Auguste Comte, G.H. Lewes – Eliot's partner – declares in his *Biographical History of Philosophy* (1857):

> The *speciality* of most scientific men, and their incapacity of either producing or accepting general ideas, has long been a matter of complaint.... The evil of speciality ... affects the very highest condition of Science, namely, its capability of instructing and directing society.[67]

Lewes complains that scientists challenge the very possibility of general or universal ideas, and that they fail to sanction the universalising doctrine of the bourgeoisie and its ambition to instruct and direct society. Lewes thus fails to heed Kant's warning that, once empiricism is accepted as the only form of knowledge, 'universality ... [becomes] only an arbitrary extension of validity'.[68] The increasing speciality of scientists is part of empiricism's move away from the universal. Though the establishment of the Chemical Society in 1841 and the Royal College of Chemistry in 1845 would seem to suggest the increasing prestige and authority of Victorian science, these institutions also represented *and* fostered what Lewes sees as the anti-social evil of speciality. Moreover, science's capacity to instruct society practically was further undermined as it moved away from what Gilmour calls 'that monument to applied science'[69] – the Great Exhibition of 1851. The Analytical Chemist is a cryptic personification of the kind of *pure* and *specialised* science that Lewes and the bourgeoisie were coming to fear.

Of all the sciences, the modern one of analytical chemistry is the most subversive of Lewes's philosophy of 'general ideas' and of any philosophy that exhorts science towards transcendental ends. Specialisation is *inherent* within analytical chemistry; analysis, by its very nature, is simply the process of separating out smaller elements, not the discovery of a general idea or *element*al truth. Indeed, the development of empiricism in chemistry depended on the very deconstitution of general ideas and abandonment of transcendental goals; as Reichen writes:

> The alchemist ... of the Middle Ages ... thought in terms of the accepted philosophical notions of the era.... Slowly [however] the

practice of chemistry began to move away from the search for the philosopher's stone to more practical and reasonable goals.[70]

Lewes and others, though, try to reimpose a moral and philosophical discourse onto chemistry. They argue for a new kind of philosopher's stone, but the pure empiricism of modern analytical chemistry is poison to any form of transcendentalism. This is why the new bourgeois order is so nervous of a science for which it is, in part, responsible. This is why, indeed, any class seeking to establish hegemony must move away from analytical chemistry and the pure empiricism it embodies – a retreat which, for Lewes and Eliot and other nineteenth-century masters, is disguised by their apparent acceptance of empiricism and empirical methodology. Marx famously compares modern bourgeois society to a 'sorcerer who is no longer able to control the powers of the nether world whom he has called up by his spells'.[71] He refers, of course, to the powers of the proletariat, but he might just as well be speaking of the powers of science in general and analytical chemistry in particular. Moreover, it becomes increasingly apparent that the nineteenth-century bourgeoisie cannot even control their own 'sorcerer' – the Analytical Chemist.

3
Slaveholders and Democrats: Combined Masters and Slaves in Thomas Carlyle, Charles Dickens' *American Notes* and Frederick Douglass's *Narrative*

Masters and slaves

> An accusation of inadequacy, which has often been laid against [the Hegelian dialectic is] ... the question of what bound the society of masters together.
>
> (Jacques Lacan, *Écrits*)[1]

> 'There are no masters here.'
>
> (Charles Dickens, *Martin Chuzzlewit*)[2]

As Hugh Thomas points out, one of the main 'causes of slavery named in [the Emperor] Justinian's Code of Laws [was] ... defeat in war'.[3] Similarly, in an article entitled 'North American Slavery' (1852), Dickens and his collaborator, Henry Morley, presuppose a past when slaves were mainly 'prisoners of war'.[4] As we have seen, Hegel provides a paradigm for such slavery in his 'Master and Slave Dialectic' (1807). For Hegel, the master's power originates in a 'life-and-death struggle'[5] with the other – the slave being the one who capitulates during this struggle. Carlyle certainly encountered Hegel's work, and, in *Chartism* (1839), invokes *and* justifies hierarchies that have their origins in violence. Here, Carlyle legitimises Hegel's model by identifying 'might and right [as] ... one and the same'. For Carlyle, 'conquest, along with power of compulsion, [which is] ... essential universally in human society, must bring benefit along with it.... The strong man ... is [also]

... the wise man.... [He] who is *fit* to administer, to direct, and guidingly command: he is the strong man.'[6] In *American Notes* (1842), however, Dickens condemns *contemporary* American slaveholders as 'cowards' – cowards who are somehow also 'merciless and unrelenting tyrants'.[7] Similarly, in the *Narrative of the Life of Frederick Douglass* (1845), Douglass describes his master, Thomas Auld, as 'cruel but cowardly'.[8] There are obvious inconsistencies here, both *between* the *Narrative*, *American Notes* and other writings on slavery, and *within* Dickens' and Douglass's accounts of slaveholders.

Any inconsistencies between the texts arise partly because of the writers' differing perspectives. Hegel's dialectic is set in what Thad Ziolowski calls a 'fabulist realm of universalist discourse', whilst, according to Ziolowski, Douglass writes 'against the grain of such unmoored universalist discourse'.[9] Douglass and Dickens are seeking to present their own specific experiences. Although Dickens' chapter on 'Slavery' in *American Notes* is written in the form of a diatribe against slavery, it is nevertheless presented in the context of a personal travelogue, and, of course, Douglass's text *purportedly* relates events in his own life. Moreover, both are discussing the specific phenomenon of North American slavery at a particular point in time. As Stanley Elkins argues, 'American slavery was unique, in the sense that ... nothing like it had ever previously been seen.'[10] Hegel's abstract discourse rationalises slavery, reducing the concept to its extreme, dialectical form; Dickens and particularly Douglass, however, come to know slavery empirically, one viewing it from without, the other from within.

The empirical details of the American master–slave experience deconstruct, to some extent, the mythology of mastery which Hegel, in part, upholds. For this reason, the differences and slippages between Hegel's paradigm and the master–slave experience in the American South are more significant than the actual points of contact. Here, Carlyle offers a useful point of mediation, between the philosophically abstract world of Hegel and the empirically specific worlds of Dickens and Douglass. Whilst Carlyle is certainly concerned with abstract and ideal notions of mastery and heroism, his writings also deal with specific issues. In 'Shooting Niagara: and After?' (1867) and his earlier essay 'The Nigger Question' (1849), he addresses the subject of American slavery directly. As Elkins remarks, 'Carlyle was much praised and widely quoted in the American South.'[11] He is, though, a usefully ambivalent figure. He was admired by both pro-slavery thinkers, such as the American philosopher George Fitzhugh, and anti-slavery writers, such as Dickens. It is certainly true, as Arthur A. Adrian notes, that it was 'especially in later years' that Dickens developed an 'increasing respect for the views of the crusty Scot', a respect that coincides with an increasing conservatism and what Brahma Chaudhuri calls a 'softening attitude to the [American] South'. Adrian makes clear, however, that Dickens 'always remained implacably set against forced servitude',[12] despite his debt to Carlyle.

As Jon Roper writes, 'Carlyle can be quarried by ideologues of all persuasions'[13] – in part, because his writings vacillate between the abstract and the empirical, the philosophical and the historical. Although a contemporary of Dickens and Douglass, Carlyle drew heavily on German Idealist and Romantic writings, and certainly knew of Hegel's work. It is not surprising, then, that Carlyle appropriates *and* modifies a Hegelian model of mastery. Both, for example, admire Napoleon Bonaparte, but, whilst Hegel's writings are contemporaneous with Napoleon's victories, Carlyle is writing in a post-Napoleonic world – and these differing historical contexts *do* have an effect on even their most abstract writings on mastery and slavery. Despite Ziolowski's criticisms, Hegel's dialectic *is* marked by the empirical, historical context in which it was formulated. The *Phenomenology of Spirit* was completed as Napoleon's armies advanced on, and then occupied, Jena in October 1806. Following Napoleon's victory, Hegel saw and described him as that 'world-soul ... who ... reaches out over the world and masters it'.[14] In this respect, there seems little doubt that Napoleon's world-mastery exemplifies the violent, confrontational mastery Hegel describes in the 'Master–Slave Dialectic'. Thirty or so years later, Carlyle uses Napoleon as just such an example. In *Heroes and Hero-Worship* (1840) he writes, 'to bridle-in that great ... French Revolution; to *tame* it ... is not this ... what [Napoleon] ... managed to do? Through Wagrams, Austerlitzes; triumph after triumph.... He rose naturally to be the King.'[15] Consciously or not, Hegel's description of violent mastery remains a vital *master*-text for Carlyle, as well as for Dickens and Douglass. Dickens, as we have seen, demonstrates an awareness of a Hegelian form of slavery in his essay 'North American Slavery'; and Ziolowski suggests that 'the dialectical movement of ... [Hegel's] ... thought provides an appropriate rhythm for a reading of ... Douglass's *Narrative* ... It is not difficult to imagine Douglass ... writing [the 'Master–slave'] ... passage [himself].'[16]

Nevertheless, the years separating Hegel and these other writers are of the utmost importance. Whilst Hegel's writings are marked by the Napoleonic era, Carlyle's are both marked and alienated from that moment. For Carlyle, the heroic past of Austerlitzes and Wagrams is to be contrasted with a contemporary 'Valet-World ... governed by the Sham-Hero [and] ... the Unheroic'. 'Napoleon,' claims Carlyle, '[was] our last Great Man!'[17] In *The Eighteenth Brumaire of Louis Bonaparte* (1852), Karl Marx argues that the contemporary Emperor of France, *Louis* Napoleon, is the example *par excellence* of a 'Sham-Hero': he is merely an 'adventurer who hides his commonplace repulsive features under the iron death mask of Napoleon'.[18] As Bonaparte's nephew, Louis Napoleon's claim to the Imperial throne does not consist in any heroism on his part, but merely in his relationship to a past hero. In this sense, Louis Napoleon is symptomatic of the 'unheroic' nature of the age. As Carlyle observes in the *Latter-Day Pamphlets* (1850), 'on the dust of our heroic ancestors we ... sit ... saying to one another, It is well, it is well! By inheritance of their noble struggles, we have been permitted to sit slothful so long.'[19] In a post-Napoleonic world, mastery is not gained by the life-and-death violence described by Hegel, but merely by inheriting the results of such heroism.

By the 1840s, it was certainly the case that most American slaveholders only inherited their mastery. Dickens' *American Notes* was written during a crucial but liminal period in the history of slavery: the slave-trade had been made illegal in the United States in 1808, yet, anomalously, the institution of slavery was legally perpetuated until 1863. Although an illegal trans-Atlantic slave-trade continued, legally no new Africans could be subjugated and made slaves; and, although an internal trade thrived, this mainly involved the sale, purchase and hiring of those who had already been made slaves. The result was that masters inherited their authority from others, and slaves were born into slavery. Both mastery and slavery depended on inheritance. By 1852, Dickens and Morley could claim that even the illegal importation of slaves had 'entirely ceased', because the rate of natural increase in the United States provided the necessary workforce. As they note, 'in 1840 the number of slaves in the United States was not quite two millions and a half. In the year 1850 there were more than three millions'.[20] These claims are generally supported by historians. Peter Parish argues that 'the ... unique ... mark of slavery in the Southern states was the natural increase of the slave population. In all other slave societies of the New World, the slave population ... was sustained ... only by constant injection of new slaves from Africa.'[21] For Dickens and Morley, this 'unique mark' of slavery in the United States seems to render it preferable to other existing systems:

> The contraband traffic in slaves is essential to the working of the slave system on its present footing in the Spanish Antilles.... [On

the other hand,] the bodily condition of the slaves under our cousins in America ... is good. They are, on the whole, fed ... amply and ... well treated.... They have therefore thriven and their stock is multiplied in the land.[22]

Despite the success in 'multiplying' the 'stock' of slaves, the slaveholders' reliance on natural increase must have weakened the system's claims to absolute legitimacy. When the vast majority of a slave population have been born into slavery, the origin or cause of that slavery must seem remote, almost pre-historical. Although, as Thomas notes, Justinian claimed that another of the 'causes of slavery ... [was] being born a slave',[23] this hardly constitutes a direct form of causation for the slave concerned. Similarly, the origin of the slaveholders' mastery vanishes into a chain of previous masters from whom the slaves were bought or inherited. In Hegelian terms, none of these masters 'proved'[24] their authority in a struggle with the other. After 1808, the absence of such proof for mastery becomes increasingly and dangerously obvious.

This is not, though, to claim a Hegelian life-and-death heroism for the Atlantic slave-traders before 1808. Douglass accuses his forefathers' enslavers of being a 'band of successful *robbers*, who had ... gone to Africa, and stolen us from our homes' (*NFD*, 33: my emphasis). Similarly, contemporary slaveholders are 'men-stealers' (*NFD*, 75) because they have merely inherited what was originally stolen. Hegel's scheme evidently cannot encompass the notion of masters as 'robbers;' but, in *Chartism*, Carlyle suggests that 'robbers' are masters who obtain obedience from slaves or servants without fulfilling the obligations on their side. As he writes,

> that Society 'exists for the protection of property' ... [is] true enough, O friends ... *Thou shalt not steal, thou shalt not be stolen from*: what a Society were that; Plato's Republic, More's Utopia mere emblems of it! ...
> And now what is thy property? ... [It includes] a god-given *capability* to be and do; [and] rights, therefore, – the right for instance to thy ... guidance if I obey thee.[25]

Carlyle's use of the term 'guidance' always implies both a form of paternalism *and* a Hegelian element of coercion; for Carlyle, is it the 'right of the ignorant man to be guided by the wiser, to be, *gently or forcibly*, held in the true course by him.... It is a sacred right and duty, on both sides.'[26] Thus, the robber-master is she/he who 'steals' obedience from the slave without any reciprocal paternalistic, or Hegelian, recognition. The trans-Atlantic slave-traders conform to this definition; John Blassingame argues that many 'African slaves were ... kidnapped by slave raiders', and Thomas asserts that '"man-stealing" accounted for the majority of slaves taken to the New World'.[27]

Clearly, '"man-stealing"' is no origin at all in Hegelian terms. Indeed, since the 'Master and Slave Dialectic' represents, for Hegel, an originary moment of history, the slave-traders have no history in Hegelian terms; their mastery has no beginning, so they have no history. Ironically, it is the European and American slave-traders who thus conform to Hegel's definition of 'the African Spirit' as 'the Unhistorical, Undeveloped Spirit'. In *The Philosophy of History* (1830–1), Hegel asserts that 'Africa ... is no historical part of the World; it has no movement or development to exhibit.... What we properly understand by Africa is ... still involved in the conditions of mere nature, and [is] ... on the threshold of the World's History.'[28] As Jacques Derrida notes, such ahistoricity is, according to Hegel, the result of Africa's 'hardheadedly keep[ing] itself on the threshold of the historico-dialectical process'.[29] It is really, though, the *slave-traders* who keep out of the historico-dialectical process, by avoiding the originary dialectical confrontation between master and slave; because of their 'men-stealing', it is the slave-traders who are ahistorical. Nevertheless, they also impose their own ahistoricity on the Africa from which they steal; by 'men-stealing', the traders rob the Africans of any Hegelian origin or history. Rather than 'hardheadedly keep[ing] itself on the threshold of the historico-dialectical process', Africa is *kept* out of this process – by slave-traders and, indeed, by European thinkers such as Hegel. The slave-traders envisaged by Douglass, and described by Thomas and Blassingame, steal or buy Africans in order to avoid the violence of the historico-dialectical process. For Hegel, as for Carlyle, the process of history is in part propelled forwards by 'Heroes' or 'World-Historical persons, whose vocation it [is] ... to be the agents of the World-Spirit'[30] – heroes like Napoleon, in fact. Given that the trans-Atlantic slave-traders were generally 'robber-masters', however, it is clear that history could *not* be made in Africa. Writing of Hegel's *Phenomenology*, Judith Shklar argues that 'the dawn of ... knowledge' – and therefore of Western history – 'is Homer's poetry' in which

> the battle of heroic competition cannot be anything less than mortal combat. Hector and Achilles never consider anything else.... However ... a moment of genuine mutual recognition does occur. For it is peculiarly human to risk one's life.... It sets men radically

apart from the beasts.... The germ of the freedom of mankind is born in the battle between heroes.[31]

The slave-traders rob their African slaves of even the limited recognition and 'germ of freedom' that inheres in Hegel's originary struggle. For the traders, Africans are not set radically apart from the beasts – but then nor are the traders themselves. Within the Atlantic slave-trade, both masters and slaves lack any kind of originary recognition.

Nevertheless, even such an unsatisfactory origin as this disappeared in 1808. Since, as Thomas asserts, 'most of the millions of slaves shipped from Africa were not members of an established slave population',[32] the causes of slavery and mastery seemed at least slightly more apparent before 1808 than in 1842. The lack of any real origin for mastery in 1842 is certainly apparent when Dickens defines what he calls the 'three great classes' of slaveholders in the United States:

> The first, are those more moderate and rational owners of human cattle.... The second, consists of all those owners, breeders, users, buyers and sellers of slaves ... [each of whom] is a more exacting, and a sterner, and less responsible despot than the Caliph Haroun Alraschid.... The third ... is composed of ... [a] delicate gentility. (*AN*, 229–30)

Of these, the first and third are constituted as capitalist and aristocratic forms of mastery, whilst the second is envisaged by Dickens as a form of despotism. None of these three types of masters is able, however, to *create* slaves: all three are merely 'upholders of slavery' (*AN*, 229). They are perpetuating a hierarchy that pre-dates them.

The fact that, in this period, slaves were not created partly explains some of the religious rhetoric used by the 'upholders' of slavery. One of the many ways in which slavery was legitimised was by reference to the book of Genesis. The right of ownership of slaves was perceived to be *inherited* from the masters' biblical forefathers. As Douglass notes, this is 'the argument that God cursed Ham, and therefore American slavery is right' (*NFD*, 14).[33] An appeal to the Old Testament is, however, inherently problematic in that it at once identifies an origin and displaces it – back to Genesis no less. The American slaveholders' appeal to Genesis also points up that mastery's distance and displacement from *any* origin.

In Douglass's *Narrative*, the reliance on any religious or biblical sanction seems to be a sign of weakness on the part of the masters. This is certainly the case for Thomas Auld, one of Douglass's masters, who 'came into possession of all his slaves by marriage' (*NFD*, 40). For Douglass, Auld's authority lacks an origin even more conspicuously than that of the slaveholders born into mastery, and so Auld's mastery comes to depend on religious and biblical sanction, in lieu of anything else:

> Of all men, adopted slaveholders are the worst.... [Auld's] airs, words and actions were the airs, words, and actions of born slave-holders, and, being assumed, were awkward enough. He was not even a good imitator.... Having no resources within himself, he was compelled to be the copyist of many.... After his conversion, he found religious sanction and support for his slaveholding cruelty. (*NFD*, 40)

Auld is described as 'cruel, but *cowardly*' (*NFD*, 40: my emphasis). His cowardice consists primarily of his reliance on past masters. His authority is apparently sanctioned by God, Noah and those who have supposedly inherited their spiritual mastery – namely, the 'three or four preachers' (*NFD*, 41) whom Auld frequently invites to his home. He is also the 'copyist' of past secular masters; he speaks at times 'with the firmness of Napoleon' (*NFD*, 40). Auld's authority is perpetuated only by deferring to a chain of past masters. Despite belonging to 'The New World' that defines itself as a break with the European past, American mastery depends ironically enough on that and other pasts. This dependence must have become increasingly and dangerously apparent during the period 1808–63, when power over slaves could only be inherited or copied.

As well as inheriting and copying mastery from *past* masters, slave-holders also sustained their power by deferring to other, contemporary masters. On a small scale, this is demonstrated by a fight Douglass has with four apprentices in the shipyard at Baltimore:

> While I kept ... [the white apprentices] from combining, I succeeded very well; for I could whip the whole of them, taking them sepa-rately. They, however, at length combined, and came on me, armed with sticks, stones and handspikes. (*NFD*, 63)

Here, white mastery is perpetuated only by the (cowardly) combination of the masters. Otherwise, it would be Douglass who was 'whipping' the masters, not the other way round. Any Hegelian struggle is pre-vented, or at least mediated, by the combination of the masters. Auld, for instance, does not relate directly to Douglass, but crowds the relationship with God, Noah, the preachers who visit him and, later, Covey the '"nigger-breaker"' (*NFD*, 42). Similarly, it is collective action which is obviously the premise behind 'Lynch law' (*NFD*, 63) and, after the Civil War, the rise of such groups as the Ku Klux Klan. Collective violence against blacks in America concerned Dickens a great deal. In *American Notes* (*AN*, 231) and in a letter to John Forster, he writes of a particular incident in St. Louis: 'A slave ... being arrested ... drew his bowie knife and ripped the constable across the body. The mob who gathered round ... overpowered him by numbers; carried him away to a piece of open ground ... *and burned him alive.*'[34] In his 'Address Before the Young Men's Lyceum of Springfield, Illinois' (27 January 1838), Abraham Lincoln refers to the same event as an example of what he calls a 'mobocratic spirit, which ... is now abroad in the land'. For Lincoln, such mob violence is a profanation against the 'Founding Fathers' of the Constitution: 'let every man remember,' he declares, 'that to violate the law is to trample on the blood of his father.' The only remedy for the mobocratic spirit, he claims, is to instil 'reverence for the laws' in all Americans: 'let reverence for the laws be breathed by every American mother, to the lisping babe.... Let it become the *political religion* of the nation.'[35] What Lincoln fails to acknowledge, however, is that the mobocratic spirit exhibited in St. Louis is not so far from his own 'political religion'. In the case of the lynching in St. Louis, the jury was told by the aptly named judge, Luke E. Lawless, that 'a bad and lamentable deed had been committed, and that if it were proved to have been the act of a few, they must be punished; but if it were the act of "the many ... it was no affair for a jury to interfere in"'.[36] Lawless's law here effectively legitimises mob action. In *American Slavery As It Is* (1839) – the book from which most of the material of Dickens' 'Slavery' chapter in *American Notes* is taken – Theodore D. Weld asserts that, by this judgement, 'the state of Missouri ... proclaimed to the world, that the wretches who perpetrated that unspeakably diabolical murder and the thousands that stood by consenting to it, were *her representatives*, and the Bench sanctifies it'.[37]

Generally speaking, the law did indeed 'sanctify' the lynching of slaves in the sense that it was notoriously difficult to gain any white's conviction for a black's murder. Referring to an episode in Douglass's *Narrative* when an overseer shoots a slave, William Lloyd Garrison writes, 'Let it never be forgotten, that no slaveholder or overseer can be convicted of any outrage perpetrated on the person of a slave ... on the testimony of coloured witnesses, whether bond or free.'[38]

By appealing to 'reverence of the laws', Lincoln is inadvertently upholding the same mobocratic spirit he is attacking – the very spirit on which American slavery seems to be based. Later in the 'Address to the Young Men's Lyceum', he attempts to justify his stance by declaring that, 'although bad laws, if they exist, should be repealed as soon as possible, still while they continue in force ... they should be religiously observed'.[39] Lincoln is entangled in a common paradox of democracy: although laws are to be revered, 'bad laws' can be recognised as such and changed. To a certain extent, this attitude can only preserve the hierarchical status quo for slaves: such reverence for 'bad laws' is another way of perpetuating the master–slave relationship. By sanctifying the law, the masters are fixing their relationships with their slaves and ensuring that the individual slave is confronted not so much with an individual master but with an almost deified institution and abstraction. The slave has to deal not so much with one master, but with the masters' sacred law. In *Latter-Day Pamphlets*, Carlyle writes that American society is '"anarchy *plus* a street-constable"' – America's 'attainments' as a nation consist, he argues, merely in its fostering an 'inveterate and ... as it were, inborn reverence for the Constable's Staff'. For Carlyle, real mastery disappears in America into an anarchy in which rule is perpetuated only by a reverence for the law. America is anarchic because it lacks any genuine mastery; its 'constables' are not masters themselves, but personifications of what Carlyle calls America's 'model institutions and constitutions'.[40] American society is based not on the risk inherent in individual mastery, but on the security provided by deified institutions.

In *Martin Chuzzlewit* (1843–4), Martin accuses the Americans of trying to '"make anything an Institution"'. He asks, '"Are pistols with revolving barrels, sword-sticks, bowie-knives, and such things, Institutions on which you pride yourselves? Are bloody duels, brutal combats, savage assaults, shooting down and stabbing in the streets, your Institutions!"' (*MC*, 534). In fact, '"pistols with revolving barrels"' *are* institutions, in the sense that the right of every citizen to bear firearms is written into the Constitution. There is no disjunction here between the *apparently* Hegelian, individualised confrontation presupposed by 'duels' and the collectivism posited by 'institutions'. In America, institutions like the Constitution are omnipresent at a microcosmic level, and are even inscribed in the violence between individuals or between masters and slaves. In a sense, duels with pistols are merely an expression of the Constitution.

Likewise, the law did not *passively* accept the individual beatings and shootings of slaves. The law was also *actively* violent, institutionalising what Dickens calls the 'cowards' weapons' (*AN*, 243) – the 'whips, chains, thumb-screws, paddles [and] bloodhounds' which Garrison claims are 'indispensable to keep the slaves down' (*NFD*, 8). Douglass makes clear, for instance, that, under Southern law, slaves could be 'taken by the constable to ... the public whipping post' (*NFD*, 51). Once again, the kind of violence Lincoln sees as a dangerous private 'substitute ... in lieu of the sober judgement of Courts'[41] is inherent within the public law. Indeed, private violence always seems to encode the public discourse of the law – the law carries out the violence that Garrison argues is 'indispensable ... to give protection to [the] ... ruthless oppressors' (*NFD*, 8). It stands in for the individual master when she/he is too 'cowardly' to perpetrate the 'indispensable' violence, and is present as a point of reference and mediation when she/he *is* willing to commit violence to the slave. In both respects, the law collectivises the masters and, in an Hegelian sense, thereby renders them invisible. The master–slave hierarchy is perpetuated as a stand-off whereby the masters avoid confrontation by a reliance on the law, whilst hoping that the slave is so terrified by this institutionalisation of mastery that she/he also avoids confrontation.

Of course, in Dickens' *American Notes*, Douglass's *Narrative* and elsewhere, slavery itself is repeatedly referred to as an 'institution' or a 'peculiar institution'. It is, however, really *mastery* which is the legal and public institution. Slaves, on the other hand, are generally denied recourse to *any* institution – not just to the law, but also, as Garrison observes, the 'marriage institution' (*NFD*, 8). Whilst masters retain their power by reference to an institutionalised chain of other masters, the disempowerment of the slave is achieved by denying him/her recourse to the society of other slaves. Douglass often recurs to this aspect of his slavery. In the *Narrative*, any bond between adult slaves is perceived as subversive. Douglass reports how one 'Sabbath school' (*NFD*, 41) he attends is broken up, and later how he is separated from the fellow slaves with whom he has planned an escape: 'I was ready for anything rather than separation' (*NFD*, 61). Douglass and the other slaves are rendered powerless at this point by separation; whilst the master avoids full confrontation with the slave by deferring to other masters, the slave has to face the master alone. Once again, the law supported this technique of mastery. As Weld notes, '*twenty lashes a piece*' would be given under Southern law 'if more than seven slaves are found together in any road, without a white person'. John Franklin and Alfred Moss observe that, under the 'Slave Codes ... slaves ... were never to assemble unless a white person was present'.[42]

In the *Narrative*, the individualisation of slaves goes beyond policing and preventing assemblies and combinations of adult slaves. From childhood, Douglass is individualised in and by his slavery because 'the ties that ordinarily bind children to their homes were all suspended'. He notes that 'my mother and I were separated when I was but an infant'. Whilst the bond between Douglass and his mother is weakened in this way, his paternal origin is wholly denied: 'the opinion was ... whispered that my master was my father; but of the correctness of this opinion, I know nothing' (*NFD*, 26, 12–13). Elkins argues that 'such equivocal relationships were never permitted to vex the law'.[43] As with Noah's cursing of Ham, Douglass's slavery seems to originate in the master's repudiation of his own son. Slavery is based wholly on a denial of origin – in this case, a denial of paternal origin. In a world where mastery is inherited, it is only such repudiation that makes slavery possible. Though half-white, Douglass cannot be allowed to appeal to a white inheritance of mastery. Within a hierarchy based on racial inheritance and division, miscegenation is deeply subversive of the whites' myths of origin. As Douglass points out:

> Every year brings with it multitudes of this class of slaves [that is, mulattos].... If their increase will do no other good, it will do away the force of the argument, that God cursed Ham, and therefore American slavery is right. If the lineal descendants of Ham are alone to be scripturally enslaved, it is certain that slavery at the south must soon become unscriptural. (*NFD*, 14)

Though scriptural slavery is based on the slaves' descent from Ham, it increasingly becomes dependent on denying patrilinear descent because of widespread miscegenation. In this sense, Douglass is both a descendant of Ham and a descendant of no one – Southern slavery relies on both the affirmation *and* rejection of male, lineal descent. As soon as there is miscegenation, racial mastery can be perpetuated only by the (emasculating) abdication of another form of mastery – fatherhood. Of course, this abdication was legally facilitated by the matrilineal nature of Southern slavery.

The slave, to some extent, is also denied masculinity and paternity. Quoting a legal case of 1811, Elkins notes 'that "the father of a slave is unknown to our law" was the universal understanding of Southern jurists'.[44] This denial of paternal lineage is fundamental to the masters' attempts to deny slaves recourse to an origin or even a history. Just as the slave-traders attempted to 'rob' the Africans of any legitimate origin, slaveholders often attempted to suppress the slaves' references to their forefathers in Africa: 'slave owners,' writes James Walvin, 'commonly assumed that most things African were inappropriate.' Elkins suggests that, even in the passage across from Africa, 'much of [the slave's] ... past [was] ... annihilated [and] nearly every prior connection ... severed'.[45] This is doubly ironic, for, although slavery was hereditary in the South, masters attempted to deny their slaves any historical inheritance; and, though American slavery, according to Parish, 'was explicitly and essentially racial',[46] the masters also sought to deny their slaves any separate racial meaning or history.

As Marian Musgrave points out, many white pro-slavery activists sought to perpetuate their mastery by rewriting African history as *anti*-history. This became a powerful means of defending slavery – and, in fact, of demanding the reconstitution of the slave-trade. Musgrave writes:

> *Anti-Fanaticism* by Martha Butts and *The Black Gauntlet* by Mrs. H.R. Schoolcraft describe Africa as a benighted land full of miserable, naked savages who worship snakes, practise cannibalism, are degraded, barbarous, and wild.... Once becoming slaves in America, however, they become submissive, docile, humble, patient, and happy, thus proving ... slavery ... a civilising institution.[47]

These writers legitimise their mastery by reference to a myth of Western *progress*: Africa has never progressed and is forever in a state of savagery, so it *needs* to be enslaved by a nation like America, which has progressed and attained civilisation. This standpoint is reminiscent of Hegel's view of African history. He writes that 'the character of the Negroes [in Africa] ... is capable of no development or culture, and as we see them at this day, such have they always been'. For this reason, though slavery is an 'injustice' in itself, it is 'a phase of advance from the merely isolated sensual existence'[48] of Africa. The problem is, however, that the myth of progress cannot be maintained where historical and patrilinear succession is denied. The kind of progress Hegel attributes to the slave within slavery is impossible because slavery is based on dehistoricisation. Although Hegel and others might argue otherwise, the very act of taking Africans away from their forefathers in Africa divests them of any possibility of 'progress' because it divests them of their African history. In the same way, slaves like Douglass, born into slavery, are denied a personal history because their paternal origins are obscured and, legally speaking, non-existent. Moreover,

American slaves are excluded from an American history and patrilinear descent – the 'Founding Fathers' invoked by Lincoln and so many others hardly recognised the existence of slaves. As Roper remarks, 'the Constitution does not mention the word ... "slavery"'.[49]

Despite this lack of historical recognition, however, Blassingame and other historians have argued that slaves developed quite separate historical, cultural, familial and social structures. Rejecting the arguments of historians like Elkins, Blassingame writes that, despite the constraints of slavery, there was usually a very strong 'sense of community in the [slaves'] quarters'. As regards family ties, 'the important thing was not that the family was not recognised legally ... but rather that some form of family life did exist among slaves'. In fact, Blassingame goes further and argues that some slaveholders actually 'tried to foster the development of strong family ties in the quarters'. In this context, 'the simple threat of being separated from his family was generally sufficient to subdue the most rebellious "married slave"'.[50] As Douglass writes, 'it is my opinion that thousands would escape from slavery, who now remain, but for the strong cords of affection that bind them to their friends' (*NFD*, 68). By exploiting 'family *ties*' or the '*cords* of affection' binding friends together, the master is still, however, using a strategy which depends on isolation. For here it is the *threat* of isolation that is debilitating for the slave. Moreover, the slave family is itself an isolated unit, small enough for the master to keep under surveillance.

The master's strategy of disempowering slaves by isolation accords with the ideas of one of the American South's foremost thinkers and apologists for slavery, George Fitzhugh. As Eugene Genovese writes, 'the most helpless of animals ... [for] Fitzhugh was the isolated, "individualised" man'.[51] Fitzhugh, though, was attacking specifically *capitalist* individualism, since it is on a rejection of such individualism that his defence of slavery depends. He proposes that the master–slave relationship should perpetuate the feudal tradition of mutual obligations – that is, the 'reciprocal rights' of 'the pre-industrial master ... [and] employee',[52] to which Alexander Harding refers. For Fitzhugh, writes Genovese,

> the labouring classes have the right to demand security against want, hunger, and abandonment to the vicissitudes of the market. Property owners must meet their responsibilities.... Slave property, like all other, carries with it the duty of public leadership and ... responsibility towards the propertyless.[53]

The defence of slavery by reference to feudal and paternal codes was, of course, very common in the South. It depended on a binary opposition between South and North – between feudalism and capitalism, paternalism and 'free labour'. Dickens frames such a defence of slavery within *American Notes* when he writes:

> The ground most commonly taken by these better men among the advocates of slavery, is this ... 'The greater part of my slaves are much attached to me. You will say that I do not allow them to be severely treated; but I will put it to you whether you believe that it can be a general practice to treat them inhumanly, when it would impair their value, and would be obviously against the interests of their masters.' (*AN*, 230–1)

The language of Dickens' advocate of slavery, however, slips noticeably between that of feudal and capitalist discourses: the appeal to the slaves' attachment to their master evidently draws on a code similar to Fitzhugh's argument, but the references to the slaves' 'value' and the masters' 'interests' seem to arise from a capitalist discourse of self-interest.

This linguistic slippage serves to deconstruct the paternalism versus capitalism opposition set up by writers like Fitzhugh. It betrays the difference between Fitzhugh's feudal ideal and the true economic relations of masters and slaves in the American South. Whether or not American slavery was constituted as a capitalist or a feudal system of labour is, of course, the subject of a debate as old as the historical study of slavery. As Parish writes, 'the first great historian of slavery ... Ulrich B. Phillips, treated the slave as beneficiary of a patriarchal but unprofitable institution.... By contrast ... Kenneth M. Stampp a generation later saw the slave as the maltreated victim of a profitable economic system.' Whilst Genovese argues for 'the premodern quality of the Southern world', Elkins writes that, 'by 1830 the commitment of the South to capitalist agriculture ... was the dominant fact of Southern life.'[54] Nevertheless, as Parish notes, slavery has more recently come to be recognised as 'a system of systems'. Indeed, Dickens prefigures such inclusiveness in *American Notes* when he asserts that 'the upholders of slavery in America ... may be divided into three great classes' (*AN*, 229): the capitalists, the 'despots' and the pseudo-aristocratic. As Parish writes:

> The complexity of the problem derives from not only the contradictions but also the variety of slavery in the American South. There

can be no greater mistake than to regard slavery as monolithic.... Behind all the generalisations ... there lies the history of millions of individuals living out their daily lives.[55]

This (belated) recognition of slavery's millions of variants underwrites the historiographical significance, or authority, of very individual accounts of the institution, such as that given by Douglass. For this reason, the peculiar implications of Douglass's *Narrative* for the economic debate can be taken seriously, despite the fact that they fail to conform wholly with either the capitalist or feudal standpoints.

The masters described by Douglass, in fact, try to enjoy the benefits of Hegelian, feudal *and* capitalist forms of mastery, without undertaking the responsibilities implied by any of those paradigms. The slave, for instance, is expected to stand in a feudal relation to his/her master: she/he is 'attached' to the master legally and – according to Dickens' advocate of slavery – emotionally as well. The master, however, fails to reciprocate such a relationship, abdicating the responsibilities detailed by Fitzhugh as fundamental to the feudal bond. Rather than providing 'security against want [and] hunger', Douglass's masters are in possession of an 'irresponsible power' (*NFD*, 29), as are those described by Dickens (*AN*, 231) – an irresponsible power whereby the mutual obligations of feudalism are frequently ignored. Of his master Thomas Auld, Douglass writes:

> Not to give a slave enough to eat, is regarded as the most aggravated development of meanness even among slaveholders.... Master Thomas gave us enough of neither coarse nor fine food.... It was not enough for us to subsist on. (*NFD*, 39)

In a sense, Douglass is measuring the 'meanness' of Auld against the kind of code to which Fitzhugh appeals. Douglass, however, finds that that code has been violated. Even Carlyle, whilst expressing 'real sympathy'[56] with the American pro-slavery lobby, acknowledged that there were problems inherent in the master–slave relationship of the South. In his essay 'The Nigger Question', he argues that, as regards the relations between whites and blacks in the South, 'there is probably much in them *not* fair, nor agreeable to the Maker of us'.[57]

Like Fitzhugh, Carlyle appeals to a feudal past as the basis of a 'fair' form of servitude. As he writes in *Chartism*,

> How much the Upper Classes did actually in any the most perfect Feudal time, return to the Under by way of recompense, in govern-

ment, guidance, protection, we will not undertake to specify.... Yet we do say that the old Aristocracy were the governors of the Lower Classes, the guides of the Lower Classes.[58]

One of the fundamental characteristics of old aristocratic rule for Carlyle is the permanency of the connection between master and servant within feudalism. This connection, he argues in 'Shooting Niagara', should be constituted as a 'contract of permanency, not easy to dissolve, but difficult extremely, – a "contract for life"'. He claims it is a mistake to believe 'that servantship and mastership, on the nomadic principle, was ever, or will ever be, except for brief periods, possible among human creatures'.[59] In Douglass's *Narrative*, however, the permanency of the pseudo-feudal contract between masters and slaves is merely one-sided, for it is only the masters who can sever the contract. Indeed, American mastery seems to depend for its perpetuation on the 'nomadic principle': after Douglass has made his first, abortive attempt to run away, he believes his masters will sell him as punishment. As he writes, 'I supposed that [the masters] ... had decided ... to ... sell me as a warning to the others that remained' (*NFD*, 61). After the slaves' transgression, their slavery is reconstituted and strengthened by reference to the very 'nomadic principle' Carlyle attacks. Whilst Douglass is fixed in his slavery, his masters can break their side of the feudal 'contract' by moving him nomadically from master to master.

Throughout the *Narrative*, the anomalous nature of the master–slave relation becomes increasingly apparent, to the point at which Douglass applies to his master 'for the privilege of hiring [his own] ... time':

He granted me the privilege, and proposed the following terms: I was to be allowed all my time, make all contracts with those for whom I worked, and find my own employment; and, in return ... I was to pay him three dollars at the end of each week.... This arrangement, it will be perceived, was decidedly in my master's favour. It relieved him of all the need of looking after me.... He received all the benefits of slaveholding without its evils; while I endured all the evils of a slave, and suffered all the care and anxiety of a freeman. (*NFD*, 67)

What is happening here is that, whilst the slave is expected to treat the master as a kind of feudal lord, the slave is exploited by the master as a capitalist subject. Douglass is certainly delineating an extreme and perhaps exceptional scenario here – but, in so doing, he brings to consciousness a paradox that is implied by many of the master–slave relationships he and others describe. For Douglass, one result of individualising the slave whilst institutionalising the society of masters is that the slave, paradoxically, becomes a more modern, capitalist figure than his master.

Although it would be nonsensical to argue that the American slave is a full-blown capitalist individual, what I am suggesting is that capitalism is 'implicit' within him/her. During the later stages of his slavery, Douglass's implicit capitalism is retarded only by his being denied the limited recognition accorded to wage-labour in the form of cash payment: the masters 'rob' Douglass of the 'reward of [his] ... toil' (*NFD*, 74, 66). As Hegel writes, 'servitude is not yet aware [of the] ... truth ... implicit in it.... Through work, however, the bondsman becomes conscious of what he truly is.'[60] For Hegel, the slave's self-realisation is a *process* through which the slave passes as she/he reaches beyond the master–slave relationship. In the *Narrative*, this is the process through which Douglass moves towards a capitalist ideal of 'free labour' – that is, from broken slave on Covey's farm, through 'independent' slave who hires his own time, to 'free' wage labourer at the end:

> I found employment ... [and] I went at it with a glad heart and a willing hand. I was now my own master.... It was the first work, the reward of which was to be entirely my own. There was no Master Hugh standing ready, the moment I earned the money, to rob me of it. (*NFD*, 74)

Douglass appeals to his Northern, bourgeois audience by reference to a capitalist code of 'self-mastery' they readily understand as the alternative to the master–slave relationship. Capitalism is represented by Douglass and many others as the escape route, both figuratively and literally, from slavery. In the 'Final Emancipation Proclamation' (1 January 1863), Lincoln expresses the hope that, now the slaves are free, they should 'labour faithfully for reasonable wages'.[61] Likewise, J.S. Mill argues in his near-contemporaneous essay *Representative Government* (1861) that 'personal slavery, by giving a commencement to *industrial life* ... may accelerate the transition to a better freedom.... A slave ... is a being who has not learnt to help himself.... [Slavery is] admissible as a means of gradually training the people to walk alone.'[62] Mill makes explicit and systematises what is implicit in the 'Emancipation Proclamation' and, apparently, Douglass's *Narrative* – namely, that capitalist free-labour, industry, self-mastery and 'self-help' form the absolute end of slavery towards which the slave works. As well as being the end of slavery, however, capitalism is also the means by which slavery is ended: Douglass escapes by becoming a kind of capitalist, as far as his slavery will allow. The connection between escape and capital is made explicit when he writes, 'I was ever on the look-out for means of escape ... [so] I determined to try to hire my time, with a view of getting money with which to make my escape' (*NFD*, 66).

As regards Douglass, it really would seem that Hegel is right in claiming that 'through work ... the bondsman becomes conscious of what he truly is'. For Hegel, the 'consciousness [of the] ... worker comes to see in the independent being [the thing on which he works] ... its *own* independence'.[63] Similarly, Carlyle writes that 'he that can work is a born king of something ... is a master of a thing or things'.[64] At the end of his *Narrative*, however, Douglass does not attain either Carlyle's or Hegel's ideal of work. Instead of being able to take up 'calking', the job for which he is trained, he is still alienated from his work:

> I went in pursuit of a job of calking; but such was the strength of prejudice against colour, among the white calkers, that ... I could get no employment. Finding my [own] trade of no immediate benefit, I ... prepared myself to do any kind of work I could get to do.... There was no work too hard – none too dirty. (*NFD*, 74)

Douglass is no 'master of a thing or things'; rather, his work is a form of non-specific wage-labour into which he is compelled by his colour. His work and 'things' are masters of him – his work subsumes his individual identity as 'calker'. Marx argues in *The Communist Manifesto* (1848) that, within modern capitalism, 'the work of the proletarians has lost all individual character'.[65] In nineteenth-century America, the free blacks of the North constitute such a proletarian class. 'In the free states,' Dickens and Morley write, 'the negro is no less forced down out of his just position as a man than when he works under the planter's whip.'[66] Indeed, Douglass's experience foreshadows a general trend following the Civil War. As Franklin and Moss write:

> White artisans and factory hands were keenly aware of the ... threat to their security.... Negro blacksmiths, bricklayers, pilots, cabinet-makers, painters, and other skilled workers met stern opposition from white artisans wherever they sought employment.[67]

Once in the North, Douglass discards his trade rather than confront this kind of opposition from the prejudiced white calkers. In this way, his arrival at capitalist subjectivity does not equate with the arrival at self-consciousness described by Hegel. Though Douglass becomes his 'own master' (*NFD*, 74), this kind of mastery does not depend on his overcoming anyone else as it does in Hegel's dialectic, in which work is the means by which the slave overturns the master–slave hierarchy. Once in the North, Douglass opposes and overcomes no one, whether by a struggle or by his work. Rather, his capitalist self-mastery represents, in part, an escape from confrontation with both slaveholders and white calkers. Douglass cannot 'become conscious of what he truly is ... through [his] work' because his work is a non-confrontational compromise. This also applies, albeit to a lesser extent, to his work as writer. As Lucinda MacKethan writes, 'the slave narratives were controlled by the aims of white abolitionist sponsors, by the scruples and tastes of "gentle" and "delicate" readers'.[68] Douglass's work, whether manual or literary, is still controlled by whites in the North.

Marx suggests that it is specifically capitalism that invalidates Hegel's idealisation of work when he writes:

> the serf, in the period of serfdom, raised himself to membership in the commune, just as the petty bourgeois, under the yoke of feudal absolutism, managed to develop into a bourgeois. The modern labourer, on the contrary, instead of rising with the progress of industry, sinks deeper and deeper below the conditions of existence of his own class. He becomes a pauper.[69]

For Marx, the work of the proletariat under capitalism serves only to perpetuate the status quo by reducing the status and conditions of the labourers. As Lacan writes, 'the work to which the slave is subjected ... we are told [by Hegel] will be precisely the way through which he will achieve freedom. There can be no more obvious lure than this, politically.'[70] Lacan states what Marx implies: for the proletarian 'slave', any idealisation of work is merely a lure, a *ruse*. Indeed, this is also unwittingly implied by Carlyle in *Chartism*, since, unlike Hegel's slave, Carlyle's worker is a master only of a 'thing', not of another master.

Capitalism and capitalist labour are, for Lincoln and Douglass, yet another means of deferring confrontation with that other master. Under American capitalism, the individualised dialectic between master and slave is subsumed into a more general racial-cum-class relation. Ironically enough, Douglass seeks to validate his freedom by reference to the same binary opposition between North and South to which Fitzhugh and others also appeal – that is, between slavery and 'free labour'. Nevertheless, just as Fitzhugh's validation of paternalistic slavery is undermined by the capitalism at work within Southern feudalism, the opposition Douglass attempts to set up is also deconstructed within his own text. The opposition is subverted, for example, by his acknowledgement of the white calkers' prejudice. Evidently, such prejudice is defined by a form of racial mastery, so Douglass's text bears witness to the infiltration of Southern mastery and slavery into Northern capitalism and free labour. Once again, Douglass's experience at the end of the *Narrative* foreshadows a general trend for blacks after emancipation. As Franklin and Moss note, 'the peace was ... lost' for blacks following the Civil War, as white supremacy gradually replaced the master–slave hierarchy. As with pre-war slavery, this was achieved by the exclusion of blacks from the nation's institutions:

> by 1910 blacks had been effectively disfranchised by constitutional provisions in North Carolina, Alabama, Virginia, Georgia, and Oklahoma.... The law, the courts, the schools, and almost every institution in the South favoured whites. This was white supremacy.[71]

Capitalism in America is haunted by the ghost of slavery – a ghost that takes the form of white supremacy. As a *complete* end to slavery, capitalism signally fails. Visiting America for the second time in 1867–8, Dickens remarks in a letter to John Forster how, in Baltimore, 'the Ghost of Slavery haunts the town'[72] and cites various examples of racial segregation he has witnessed. He seems to agree with Carlyle when he writes:

> I have come to the sad conclusion that SLAVERY, whether established by law, or by law abrogated, exists very extensively in this world ... and, in fact, that you cannot abolish slavery by act of parliament, but can only abolish the *name* of it, which is very little! (NQ, 359)

As Alexis de Tocqueville remarks in *Democracy in America* (1835), 'although the law may abolish slavery, God alone can obliterate the traces of its existence'.[73]

For Marx, only revolution can obliterate the traces of slavery: 'the Communists ... declare that their ends can be attained only by the forcible overthrow of all existing social conditions.'[74] Like Carlyle, Marx emphasises the importance of Hegel's life-and-death struggle. However, whilst Carlyle envisages the struggle as the beginning of true mastery, Marx sees it as the self-destructive object and end of bourgeois rule. This final confrontation with power is absent from Douglass's narrative. He does not and cannot go beyond alienated wage-labour, since otherwise further confrontations would become necessary, with the white calkers and with his white sponsors and readers.

Douglass's text does, though, *allude* to the threat of black violence within Northern capitalism:

> A coloured man and a fugitive slave were on unfriendly terms. The former was heard to threaten the latter with informing his master of his whereabouts. Straightway a meeting was called among the coloured people.... The betrayer was invited to attend. The people came at the appointed hour, and organised the meeting by appointing a very religious old gentleman as president, who ... addressed the meeting as follows: *'Friends, we have got him here, and I would recommend that you young men just take him outside the door and kill him!'* (NFD, 73).

What is notable about this 'meeting' is that it seems to imitate such white institutions as the Constitution of Lincoln's America – the *'president'* of the meeting is appointed democratically by the people, just like the President of the United States himself. This president, though, makes explicit what is implicit in American mastery elsewhere; he explicitly represents the sanction for mob violence, which is encoded in the roles of, for example, the US President and Judge Lawless. The *black* mob violence threatened in and by this scene is reminiscent of the kind of *white* mob violence directed against the black Francis McIntosh, violence 'sanctified' by Judge Lawless and unwittingly upheld by Lincoln in his 'Address to the Young Men's Lyceum of Springfield'. The blacks' 'Lynch Law' merely recycles the whites' form of mob-mastery, whereby the individual is overcome by force of numbers.

Of course, the difference between the white and black 'Lynch Laws', as described by Douglass, is that, whilst white violence is *inter*-racial, black mob violence is directed only against other blacks. As Musgrave observes, in anti-slavery literature of the time, there are 'few cases where the Black is directing violence outward.... [Such] violence is directed against ... other slaves, or against himself.'[75] Nevertheless, though the meeting in Douglass's *Narrative* partly adheres to this pattern, it also conveys a veiled threat to the Northern, white reader, a threat which operates in various ways. The meeting is cited as an example of the black workers' 'determination to protect each other'

(*NFD*, 73), and, indeed, the very fact of blacks meeting together in this way must be deeply subversive to a power structure reliant on combinations and institutions of white 'masters', be they capitalist calkers or Southern slaveholders. Furthermore, inter-racial mob violence is surely the unwritten text of the scene and the unrealised possibility encoded in it. In this sense, the threat posed by the blacks' meeting is analogous to the threat posed to the bourgeoisie by early proletarian unionisation or *combination*. Marx observes that at first these 'bodies ... do not fight their enemies, but the enemies of their enemies, [such as] the remnants of ... the landowners' – that is, proletarian combinations initially fight the enemies of the bourgeoisie *for* the bourgeoisie. Similarly, the blacks in the *Narrative* combine to fight the enemies of *their* enemies, such as Southern masters and representatives of the South like the 'betrayer'. In the North, however, it is clear that the 'free' blacks' most obvious and immediate enemies must be the prejudiced whites, such as the calkers – even though Douglass seems unwilling to acknowledge this openly. Instead, Douglass and the other blacks in the *Narrative* direct their violence and anger against the enemies of the text's implied white readers. After 1863, however, a capitalist, class-based white supremacy became impossible to ignore. Following the defeat of the enemies of the blacks' enemies in the Civil War, the division between blacks and whites in America became increasingly based on the kind of class hierarchy implied by Douglass at the end of his *Narrative*. A capitalist code of class relations is substituted for the Southern master–slave relation, so that the relationship between combined masters and the individualised slave is gradually replaced by the relationship between combined masters and combined blacks. This is the class confrontation that is foreshadowed at the end of Douglass's *Narrative*. According to Marx, the unfocused violence perpetrated by early proletarian combinations is merely the precursor of an inevitable confrontation between the bourgeoisie and proletariat; as he writes, 'the workers begin to form combinations (Trades Unions) *against* the bourgeois'.[76] Similarly, the unfocused violence threatened in the blacks' meeting in Douglass's *Narrative* is the precursor of an inter-racial confrontation between combinations, a confrontation that blacks eventually attempt to bring about in the twentieth century as the Civil Rights Movement.

Masters, slaves and animals

> The alleged justification of *slavery* (with ... its ... explanations in terms of physical force, capture in time of war, ... the slave's

> own acquiescence, etc.) ... depend[s] on regarding the human
> being simply as a *natural being*.
>
> (Hegel, *Elements of the Philosophy of Right*)[77]

In their essay 'North American Slavery', Dickens and Morley berate the
Southern slaves' failure to confront their masters:

> It is the greatest horror of the slave system to our minds, when men
> can live contented under so complete an abnegation of their
> manhood.... It is pleasanter to think of slaves in Cuba flying before
> bloodhounds, than to know that the slaves of North America learn
> to ... lie down contented with their place among farm animals.[78]

Dickens sees the alternative to slavery as escape; he leaves unsaid the
other alternative of violent confrontation between master and slave.
Chaudhuri remarks that, in *Barnaby Rudge* (1841), Dickens 'appears to
support even mob violence and revolution'.[79] Eleven years later,
however, he refuses to acknowledge the possibility of insurrection, let
alone black rebellion against whites. Instead, he implies that running
away involves its own form of confrontation – that of slave with
'bloodhound'. In this sense, Dickens is as guilty of placing slaves
'among farm animals' as the slaveholders. He refuses to envisage a
direct struggle between white master and black slave; instead the
contest is seen as that between runaway slave and dog: 'we have all
heard of the Cuban dogs trained to hunt men.... When they have
hunted down their prey, they do not injure him, unless the black man
should dispute the dogs' superiority.' In this scenario, the slave can
hardly prove what Dickens calls his 'manhood'; rather, the slave can
prove his superiority–or lack of it–only against a dog. Dickens' thought
is rendered inconsistent by his own, white prejudice: whilst condemn-
ing slaves for acquiring 'the hearts and brains of horses and of oxen',[80]
he cannot place blacks on the equal plane with whites, which is the
Hegelian life-and-death struggle.

For Douglass, on the other hand, escape *might* well involve confrontation with human masters, and even with what Hegel calls 'the
fear of death, the absolute Lord'.[81] Although, ultimately, it is capitalism
that constitutes the means and end of Douglass's escape from slavery,
other, more confrontational modes of escape are alluded to in the
Narrative. Concerning the fears he and his friends experience before his
first attempt, he writes that 'on either side we saw grim death, assuming the most horrid shapes.... We were overtaken by our pursuers, and,

in our resistance, we were shot dead on the spot!' (*NFD*, 57: my emphasis). The phrase 'in our resistance' serves only to reinforce the potential for life-and-death confrontation inherent in the attempt to escape. Franklin and Moss evidently agree with Douglass when they write that 'fleeing from the institution [of slavery] was one of the slaves' most effective means of *resistance ... against their masters*'.[82] Douglass seems almost Hegelian when he describes his attempts at escape as 'a matter of life and death' or of 'liberty and death' (*NFD*, 58, 57).

For Dickens and Morley, those slaves who, unlike Douglass, do not attempt to escape, learn 'to lie down contented with their place among farm animals'. Under North American slavery, Dickens and Morley suggest, 'negroes have been depressed ... [to] the state of simple beasts of burden'.[83] The analogy is a common one, reappearing in both abolitionist and pro-slavery texts, because it is fundamental to very notion of American slavery. As Houston Baker, Jr. notes, 'American slavery's chattel principle ... equated slaves with livestock'.[84] Likewise, Henry-Louis Gates suggests that, according to the hierarchy established within Douglass's *Narrative*, 'the slave's closest blood relations [are] the horses',[85] and Douglass himself notes that, under Covey the 'nigger-breaker', he is 'transformed into a brute' (*NFD*, 45). For Dickens and Morley, slaves are brutalised by acquiescence in their slavery. Douglass implies much the same. He is 'made a man' only when his 'cowardice departed'; it is his fight with Covey which, Douglass claims, 'revived within me a sense of my own manhood' (*NFD*, 47, 50). Such an attitude accords to a certain extent with Hegel's paradigm. As Shklar notes of Hegel's life-and-death struggle, 'it is peculiarly human to risk one's life.... It sets men radically apart from the beasts.'[86] According to Hegel, *not* being willing to risk one's life in 'mortal combat' brutalises and dehumanises the slave in the way assumed by Dickens and Morley. As Alexandre Kojève notes in connection with Hegel's dialectic, 'by refusing to risk his life in a fight for pure prestige, [the slave] ... does not rise above the level of animals'.[87]

The problem with Hegel's dialectic, however, is that it is unable to comprehend anything except what Foucault terms the 'law of all or nothing'. Though Dickens and Morley emphasise escape rather than struggle, they are similarly blind to what Foucault calls the '"micropowers"' that 'define innumerable points of confrontation [and] focuses of instability'.[88] Dickens and Morley complain that, 'in the year 1850, out of three million slaves only a thousand fled away in search of liberty',[89] but they seem unable to comprehend the diverse forms resistance might assume *within* slavery. Franklin and Moss, however, are able to do so; though 'the most sensational and desperate reaction of Negroes to their status as slaves was the conspiracy to revolt', they also cite, as means by which the slaves expressed 'dissatisfaction with their worldly status', religion, suicide, poisoning, murder and, of course, music, a means of subverting and/or upholding various kinds of slavery. (This is discussed in detail in Chapter 4.) As Parish observes,

> Slaves were obliged to strike their own balance between resignation and rebellion.... They could fight or take flight or they could lapse into total submissiveness, but for most of the time most slaves steered a complex ... [and] devious course between those two extremes.[90]

By steering a 'devious' course between fight and flight, slaves come to exemplify what Carlyle calls 'sham-subjects' (NQ, 363). After winning his fight with Covey, Douglass becomes the extreme example of a sham-subject. He allows Covey to reassert the illusion of mastery, but declares to himself that, 'however long I might remain a slave in form, the day had passed forever when I could be a slave in fact' (*NFD*, 50).

In becoming a sham-subject, Douglass is also becoming a sham-animal. A well-documented example of slaves' 'deviousness' is the way in which the slave-animal analogy was subverted by the slaves themselves. In the Brer Rabbit folk-tales, for instance, the blacks associated themselves with the weaker animal, which gains control of others by trickery. 'The tales,' Lawrence Levine writes, 'encouraged trickery and guile; they stimulated the search for ways out of the system; they inbred a contempt for the powerful and an admiration for the perseverance and even the wisdom of the undermen.'[91] Douglass himself, MacKethan observes, uses 'many ... sly, Brer-Rabbit-like tricks' in his *Narrative*. MacKethan argues that 'the "trick" as a satisfying metaphor of mastery for the slave storyteller is certainly a significant feature of the animal tales'.[92] In fact, 'the "trick"' is fundamental to the mastery of sham-masters and sham-slaves, as a means of modifying the 'micro-powers' of the relations between them. Southern slaveholders institutionalise their mastery and thus 'trick' their slaves out of an Hegelian struggle. Their slaves, though, copy and reciprocate such tricks and *ruses*, thereby undermining mastery without resorting to direct confrontation.

There *are*, however, some instances of direct confrontation within Douglass's *Narrative* – instances where black violence is directed against *Southern* whites. At one point, Douglass is sent to the '"nigger-breaker"' Covey, the apparent apotheosis of white mastery. At first, Covey seems to succeed in 'breaking' Douglass, but after six months Douglass confronts his master. Significantly, Covey's initial reaction is to attempt to involve others in the fight – he 'soon called out to Hughes for help' (*NFD*, 50). Finally, however, he is forced to fight Douglass on his own, in a kind of life-and-death struggle; as Ziolowski remarks, 'Hegel ... provides an appropriate ... philosophical gloss on ... [Douglass's] confrontation with the overseer Covey.'[93] Douglass writes of the struggle:

> We were at it for nearly two hours. Covey at length let me go ... saying that if I had not resisted, he would not have whipped me half so much. The truth was, that he had not whipped me at all. I considered him as getting entirely the worst end of the bargain (*NFD*, 50).

Having been reduced to the last resort of one-to-one combat, and having been beaten, Covey seeks to reinstate his mastery over his slave by a trick or *ruse*. The *ruse* on which slavery is based is that slaveholders pretend to represent life-and-death to their slaves. Nevertheless, it becomes clear in Douglass's *Narrative* that this *individual*, life-and-death power is absent from Southern mastery. Douglass is transferred from one master to another, yet none of them successfully manages to control him.

At the same time, the masters themselves are neurotically aware of the absence of absolute, individual power. Following Douglass's and Covey's fight, what is so peculiar about the latter's reinstatement as master is that not only do both of them know his mastery is no more than a *ruse*, but Covey must know that Douglass knows – indeed, Covey must know that Douglass knows that Covey knows. As Douglass writes,

> The whole six months afterwards, that I spent with Mr. Covey, he never laid the weight of his finger on me in anger. He would occasionally say, he didn't want to get hold of me again. 'No,' thought I, 'you need not; for you will come off worse than you did before.' (*NFD*, 50)

Covey's threat is simultaneously an admission of fear. He really does not want to get hold of Douglass again; he really does not want to expose his own failure again. Though a master, Covey is afraid of the life-and-death struggle described by Hegel. The fear of confrontation is surely one of the fears, or neuroses, Douglass is referring to when he claims that there are 'faults peculiar to slaveholders, such as being very ... fretful' (*NFD*, 46).

The fear of confrontation and direct struggle within slavery was usually verbalised in terms of the fear of insurrection. As Franklin and Moss note, 'even rumours of insurrections struck terror in the hearts of the slave-holders'. They argue that both the fear of insurrection and actual revolts were a fundamental and inevitable 'part of the institution, a kind of bitterness that the whites had to take along with the sweetness of slavery'.[94] Nevertheless, weak white masters like Covey do possess one, vital form of physical supremacy to keep such revolts at bay – the might of the instruments and technology of slavery, in the form of 'whips, chains, thumb-screws, paddles [and] bloodhounds'. Their ultimate expression is the rifle. Douglass masters Covey in a direct, physical battle. By contrast, the overseer, Mr Gore, seeks to prove his mastery over the rebellious slave Demby simply by recourse to his 'musket': 'Mr. Gore ... raised his musket to his face, taking deadly aim at his ... victim, and in an instant, poor Demby was no more.... A thrill of horror flashed through every soul on the plantation' (*NFD*, 24).

The 'thrill of horror' Douglass describes is similar to the 'absolute fear' experienced by Hegel's slave on being mastered – but the slaves in the *Narrative* are mastered by fear not so much of the overseer himself, but rather of his rifle. In Harriet Beecher Stowe's *Uncle Tom's Cabin* (1852), Augustine St Clare asserts that it is 'the ever-necessary whip [which is the] first, last and only argument' for slavery; it is on the whip alone that rests '*the right of the strongest*'.[95] This 'right' is hardly the same, though, as Carlyle's equation of right and might with legitimate mastery: right is merely a fiction superimposed on strength which is, in itself, merely a fiction imposed on the technology of violence. In Douglass's *Narrative*, the whites have neither absolute might nor absolute right – just whips and rifles. In fact, despite Carlyle's claim that 'the Almighty Maker has appointed ... [the black] to be a Servant' (SN, 5), the fear that white supremacy might be constituted merely by the technology of its weapons seems to be encrypted in the title of his essay, 'Shooting Niagara'. The phrase is uncomfortably close to 'Shooting "Niggers"'.

In 'Shooting Niagara' and 'The Nigger Question', however, Carlyle attempts to argue that it is through emancipation, not slavery, that murderous violence is done to blacks. This is because the chaos of a deadly struggle exists *outside* the master–slave relationship, as its *other*. Like Marx, Carlyle believes that such deadly struggles exist as the *end* of mastery and servitude:

Well, *except* by Mastership and Servantship, there is no conceivable deliverance from Tyranny and Slavery.... Where folly is 'emancipated,' and gets to govern ... all is wrong.... No man reverences another ... each man ... clutches [the other] ... by the throat, with 'Tyrannous son of perdition, shall I endure thee, then, and thy injustices forever?' (NQ, 362).

Emancipation is envisaged here in terms of a murderous struggle – and Carlyle has a point in so far as racist murders and lynchings *did* supersede the other instruments of violence, after the Civil War, as important means of maintaining white supremacy and as a means of racial control. As Franklin and Moss observe:

> As early as 1866 ... a kind of guerrilla warfare was carried on against ... blacks.... Secret societies grew and spread.... There flourished [for example] the ... Knights of the Ku Klux Klan ... and the *Rifle* Clubs of South Carolina.... Armed with *guns*, swords, or other weapons, their members patrolled some parts of the South day and night.... They used intimidation, force, ostracism ... arson, and *even murder* to accomplish their deeds.[96]

For Carlyle, however, emancipation will not result merely in the murder of individual blacks or even in inter-racial 'guerrilla warfare'; rather, the act of emancipation is an act of racial genocide in itself. In 'Shooting Niagara', Carlyle writes:

> The Nigger ... is the only Savage ... [who] can actually live beside [the 'White Man'] and work ... [as] a Servant.... [In America] three million absurd Blacks ... are completely 'emancipated'; launched into the career of improvement, – likely to be 'improved off the face of the earth' in a generation or two! (SN, 5–7)

Carlyle suggests that, once the blacks are no longer slaves, the only *improvement* possible in their situation is their annihilation. The peculiar subtext here involves the related and different discourses of progress and evolution. Carlyle's attitude towards the nineteenth century's myth of progress is ambivalent, to say the least. Le Quesne notes that 'the theme of progress does sometimes occur in Carlyle's writings ... but it is very muted and eventually disappears altogether'. For Carlyle, history is really 'a gospel, the revelation of a just providence working in human affairs.... History [is] ... a theatre for the workings of a providence which itself remains firmly outside history.'[97] In other words, though the history of 'human affairs' develops, the ideal exists as a transcendental code 'outside history'. For Carlyle, this ahistorical ideal consists of the master–slave bond, which he defines as the 'perennial ... element of human Society'. As he writes, 'the Noble in the high place, the Ignoble in the low; that is, in all times ... the Almighty Maker's Law.... It is the everlasting privilege of the foolish to be governed by the wise.'[98] For Carlyle, the law binding master and slave is not subject to progress or evolution. It is only when blacks are emancipated that they are exposed to the quasi-genocidal forces of 'improvement'.

In this, Carlyle is oddly out of step with most other pro-slavery propaganda, which usually depends on slavery itself being an improving institution. Carlyle seems to suggest that 'the Nigger' is necessarily and unchangeably 'a poor blockhead' – and that is why 'the Almighty Maker has appointed him to be a Servant' (SN, 5). Since 'the Nigger' cannot improve, he *has* to be a servant. For Hegel, on the other hand, slavery is partly justified because it represents a necessary, transitional stage in a race's development. 'The subjection of the slave,' he notes, 'is a necessary moment in the education of all men.... Servile obedience forms ... the *beginning* of freedom.'[99] Unlike Hegel *and* Carlyle, however, many pro-slavery propagandists, such as those cited by Musgrave, are inconsistent because they are caught between these two positions – they justify the necessity *and* permanency of slavery by portraying it as a 'civilising institution'. They appropriate Hegel's progressive discourse as an argument for slavery, without acknowledging that the idea of progress loses all meaning if deprived of its teleology. For Hegel, 'servile obedience leads to freedom'; for Martha Butts and Mrs H.R. Schoolcraft, servile obedience leads to servile obedience.

By contrast, Dickens and Morley are closer to Carlyle when he argues that it is emancipation that will serve as a means of 'improvement' for blacks – though Dickens and Morley apparently perceive this improvement in positive terms. For Dickens and Morley, emancipation will raise blacks from the static level of 'simple beasts of burden'. They argue that 'if, step by step, the degraded race be raised, their higher impulses awakened [and] their minds developed ... there will arise out of the present multitude of slaves, by slow degrees, a race of free labourers'.[100] It is just such a progressive view of slavery and emancipation that Carlyle derides in 'Shooting Niagara', but Dickens is closer here to Carlyle than may first appear. Dickens and Carlyle both affirm specifically white ideals; whilst Carlyle seeks to reaffirm white, feudal mastery, Dickens' blacks develop towards the kind of white, middle-class ideal of free labour – an ideal of capitalist self-mastery, 'self-help' and 'industrial life' which, as we have seen, was later envisaged for ex-slaves in Lincoln's 'Emancipation Proclamation' and Mill's supposedly liberal *Representative Government*. As Chaudhuri points out, 'in their over-zealousness to civilise and educate the Africans, Victorians expected from them the same respectability, success and gentility as they did from their own ... rising middle-class society'.[101] In a sense, Dickens and other Victorians want blacks to improve and develop into whites, and the kind of progress envisaged in 'Shooting Niagara' is a typical form of white wish-fulfilment, whereby blacks are '"improved off the face of the earth"'. This phrase verbalises the unconscious of 'liberal' texts such as 'North American Slavery' – and perhaps even *Representative Government* – where blacks and slaves gradually disappear by conforming to white ideals.

This is why Dickens' later writings on slavery so easily slip ever closer to Carlyle's. In 1865–6, Carlyle and Dickens both supported Governor John Eyre, who, following a major insurrection, sought to reinstate white supremacy in Jamaica by the hanging and shooting of blacks. As Chaudhuri writes, Dickens was utterly opposed to the 'section of the British public [who] tried to indict John Eyre ... for unlawfully hanging a black leader, George William Gordon, killing 439 blacks, flogging 600 men and women, and burning more than 1000 houses'.[102] Support for Eyre's killings in Jamaica forms the subtext of Dickens' endorsement, during his second visit to America, of Carlyle's theory of racial selection. Writing to Forster from America in 1868, Dickens asserts that the blacks 'will die out of this country fast. It seems ... so manifestly absurd to suppose it possible that they can ever hold their own against a restless, shifty, striving, stronger race.'[103] For Dickens, as for Carlyle, emancipation brings about a racial and capitalist struggle in which blacks do not stand a chance.

At times, Carlyle explicitly affects the language of evolution to convey this process of racial selection:

> In the *progress* of Emancipation, are we to look for a time when all the Horses also are to be emancipated, and brought to the supply-and-demand principle? ... Small kindness to ... horses to emancipate them! The fate of all emancipated horses is, sooner or later, inevitable. To have in this habitable Earth no grass to eat, – ... to roam aimless ... and be hunted home to Chaos.[104]

In fact, the 'Chaos' to which Carlyle refers seems to be exactly the kind of Godless (and thus masterless) evolutionary process described by Darwin in *The Origin of Species* (1859). Carlyle's argument sets a

genuine master–slave hierarchy in opposition not only to emancipation and capitalism, but also to Chaos and an evolutionary, life-and-
death struggle. Darwinian evolution, however, deconstructs such
oppositions, since Darwin asserts that '*all* organic beings are exposed to
severe competition ... [in] the universal struggle for life'. In this
context, Carlyle's argument that the master–slave relation represents
an ideal, and struggle is precipitated only by its dissolution, is unsustainable. From a Darwinian perspective, the master–slave relation is
just another symptom of the struggle between two races for survival.
As Darwin himself notes, 'I use the term Struggle for Existence in a
large and metaphorical sense, *including dependence of one being on
another.*'[105] As Douglass and Garrison make clear, struggle and violence
are not extrinsic, or alien to the master–slave relation, but rather form
a fundamental part of it. Garrison writes of the 'scenes of pollution and
blood', which, he asserts, are 'all ... the *natural* results of slavery!' (*NFD*,
8: my emphasis). Even 'murderous cruelty' (*NFD*, 8) is in the *nature* of
the institution, according to Garrison and Douglass.

This 'murderous cruelty' is not the same as Hegel's life-and-death
struggle. For Hegel, life-and-death violence represents the origin of
slavery; for Garrison, violence is one of 'the natural *results* of slavery'. For
Hegel, the life-and-death struggle is a first stage in the progress towards
freedom; for Garrison, the violence of the master–slave relation progresses towards nothing, but merely perpetuates the relation. As he
writes, such violence 'is indispensable to keep the slaves down'. In
Hegelian terms, the violence of the North American master–slave hierarchy is amoral because it progresses nowhere and 'improves' no one. In
this sense, the struggle between master and slave is, again, closer to a
Darwinian struggle. As Robin Gilmour points out, 'evolution by natural
selection was not a theory about progress but about the machinery ...
driving the development of life.... In the Age of Progress something so
directionless was troubling.'[106] The kind of Darwinian struggle for
existence inscribed in the master–slave relation is, in Hegelian terms,
troubling *and* amoral precisely because it is so directionless.

Darwinian evolution legitimises neither Hegel's nor Carlyle's attribution of 'right' to the master–slave relation. Whilst its lack of direction
hardly conforms to Hegel's teleological view of mastery, its universality
refutes Carlyle's belief in the master–slave relation as the transcendental
truth outside struggle and history. Darwin's system acknowledges no
such 'outside', no such truth or *right*. Racial mastery is not, then, constituted by 'might and right', but merely by an amoral and contingent
'might', which is always in flux and always in dispute. The amoral might

of the whites in America is constituted merely by the technology of its weapons. As far as a Darwinian struggle is concerned, white 'progress' is merely the history of the technological advance in weaponry. The fear encoded within writings like 'Shooting Niagara' is that, once emancipated, blacks will not necessarily be '"improved off the face of the earth"', but might get hold of such technology; if whites do not have absolute right for their supremacy, their absolute might could also be disputed.

In this sense, the apocalyptic 'consummation … [of] *shooting* Niagara to the bottom' (SN, 14) would seem to involve not only the shooting *of* 'niggers' but also emancipated 'niggers' who do the shooting themselves. The consciousness that white superiority may be dependent on its weapons means that the seizure of guns by blacks is greatly feared. This is one reason why, according to Franklin and Moss, 'the Confederacy was outraged by the Northern use of Negro troops' during the Civil War. As Franklin and Moss observe, 'Some white Southerners … wanted to arm Negroes…. Public opinion, however, was generally against arming Negroes. There was, of course, the fear that they would turn on their masters.' By contrast, in the North 'Negro enlistment was … a notable success', according to Franklin and Moss; indeed, 'leading Negroes like Frederick Douglass served as recruiting agents'.[107] Nevertheless, though armed, other means of maintaining white supremacy were employed – black regiments were paid less than their white counterparts, for example. Moreover, Northern commanders tried various techniques of diverting black violence, in an attempt to avoid black versus white confrontation. Franklin and Moss note that 'Negro soldiers … were engaged so much in menial tasks, instead of fighting, that their officers made numerous complaints'.[108] Of Robert Gould Shaw and the troops under his command – 'the 54th Massachusetts Colored Volunteers' who were 'the first regiment of free black men' – Marianne Gilchrist writes:

> On 11 June 1863, he and his troops were made unwilling participants in Colonel James Montgomery's burning of the defenceless Georgia town of Darien. The incident deeply disturbed Rob [Robert Gould Shaw], who had a strong sense of honour, and did not wish to see the reputation of black troops damaged by such incidents.[109]

Here, the kind of violence practised by black troops is differentiated from 'honourable' white forms of warfare. Colonel Montgomery's use of the 54th adheres to a discourse in which black violence is perceived as savage, unheroic and thus *animalistic*. Carlyle argues that Haiti, for instance, is 'nothing but a tropical dog-kennel' with 'black Peter exterminating black Paul'. Heroism, for Carlyle, is specifically 'European' – he acknowledges only 'heroic white men' (NQ, 376–7). He would not, therefore, have been able to recognise the heroic *black* men of the 54th regiment whom Shaw subsequently led into bloody confrontation with white Southerners. As Gilchrist writes,

> on the night of 18 July, the 54th Massachusetts regiment led an infantry assault on Battery Wagner on Morris Island in Charleston harbour.... When the 54th began their attack, the Rebels opened fire with artillery and rifles, but the regiment did not falter.

Interestingly, Gilchrist points out that 'among the heroes of that night were Frederick Douglass's son, Sergeant Major Lewis Douglass' – as was Private Charles R. Douglass, another of Douglass's sons. She goes on to remark that 'news of the heroism of the 54th ... shook public opinion, especially among those Northerners who had believed that black men could not make good soldiers'.[110] Carlyle's equation of black violence with bestial savagery and white violence with heroism is clearly undermined by the 54th regiment. Indeed, since, for Hegel, 'the battle of heroic competition' is the beginning of human consciousness, the black troops of the 54th are, in both Hegelian and Carlylean terms, 'set ... radically apart from the beasts' – they shoot their way into human existence.[111]

Masters, slaves and democracy

> *Vox Populi vox Dei.*
>
> (Carlyle, 'Shooting Niagara')

The fact that the 54th regiment 'shook public opinion' is particularly significant in a democratic state where the law that perpetuates slavery or racial segregation is *made* by public opinion. As Weld observes in *American Slavery As It Is*, 'in a republican government the people make the laws, and those laws are merely public opinion *in legal forms*',[112] Dickens' attack on slavery in *American Notes* takes the lead from Weld by attacking public opinion in the South:

> Why, public opinion in the slave States *is* slavery, is it not? Public opinion, in the slave States, has delivered the slaves over, to the

gentle mercies of their masters. Public opinion has made the laws, and denied the slaves legislative protection. (*AN*, 231)

For Dickens, public opinion and its expression in the institutions of modern democracy are *not* the alternative to, or opposite of, slavery; rather, they perpetuate slavery. Ironically, the pseudo-feudalism of the slaveholders is dependent on democracy, its supposed antithesis. It should be noted that Hegel perceives no opposition between democracy and slavery; indeed, Peter Singer argues that, for Hegel,

> the Greek form of democracy positively required slavery if it was to function at all. If, as was the case in Athens, every citizen has the right and duty to take part in the public assembly that is the supreme decision-making body of the city-state, then who is there to do the daily work of providing the necessities of life?[113]

In the same way, since democratic America is 'a land where voluntary servitude is shunned as a disgrace', Dickens argues that there are many who 'must be ministered to by slaves ... whose inalienable rights can only have their growth in negro wrongs' (*AN*, 230). In *Uncle Tom's Cabin*, Augustine St Clare's brother believes that '"there must ... be a lower class, given up to physical toil and confined to an animal nature; and a higher one thereby acquires leisure and wealth for a more expanded intelligence and improvement"'.[114] Liberty and democracy seem here to depend on slavery – the 'freedom' of the voters seeming to require the slavery of some who cannot vote.

Within nineteenth-century American democracy, the process of democratic enslavement involved the dehumanisation of non-voters – public opinion had the power to confer or withhold recognition of the individual subject's *human* consciousness. Human consciousness could not be recognised on an individual basis within American democracy; it could only be recognised by the majority opinion – and, for blacks in the nineteenth century, such recognition was not forthcoming. According to Roper, the American Constitution implied that 'slaves ... were to count for 60 per cent of a free individual'. Public opinion and democracy constituted blacks as non- or semi-human. As Weld writes, 'it was public opinion that ... sunk [blacks] ... from men to chattels'.[115] This was particularly the case during the Civil War. Though, in 'the battle of heroic competition', recognition occurs between two individual warriors, during the Civil

War the public opinion of the South withheld such recognition for blacks fighting with the Union troops. As Franklin and Moss write,

> The vast majority of white Southerners viewed black soldiers as rebellious slaves and insisted that they should be treated as such.... The worst case was the Fort Pillow affair.... [There] Negroes ... were not permitted to surrender; they were shot, and some were burned alive.[116]

The 'vast majority' withholds recognition of the blacks' status as anything but 'chattels' and 'rebellious slaves'. In this case, the kind of individual recognition implied by Hegel's 'battle of heroic competition' is impossible. By combining the masters into 'vast majorities', the modern, democratic state prevents masters from recognising on an individual basis anyone whom the state itself does not recognise.

For example, Dickens and Morley observe that the slave-owners *collectively* deny their slaves the human recognition of education: 'negroes have been depressed ... towards the state of simple beasts of burden,' they argue, by 'rational education of their minds [being] ... jealously withheld.'[117] In the South, it was the slave codes in particular, and the law in general, which 'jealously withheld' such recognition, by preventing individual masters, like Augustine St Clare, educating their slaves; as he declares, '"I don't think my feelings about slavery are peculiar. I find many men who ... think of it just as I do.... Yet our laws positively and utterly forbid any efficient general education system."'[118] The individual behaviour of each master was defined not by his conscience or his personal relationship with a slave, but by public opinion and the law it created. As Dickens observes, 'the slave-owners ... defer to public opinion in their conduct, not to their slaves but to each other' (*AN*, 237). In American democracy, masters were compelled to defer to other masters, to public opinion and to the expression of that opinion in the form of law. In a way, all individual masters were *slaves* to public opinion – as Dickens states, 'public opinion in the slave States *is* slavery'.

For Dickens, indeed, even those whom American democracy raises as masters *of the masters* must defer to others: 'Before whom do the presidential candidates bow down the most humbly ... and for whose tastes do they cater the most assiduously in their *servile* protestations? The slave-owners always' (*AN*, 232: my emphasis). American political masters, it seems, are really no more than slaves to the public opinion of the slave-owners. This explains why Elijah Pogram, the Member of Congress in *Martin Chuzzlewit*, seems unable to talk without 'looking round on the group' (*MC*, 533) to whom he is speaking: he is always deferring to his listeners. Likewise, Douglass compares the behaviour of slaves wishing to 'do errands at the Great House Farm' with those '*slaves* of the political parties' who 'seek to please and deceive the people' (*NFD*, 18: my emphasis). American political 'mastery' is thus the exact reversal of Carlyle's notion of mastery, or 'Kingship', according to which the individual commands the group. For Carlyle, 'the Commander over Men [is] he to whose will our wills are to be subordinated, and loyally surrender themselves.... [He is] here to *command* over us, to furnish us with constant practical teaching.'[119] This kind of mastery is impossible within democracy; indeed, Carlyle argues that genuine 'Commanders over Men' like Napoleon and Cromwell 'had to chain democracy under their feet, and become despots over it, before they could work out the earnest obscure purpose of democracy itself'.[120]

Such claims, though, are nonsensical for another contemporary observer of democracy, Leo Tolstoy. Writing in *War and Peace* (1865–8) of Napoleon's ability to command, he argues that such power

> cannot be the direct physical ascendancy of a strong creature over a weak one.... nor can it be founded on the possession of moral force, as ... some historians suppose, who say that the leading figures in history are cast in heroic mould.... [Rather] power is the collective will of the masses, transferred by their expressed or tacit consent to their chosen rulers.[121]

Tolstoy seems to be arguing here that *all* societies function, to a lesser or greater extent, like democracies: power is never appropriated by a heroic individual, but is merely conferred by those who are willingly and self-consciously subjugated. For Tolstoy, it is the will of the masses that confers mastery on an individual. Carlyle at times appears to agree: 'what are all popular commotions and maddest bellowings from Peterloo to the Place-de-Grève ... ? Bellowings, *in*articulate cries.... To the ear of wisdom they are inarticulate prayers: "Guide me, govern me!"'[122] The difference, however, between Carlyle's and Tolstoy's conceptions of power is betrayed by Carlyle's description of the prayers of the masses as 'inarticulate'. Though they demand leadership, they are unable to *articulate* that leadership themselves, and must have it imposed on them. Whilst all societies function like democracies for Tolstoy, all successful societies are dictatorships for Carlyle, even if they are *supposed* to be democratic. Of the 'model democracies' of Rome and Athens, Carlyle writes, 'we ... find that it was not by loud voting and debating of many, but by wise insight and ordering of a few that the work was done'.[123] For Carlyle, mastery remains an almost unconscious desire of the masses – a desire they themselves cannot express, within or without the democratic process. The Carlylean master is he who knows the masses better than they know themselves – he who comprehends their unconscious desire for leadership and *articulates* it himself. Carlyle's Napoleon is 'naturally ... the King' because he has 'an eye to see'[124] – and what he sees are, presumably, the masses as they really are.

Since, for Carlyle, the masses cannot see and cannot articulate their desire for leadership, rule by the masses, whether in the Tolstoyan or democratic sense, must be 'a self-cancelling business [which] ... gives in the long-run a net result of *zero*'. Furthermore, the problem is that the masses are often not only 'inarticulate', but also 'foolish, slavish, wicked, [and] insincere', whilst the 'noble-minded' are certainly 'not [in] the majority' – so whomever the masses recognise will necessarily themselves be similarly slavish, wicked and insincere. For Carlyle, the majority must always be wrong: true leadership is necessarily constituted by the minority, by a 'corporation of the Best, of the Bravest'.[125] The fear that runs throughout Carlyle's critique of democracy is what de Tocqueville famously calls the 'tyranny of the majority.'[126] As Carlyle writes,

> Minority, I know, there always was: but there are degrees of it, down to [a] minority of one, – down to suppression of the unfortunate minority, and reducing it to zero.... The flunky-world [then] has peace; and descends, manipulating its ballot-boxes ... into the throat of the Devil. (NQ, 360)

The 'suppression of the unfortunate minority' within democracy is here represented in almost murderous terms; indeed, the tyranny of majority seems to represent, for Carlyle, the political correlative of the 'mobocratic spirit' which Lincoln fears so much. The dangerous possibilities inherent in majority rule were first recognised in America. As Ian Shapiro writes, 'Americans would be first to confront the fact that the minority harmed by the workings of majoritarian process need not be a rich and powerful élite, it could be a dispossessed racial ... minority.'[127] This was certainly the case in the American South, both pre- and post-Civil War. It almost goes without saying that, in the period following Emancipation, the cause of white supremacy was strengthened by the fact that the blacks formed a minority of the voters in the South; indeed, it was majoritarian rule that eventually made the disenfranchisement of blacks possible. Likewise, in the antebellum period, white mastery was also analogous to this form of democratic tyranny, even though the slaves were placed firmly outside the democratic process. What made American slavery almost unique was the fact that the blacks always formed a racial minority: in 1860, for instance, there were probably about twice as many whites in the South as there were black slaves. In contrast, as Walvin notes, 'the Caribbean islands, with their overwhelming slave populations' were ruled by 'small white minorities'.[128] In the United States, the 'tyranny of the majority' was fundamental to mastery inside and outside democracy.

For many of Dickens' contemporaries, however, the problem posed by the rule of the majority was not simply a matter of the 'tyranny of the many over the few'. De Tocqueville himself suggests that 'in America, as long as the majority is still undecided, discussion is carried on; but as soon as its decision is irrevocably pronounced, a submissive silence is observed, and [even] ... the opponents of the measure unite in assenting to its propriety'.[129] It would seem, as Horwitz argues, that '"tyranny of unanimity" would be a more appropriate concept for the American scene'.[130] Unanimity is inscribed within the structure of democracy: once a vote has been taken on any given issue, the decision made cannot reflect the previous division of opinion. The decision, one way or the other, is necessarily monolithic. In nine-teenth-century America, however, several critics found such mono-lithic unanimity within the democratic process itself – that is, even before the decision had bee made. In *Society and America* (1837) – another book Dickens had certainly read – Harriet Martineau com-plains of the Americans' 'worship of [popular] Opinion [which fosters] ... a fear of singularity'.[131] This 'fear of singularity' is the fear of being what Carlyle calls a 'minority of one'.

Dickens' comment that 'public opinion in the slave States *is* slavery' reveals the ambivalence of the relationship between unanimity and individuality: unanimity of opinion certainly tyrannises and enslaves the independent-minded individual, yet the adherence or deference to such unanimity is a form of slavery in itself. To put this another way, unanimity of opinion enslaves both the individual who resists that unanimity and the individual who conforms to it in order to achieve public recognition. All men who wish to 'climb to any public distinc-tion,' writes Dickens, '[must] first grovel ... down on the earth ... bending the knee before ... [the] monster of depravity' that is the American press – and it is this press that constitutes 'the tone of public feeling' (*AN*, 247).

In 'The Nigger Question', Carlyle describes what he sees as the paradigmatic confrontation between the individual and the unanimous majority – namely, that between Carlyle's ultimate hero, Christ, and the Jews: 'Did you never hear of "Crucify him! Crucify him!" That was a considerable feat in the suppressing of minorities' (NQ, 360). Again, in the *Latter-Day Pamphlets*, he writes: 'A certain People, once on a time, clamorously voted by overwhelming majority, "Not *he*; Barabbas, not he!"'[132] Carlyle clearly equates Christ with the 'minority of one' that is suppressed, persecuted and crucified by the 'overwhelming majority'. Ironically, this equation is echoed by abolitionists, who frequently associate Christ with the individual slave – the slave, that is, who is suppressed by an institutionalised and majoritarian American mastery. In *American Notes*, Dickens rails against 'those who ... break ... living limbs as did the soldiery who mocked and slew the Saviour of the world' (*AN*, 243). Likewise, in *Uncle Tom's Cabin*, Tom becomes increasingly Christ-like the more he is persecuted. As he is tortured to death by Legree and two overseers, he becomes just 'like his Master',

> whose suffering changed an instrument of torture, degradation, and shame, into a symbol of glory, honour, and immortal life; and, where his spirit is, neither degrading stripes, nor blood, nor insults can make the Christian's last struggle less than glorious.[133]

Through his suffering and persecution, Tom becomes like the 'One' who is Christ; that is, he becomes Christ-like because he becomes a victimised *individual*. American mastery disempowers and suppresses the slave by individualising him/her – but, in so doing, it also invites a comparison between the slave and that ultimate, individualised victim and hero, Christ.

In 'The Nigger Question' and the *Latter-Day Pamphlets*, however, Carlyle does not merely emphasise the Christ-likeness of the suppressed individual. Rather, Carlyle also stresses the Jewishness of the persecuting 'overwhelming majority'. In doing so, he makes explicit the unspoken implications of Stowe's near-deification of Tom: since the persecuted 'minority of one' is Christ-like, those who persecute him must necessarily be re-enacting the original deicide for which Jews have traditionally been blamed. One of Marcus Stone's illustrations for the 1850 edition of *American Notes* conveys a similar impression. The illustration is entitled 'Black and White' and depicts a mother and child, along with the slave-trader who has separated them from their home and family. The trader's countenance is strikingly reminiscent of contemporary caricatures of Jews. He possesses all the characteristics listed by Anne Aresty Naman as 'marks of the [stereotyped Victorian] Jew': he has, in particular, the necessary 'aquiline nose, black eyes [and] beard'.[134] Perhaps Stone is unconsciously attempting to *other* the slave master-cum-trader in order to absolve the white American or European Christian from any responsibility for slavery.

The case of the slave-trader in *American Notes* is, though, complicated by Dickens' text. As well as being portrayed as stereotypically Jewish, he is ironically described as 'the *champion* of Life, Liberty, and the Pursuit of Happiness' (*AN*, 141: my emphasis). The trader is at once alien to, and the same as, the American, white democratic 'champion'. If Stone's illustration represents an attempt to defer responsibility from the white, Christian American, Dickens' text undercuts the attempt, placing the slave-trader's Jewish *otherness* at the centre of American democracy. In this, he is close to Carlyle, who suggests that democracy can never endorse Christ or Christ-like heroes, but only ever produces masters like the Jewish Barabbas. According to Carlyle, it was Barabbas for whom the Jews 'clamorously voted', declaring: '"To the gallows and the cross with him [Jesus Christ]! Barabbas is our man; Barabbas, we are for Barabbas!".... Well, they got Barabbas; and they got, of course, such guidance as Barabbas and the like of him could give them.' Carlyle declares of democracy in general: 'To raise the Sham-Noblest, and solemnly consecrate *him* ... is, in all times and countries, a practical blasphemy, and Nature will in no wise forget it. Alas, there lies the origin, the fatal necessity, of modern Democracy everywhere.'[135] For Carlyle, the 'fatal necessity' of modern democracy is that it replays over and over again its deicidal origin. Based as it seems to be on the 'suppression of minorities' and the 'tyranny of the majority', democracy repeats again and again the original vote of the Jews, sacrificing the true, individual, Christ-like hero in favour of the popular, demagogic, Barabbas-like 'Sham-Noblest'.

For Carlyle, the democratic 'Sham-Noblest' always slips, it seems, into the '*Shem*-Noblest'–Shem being Noah's eldest son and father of the Semites. Encrypted in Carlyle's loathing of democracy is a paranoiac fear of Jewish mastery and the Jewish infiltration of the state, a paranoia that is a recurrent theme of Christian history. For Carlyle, it is the modern, democratic state that is peculiarly vulnerable to Jewish infiltration, since democracy is not just marked by Jewishness, but is also literally susceptible to Jewish mastery. This fear is, of course, inconsistent with the notion that democratic mastery is defined by the 'tyranny of the majority' since Jews, evidently, formed a minority of American and, later, British voters. Carlyle was right, though, in the sense that the

Black and White, by Marcus Stone
Reproduced by permission of The British Library (012614.a.53/7).

gradual movement in nineteenth-century Britain towards full democracy *did* bring about a Jewish presence in the Houses of Parliament, with
Lionel de Rothschild becoming the first openly Jewish Member of
Parliament in 1858. Likewise, Howard Sachar notes that America had
always promised the 'comprehensive emancipation [of Jews].... A new
political freedom was implicit in the very phraseology of the
Declaration of Independence, '"that all men are created equal"'.[136]

It is exactly this kind of democratic equality which is derided by
Carlyle. In 'The Nigger Question', he declares that 'by any ballot-box,
Jesus Christ goes just as far as Judas Iscariot; and with reason, according to the ... Talmuds ... of these days' (NQ, 363). Again, in 'Shooting
Niagara', he attacks the notion of the '"the equality of men"', whereby
'any man [is] equal to any other; Quashee Nigger to Socrates or
Shakespeare; Judas Iscariot to Jesus Christ' (SN, 4). Since 'Judas' was
almost a synonym for 'Jew', the position of the Jew and the black are
here almost explicitly equated. White, Christian mastery seems to
equate and homogenise the other 'slave races'; as T. Peter Park notes,
for Carlyle, 'the Black could "not be emancipated from the laws of
Nature," which had pronounced a "very decided verdict on the question," and "neither could the Jew"'.[137] It seems that both democracy
and the emancipation of these 'slave races' go against a *natural* hierarchical opposition between whites and everyone else. Carlyle's idealisation of heroic, Christian, white, non-democratic mastery is very
obviously based on the opposition with a *homogenised* racial *other* –
'Quashee Nigger' is much the same as 'Judas Iscariot'. As Frantz Fanon
asserts, 'an anti-Semite is inevitably anti-Negro'.[138] Bryan Cheyette
develops this idea, arguing that 'particular histories of victimisation'
can be seen to 'intertwine'; he points out, in particular, 'the pitfalls of
constructing either an exclusively "black" victimhood or, its mirror
image, an exclusively "white" all-prevailing European culture.... "The
Jew" ... throws both of these manichaean categories into disarray.'[139]
Indeed, in nineteenth-century America, it would seem that Jews and
blacks were at least partly conscious of the ways in which black racism
and anti-Semitism might be interrelated. As Levine remarks, 'there
seems to have been an unstated bond of empathy between the two car-
icatured groups, who ... were always carefully distinguished from the
"white man".'[140] In this way, the homogenisation of other races is not
only a means of controlling and containing racial *otherness* – it also
produces a homogenised resistance to white, Christian mastery, a
homogenised resistance which, in an apparently cosmopolitan nation
like America, must seem to threaten an *other* majority.

For Carlyle, this is precisely the danger posed by democracy. By making the racial *other* the same as, or 'equal' to, Christ and the Christian master, democracy threatens to place racial *otherness* at the centre of Western civilisation, making everyone, even Christ, the same as that *other*. According to Carlyle, Jews and blacks should be excluded from mastery, which is, ideally, the province of the white, Christ-like hero. Carlyle's concern, though, is that democracy threatens to *include* Jews and blacks, and, by doing so, somehow equalises and homogenises everyone, making everyone, even the Christ-like hero – even Christ himself – both Jewish *and* black. This, according to Carlyle, is the apocalyptic end result of total democracy and equality:

> Let all men be accounted equally wise and worthy ... and then ... decide by count of heads, the vote of a Demerara Nigger equal and no more to that of a Chancellor Bacon: this, I perceive, will ... give the minimum of wisdom in your proceedings.... Folly in such million-fold majority, at length ... supreme in this earth.... Rushing ... in wild *stampede* ... fast and ever faster ... – to the sea of Tiberias, and the bottomless cloacas of Nature. (NQ, 361–2)

For Carlyle, the 'million-fold majority' will always rush 'in wild stampede' towards the sea of Tiberias and, therefore, *Israel*; total democracy brings about an apocalyptic stampede towards racial *otherness*.

In this respect, the name of the Member of Congress in *Martin Chuzzlewit*, Elijah Pogram – 'one of the *master*-minds of [the] ... country' (*MC*, 531: my emphasis) – seems to echo Carlyle's cryptic demonisation of democracy and democratic mastery as Jewish. The name, though, brings into uncomfortable proximity both Semitic ('Elijah') and anti-Semitic ('*Pogrom*') signifiers; as Philip Allingham writes, the designation is constructed according to a 'technique of iron-ically undercutting a character's first name by juxtaposing it with a contradictory surname'.[141] The surname seems to connote the genocide of the minority that is, for Carlyle, the final, terrible consummation of democracy's empowerment of the majority and suppression of the minority; just as the 'three million absurd Blacks' in America are 'likely to be "improved off the face of the earth"' as a result of their emanci-pation, so the very name of democratic mastery in Dickens' novel seems to threaten an anti-Semitic massacre. As a democratic master, Pogram's name seems to encode the massacre of the minority which, Carlyle suggests, is implied by such mastery, by the 'tyranny of the majority'. Indeed, Pogram's name uncannily foreshadows the anti-Semitic violence which, in the twentieth century, was legitimised by majoritarian rule in Germany; Hitler's National Socialist Party gained power through the democratic process. The section in which Pogram features is headlined 'Pogrammania' (*MC*, 852) – a title suggestive of mass, anti-Semitic hysteria, especially for twentieth-century readers.

Pogram is also 'Elijah', however, and somehow democratic mastery is here at once Jewish *and* violently anti-Jewish. This paradox is fundamental to Carlyle's view of democracy. For Carlyle, though it was the Jews who voted for Christ to be crucified, the vote was simultaneously an act of self-destruction – in voting for Barabbas, 'they got ... such guidance as Barabbas and the like of him could give them; and, of course, they stumbled ever downwards and devilwards.' For Carlyle, the Jews' act of deicide is also an act of self-crucifixion – he describes the Jews as 'a singular People; who could both produce ... divine men, and then could ... stone and crucify them'.[142] Carlyle fails, though, to follow up the implications of this paradox. If the Jews both produce divine men and crucify them, then divine men like Christ are both Jewish *and* non-Jewish. Though Christ is Carlyle's ultimate hero, Christ embodies the point at which the seemingly stable opposition between Christian mastery and Jewish 'slavery' is deconstructed. For Carlyle, white, Christian mastery is ideally based on an absolute opposition with its racial *other*, but, as is the case with Christ, such mastery is always also marked by its Jewish *other*. In this context, Jews are both alien to and the same as Western mastery. This 'doubleness' of the Jew, Cheyette observes, 'points to a received Christological discourse which has constructed Jews as *both* "a deicide nation [*and*] also a nation ... on whose redemption the fate of mankind hangs"'.[143]

For Carlyle, the modern democracies of Britain and America are also deicide nations – deicide nations, that is, which promise the redemption of mankind, but can really bring only ruin. Carlyle believes that 'the origin, the fatal necessity, of modern Democracy everywhere' is deicide and its displaced form, *heroicide*; he believes this because democracy is always asserting the equality of Christ and Judas, always asserting masterlessness. At the same time, though, democracy always seems to *promise* redemption. As Carlyle writes in the *Latter-Day Pamphlets*, 'perhaps Democracy ... will ... make a new blessed world of us by and by? – To the great mass of men, I am aware, the matter presents itself quite on this hopeful side.' The 'great mass of men', Carlyle argues, are 'marching ... [along] the *broad* road [of democracy], that leads direct to Limbo and the Kingdom of the Inane. Gifted men, and once valiant nations ... are marching thither, in melodious triumph'.[144] Just as the Jewish race, according to Carlyle, has 'stumbled ever downwards and devilwards' whilst 'they prophetically sing', so democratic nations also wander to 'Limbo' in 'melodious triumph'. Though *seeming* to head towards a Promised Land, Carlyle believes that democracies, like the Jews in the wilderness, are merely wandering, going nowhere. Democratic nations stampede towards the 'sea of Tiberias' and the Promised Land of Israel – but, of course, Israel did not exist in the nineteenth century, so democracies are really stampeding nowhere.

Most of the Americans in *Martin Chuzzlewit* see the United States as a democratic Promised Land. 'As a body,' Dickens observes, Americans 'are ready to make oath ... at any hour of the day or night, that it is the most thriving and prosperous of all countries on the habitable globe' (*MC*, 269). Dickens, however, repeatedly denounces these *'Pharisees'* who 'treat of happiness and self-respect, innate in every sphere of life' (*MC*, 226: my emphasis). As Meckier writes, Dickens criticises those who 'erect ... utopian castles in the air by imagining slaveholding America as "that regenerated land"'.[145] This view of America is the belief in the absolute right of democratic mastery and majoritarian rule – the belief, as Carlyle puts it, that America is 'a sign of hope for all nations, and a "Model Republic"', an 'instance of Democracy nearly perfect'. For Carlyle, as for Dickens, this belief in democratic America as the Promised Land, or '"Model Republic"' is, though, unsustainable, precisely because democracy disavows and destroys the possibility of transcendental mastery. For both writers, a Promised Land is inconceivable without Christ or Christ-like human mastery – exactly the kind of mastery which democracy seems to disavow. According to Carlyle, it was the undemocratic Cromwell who came closest to establishing a kind of Promised Land in England, since Cromwell's heroic mastery made it possible for

> the Law of Christ's Gospel [to] ... establish itself in the world.... The Theocracy which John Knox in his pulpit might dream of ... [Cromwell] dared to consider as capable of being *realised*.... I account [this] ... the most heroic phasis that 'Faith in the Bible' was appointed to exhibit here below.[146]

Cromwell's heroic mastery is a theocracy, based on the transcendental authority of Christ and the Bible. For Carlyle, England is transformed under Cromwell's mastery into a Promised Land precisely because its hierarchy is based on a theocratic-cum-militaristic combination of 'might and right'. Such a theocracy is inconceivable for democratic masters; unlike Cromwell, Elijah Pogram's mastery makes no reference to God or Christ. Pogram's mastery has no ideal *program*, has no real direction and upholds no transcendental authority, being subject wholly to the authority of public opinion.

Democracy and majoritarian rule cannot produce Cromwells; they can only produce masters who, like Barabbas or Elijah Pogram, merely embody the 'stampede' of popular opinion and mobocracy. Pogram is not so much a master as a '"public servant"' (*MC*, 532), a slave to public opinion. Comparing Elijah Pogram to his biblical namesake, Allingham writes,

> whereas the biblical figure journeyed across Sinai to Horeb and thence to Beersheba in order to avoid the repression of government, the American Elijah employs his trip to sound public opinion and contribute to the ignorance of government.[147]

The American Elijah represents, in fact, the very opposite to the Carlylean ideal of the master-as-educator. Carlyle argues that the 'right of the ignorant man to be guided by the wiser ... is the indisputablest', and the biblical Elijah certainly conformed to this definition, in that he caused the slaughter of the prophets of Baal (1 Kings 18), whom almost all of his people were misguidedly worshipping. The biblical Elijah thus saved his people by confuting public opinion. The modern Elijah, however, saves no one and confutes no misconceptions – rather, he encourages and perpetuates the ignorance of his people and his government, being himself no wiser than those people. Pogram's 'mastery' thus embodies the dangerous equalisation that Carlyle sees in democracy: though a master, his ignorance is *equal* to that of his people. This was a common fear of democracy in the nineteenth century, even for a pro-democratic thinker like Mill, who writes in *On Liberty* (1859) that, 'governments [now] ... make themselves the organ of the ... masses.... [and] the mass ... now take their opinions ... [from] *men much like themselves*.... No government by a democracy ... [like this] ever did or could rise above mediocrity.'[148] Likewise, though a rising political master, Dickens' Major Pawkins is also '*a man of the people*' who could

> hang about a bar-room, discussing the affairs of the nation, for twelve hours together; and in that time could hold forth with more intolerable dulness, chew more tobacco, smoke more tobacco, drink more rum-toddy, mint-julep, gin-sling and cocktail, than any private gentleman of his acquaintance. (*MC*, 269: my emphasis)

Major Pawkins is a political master and 'man of the people' because he is actually *more* like the people than the people themselves. For Carlyle, democratic '"Liberty and Equality" [is] ... the faith that, wise great men being impossible, a level immensity of foolish small men would suffice.... [and] "no Authority [is] needed any longer"'.[149] Dickens, though, seems to go further and implies that American democracy produces leaders who are actually *worse* than the 'level immensity of foolish small men' they represent.

In this way, the mastery and guidance of leaders like Major Pawkins and Elijah Pogram can make the people only *more* foolish and ignorant. Indeed, Pogram even supports and encourages his people's self-destructive violence, suggesting that the violent '"Mr. Chollop and the class he represents [are] ... an Institution"' (*MC*, 534). As Allingham observes, 'the American Elijah supports the forces of barbarity and violence and the worshippers of Baal (in the person of Hannibal Chollop) rather than confutes them'.[150] Martin seems to gesture towards the destructive potential of such leadership when he tells Pogram,

'The mass of your countrymen begin by stubbornly neglecting little social observances.... You abet them in this, by resenting all attacks on their social offences as if they were a beautiful national feature. From disregarding small obligations they come in regular course to disregard great ones.... What they may do ... next, I don't know; but any man may see if he will, that it will be something following in natural succession, and a part of one great growth, which is rotten at the root.' (*MC*, 536)

Neither does Pogram know what his countrymen 'may do ... next'; by 'abetting' the mass of his countrymen in their faults, Pogram does not lead his people anywhere, but merely *guides* and encourages them towards 'Pogrammania' and a dangerously unknown future – a 'Limbo' where they *may* do anything.

In this way, Elijah Pogram would seem to foreshadow Benjamin Disraeli – another 'Hebrew Conjuror' who, according to Carlyle, was to lead the British 'rabble' to the brink of a kind of Pogrammania in 1867;[151] as Carlyle writes,

this delirious 'new Reform Measure' ... pushes us at once into the Niagara Rapids.... Traitorous Politicians, grasping at votes, even votes from the rabble, have brought it on.... A superlative Hebrew Conjuror, spell-binding all the great Lords, great Parties, great Interests of England ... [is] leading them by the nose, like helpless mesmerised somnambulant cattle to such issue. (*SN*, 10-11)

In the Second Reform Act of 1867, Disraeli is leading Britain towards what Carlyle sees as its own 'Pogrammania', a Pogrammania, or 'consummation' which is the 'Niagara Leap' (SN, 11) into what Bruce Robbins tellingly calls an 'apocalyptic democracy'.[152] The Niagara Falls are, of course, on the border between the British Empire and the United States – so what Carlyle is afraid of is that, in leading Britain into the Niagara Rapids of increased enfranchisement and emancipation, Disraeli is figuratively leading Britain towards America and the American Constitution. The new Reform measure takes Britain that much closer to that democratic sham-Israel, America – a sham-Israel which, for Carlyle, is mere godless anarchy. Whereas, for Dickens, American politics *threatens* an apocalypse, for Carlyle, writing in the aftermath of the Civil War, American-style democracy *is* apocalyptic. For Carlyle, Britain is similarly heading towards such apocalyptic anarchy, towards a sham-Israel where '"there are no masters"', heroes or Christs, just emancipated and equalised mobs made up of 'absurd blacks' and 'Hebrew Conjurors'.

4
Heroes, Hero-Worshippers and Jews: Music Masters, Slaves and Servants in Thomas Carlyle, Richard Wagner, George Eliot and George Du Maurier

Heroes and hero-worshippers

> Music is well said to be the speech of angels.... Serious nations
> ... have prized song and music as the highest; as a vehicle for
> worship, for prophecy, and for whatsoever in them was
> divine.... To 'sing the praise of God,' that ... was always, and
> will always be, the business of the singer.
>
> (Thomas Carlyle, 'The Opera')[1]

In his essay 'The Opera' (1852), Carlyle argues that the ideal music
master is a kind of 'priest' who is 'a friend of the gods, and choicest
benefactor to man' (O, 398, 397). The musician is at once on a level
with 'the gods' *and* the benefactor or servant of 'man'. For Carlyle,
there is no real contradiction here: the master-musician is 'a friend of
the gods' precisely *because* he benefits and serves 'man'. In *Past and
Present* (1843), Carlyle clarifies this paradox when he suggests that

> he that cannot be servant of many, will never be master.... Is he not
> their servant ... who can suffer from them, and for them; bear the
> burden their poor spindle-limbs totter and stagger under: and, in
> virtue of being their servant, govern them, lead them out of ...
> defeat into victory![2]

For Carlyle, one such servant-master was the Ancient Greek musician
Tyrtaeus (seventh century BC), who, as Carlyle notes, *served* his fellow
countrymen by singing of 'the need of beating back one's country's
enemies'. Carlyle declares that this was 'a most *true* song, to which the

hearts of men did burst responsive into fiery melody, followed by fiery strokes before long' (O, 398). Through his music, it seems, Tyrtaeus served his countrymen by leading 'them out of weakness into strength [and] ... victory'.

There is another paradox here: whilst Tyrtaeus *served* his countrymen with his singing, his music also implied the physical strength of the Spartan warriors it inspired, and the consequent military mastery of one country over another. In this sense, Tyrtaeus himself was at once musical servant and military master. This paradox is fundamental to Carlyle's notion of heroism in general: whilst the servant-master is, for his subjects, he 'who can suffer from them, and for them', that Christ-like mastery is at the same time a physical ascendancy. In Tyrtaeus, the spiritual *right* of servant-mastery is united with the *might* of Sparta's physical mastery; the spiritual *right* of his music is united with the physical *might* of the Spartans he leads. As Carlyle writes in *Chartism* (1839), 'might and right ... are ever in the long-run one and the same'.[3]

In 'The Opera'. Carlyle is postulating an originary moment when the right of musical servant-mastery and the might of physical heroism were almost 'one and the same'. Historically speaking, it certainly seems to have been the case that music and poetry were encouraged in Sparta in so far as they *served* physical mastery; as J.C. Stobart notes, 'At Sparta ... Tyrtaeus ... was there to conduct martial dances and to train the boys of Sparta in their musical drill. Thus there was no contradiction in early times between strict military discipline and a love of choral lyric poetry.'[4] In his fusion of the militaristic and the musical, Tyrtaeus is representative of what Carlyle's contemporary, Richard Wagner, finds to be generally true of Ancient Greek music and drama. In his essay *Beethoven* (1870), Wagner argues that, for the Greeks, '[even] the order of war, the fight itself, the laws of Music led as surely as the dance'.[5]

This is also the case, Carlyle suggests, for the mythical, heroic past of Germany. In his essay 'The Nibelungen Lied' (1831) – a lengthy review and synopsis of the thirteenth-century German epic poem – Carlyle cites another, even clearer, example of the hero who combines musicianship with military prowess:

There is a certain Volker of Alsace here introduced.... [He] is ... a *Spielmann* (minstrel), a *Fidelere gut* (fiddler good); and surely the prince of all *Fideleres*, ... for ... in the brunt of battle he can play tunes; and with a *Steel Fiddlebow* beats strange music from the cleft helmets of his enemies. There is, in this continual allusion to

Volker's *Schwert-fidelbogen* (Sword-fiddlebow) ... a barbaric greatness and depth.... Is he not the image of every brave man fighting ... [a] duel ... [and] smiting the fiend with giant strokes, yet every stroke *musical*?[6]

For Carlyle, it would seem that genuine music mastery is 'a duel ... [with] the fiend', just as 'a duel ... [with] the fiend' is necessarily 'musical'. In other words, the equivalence Carlyle sets up of 'might and right' is not simply the *alliance* of the right of music with the might of physical mastery. Rather, he comes close, especially in the case of Volker, to positing a mythical moment in which music is also might, and physical mastery is also right. In Volker's 'duel ... [with] the fiend', might and right are so combined as to be one and the same; Volker's 'duel' is with 'the fiend', so it is *right* and musical, and it is right and musical because it is a duel.

On this reasoning, the Spartan Tyrtaeus's music is 'a most *true* song' because it is 'followed by fiery strokes': the truth and *right* of Tyrtaeus's music inheres in its physical results. Carlyle believes that music should have 'to do with sense and reality' (O, 398), and it would seem that the ultimate expression of such reality is the heroism of fighting. In *Heroes and Hero-Worship* (1840), Carlyle asserts, 'You may see how a man would fight, by the way he sings.' He declares that 'The Poet ... could not sing the Heroic warrior, unless he himself were at least a Heroic warrior too.... The grand fundamental character is that of Great Man; that the man be great. Napoleon has words in him which are like Austerlitz Battles.'[7] Whether they be musicians, poets or warriors, all heroes are potential Napoleon Bonapartes, and Napoleon is himself a potential poet; for Carlyle, heroic violence is, ideally, identical with the poet's or musician's truth. This affirmation of heroic violence as the transcendent truth of mastery is prefigured in Hegel's 'Master–Slave Dialectic' (1807). Just as, for Carlyle, artistic mastery is legitimised by its reference to heroic violence, so for Hegel the master's power is the result of his having 'proved' himself in a 'life-and-death struggle'. According to Hegel, the participants 'must engage in this struggle, for they must raise their certainty of being *for themselves* to truth'.[8]

If, in the original *Nibelungenlied*, Volker's masterful and musical truth would seem to be constituted in this way, the relationship between music mastery and heroic violence is also everywhere implicit in Wagner's *Der Ring des Nibelungen* (completed 1874). Throughout the third part of the *Ring*, Siegfried's power is conceived in physical *and* musical terms, though the nature of the relationship between these terms is continually reassessed and reimagined in very different ways and images. For instance, although Wagner dispenses with the character of Volker, Siegfried's sword *Nothung*, like Volker's *Sword-fiddlebow*, is used as a kind of musical instrument during the forging song in Act I of *Siegfried* – '*Nothung! Nothung! / Neidliches Schwert*' ('Notung, Notung, / trusty sword!'). As Charles Osborne writes, this scene is 'a celebration of brute strength'[9] in music. Again, in Act II, Siegfried summons the dragon Fafner to battle with his melodious hunting horn; this 'duel ... [with] the fiend', to use Carlyle's phrase, is certainly musical. After Siegfried has killed Fafner, however, he gains a different kind of mastery through music – he learns to hear and understand the 'song of [a] ... forest bird' and so is apprised of the nature of the Ring, which has the potential to make him 'lord of the world'.[10] Siegfried's potential world-mastery is attained through physical violence *and* musicianship – just like Carlyle's ideal musicians.

There is a fundamental difference, however, between Wagner's Siegfried and Carlyle's Tyrtaeus. Whilst, according to Carlyle, Tyrtaeus *served* the Spartans with his music, Siegfried's power, whether musical or not, serves no one but himself: he sings the forging song to and for himself. Siegfried is obviously problematic in *Carlylean* terms, since his heroism consists only of itself and exists only for itself – he neither serves nor hero-worships anyone else. Indeed, his mode of heroism is, in some ways, the antithesis of hero-worship in that he challenges the god Wotan, and subsequently 'strikes ... the Wanderer's [that is, Wotan's] spear in two'.[11] Siegfried does not even serve or worship the gods. Nevertheless, whilst apparently disqualifying him as a Carlylean hero, it is exactly this autonomy and egocentricity that make Siegfried a paragon of heroism for Wotan, who, in *Die Walküre*, has already defined the ideal hero as 'a man ... / [who is]... foe to the gods / free of soul, / fearless and bold, / who acts alone, / by his own design.... / One at war with all gods.'[12]

There is, though, one such hero in Carlyle's *Heroes and Hero-Worship* – and, ironically, it is 'the hero as divinity' (*HHW*, 1). Despite and because he is 'at war with all gods', Siegfried comes closest to Carlyle's 'hero as divinity', for, of all Carlyle's heroes, 'the hero as divinity' is the only one who worships himself as Siegfried does. As Carlyle writes,

This man Odin [might] ... have felt that perhaps *he* was divine; that *he* was some effluence of the ... Supreme Power and Divinity.... With all men reverently admiring him; with his own wild soul full of noble ardours and affections.... what could he think himself to be? (*HHW*, 25)

Even Odin, though, is really just a '*man*' according to Carlyle, his divine status being accorded him only by the reverent admiration of his people. It is hero-*worship* which deifies, which confers divine meaning, on Odin; the 'hero as divinity' is constituted as such only by the hero-*worship* of a man as divinity. As Carlyle remarks, 'we might rationally ask, Did any set of human beings ever really think the man they *saw* standing beside them a god, the maker of this world? Perhaps not: it was usually some man they remembered, or *had* seen.' In this sense, the hero-as-divinity-*in*-himself and *for*-himself has only ever been a fiction. It is not just that 'the Hero as Divinity [is a] ... a production ... of old ages; not to be repeated in the new' (*HHW*, 42, 78), but, rather, that the hero-as-divinity was always already a production of still old*er* ages.

In his theorisation of the hero-as-divinity, Carlyle makes explicit what is implicit throughout *Heroes and Hero-Worship*: namely, that heroism-in-itself has never existed, that heroism is always constituted by the recognition of hero-*worship*. It is not just divinity that is constituted by worship, but heroism in general. 'Any sincere soul,' comments Carlyle, 'knows not *what* he is.... [He] can, of all things, the least measure – Himself' (*HHW*, 25), so the hero is, in himself, meaningless; he cannot judge himself, but can gain meaning only from others. As Carlyle observes, the hero 'is ever the same kind of thing: Odin, Luther, Johnson, Burns; I hope to make it appear that these are all originally of one stuff; that only by the world's reception of them ... are they so immeasurably diverse' (*HHW*, 43). It is the 'world's reception' which differentiates the original 'stuff' of the hero; it is hero-worship which confers meaning on this otherwise undifferentiated stuff. Carlyle at once implies and tries to retreat from this standpoint when he writes,

> To welcome ... a [Robert] Burns as we did, was that what we call perfect? ... A man of 'genius' ... we waste away as an idle artificial firework, sent to amuse us a little, and sink it into ashes, wreck, and ineffectuality.... To fall into mere unreasoning ... admiration, was not good; but such unreasoning ... supercilious no-love ... is ... worse. It is a thing for ever changing, this of Hero-worship ... difficult to do well in any age. Indeed, the heart of the whole business of the age ... is to do it well. (*HHW*, 43)

As the 'heart of the whole business', hero-worship is more important than heroism itself: Burns's potential as a 'Great Man' is unrealised because of the eighteenth century's inability to worship him adequately. Instead of being an all-conquering hero, he is merely the 'ashes, [and] wreck' of one, because he is not recognised or properly hero-worshipped by his contemporaries.

In one sense, heroism *is* hero-worship for Carlyle: it is not merely the case that the hero is constituted as such by the hero-worship of others, but that the hero is simultaneously the hero-worshipper. In *Heroes and Hero-Worship*, the most extreme demonstration of this is James Boswell, of whom Carlyle writes,

> he passes for a mean, inflated, gluttonous creature.... Yet the fact of his reverence for [Samuel] Johnson will ever remain noteworthy.... It is a genuine reverence for Excellence; a *worship* for Heroes, at a time when neither Heroes nor worship were surmised to exist. (*HHW*, 183)

What is 'noteworthy' about Boswell's reverence is that it is as an extreme example of the heroism inherent in hero-worship; Boswell is not just a 'mean, inflated, gluttonous creature'; he is also a hero himself because of his hero-worship. As Carlyle argues,

> We will ... take the liberty to deny ... [the notion] that no man is a Hero to his valet-de-chambre.... It is not the Hero's blame, but the Valet's: that his soul, namely, is a mean *valet*-soul! ... The Valet does not know a Hero when he sees him! Alas, no: it requires a kind of *Hero* to do that. (*HHW*, 183–4)

Only heroes can recognise heroes, Carlyle suggests, so hero-worship ideally represents a kind of mutual recognition. The hero-worshipper recognises the hero and is, therefore, himself recognised as heroic.

Furthermore, ideally speaking, the hero-worshipper recognises the hero recognising the hero-worshipper: the hero himself is a hero-worshipper of the hero-worshipper. Just such a dialectical and reciprocal arrangement is encoded in the relationship between Tyrtaeus and the Spartans, since Tyrtaeus's lyrics certainly recognised the Spartans' heroism:

> Come, ye sons of dauntless Sparta,
> Warrior sons of Spartan citizens ...
> Stoutly brandish spears in right hands,
> Sparing not your lives for Sparta
> Such is not the Spartan custom.[13]

In his songs, Tyrtaeus recognised and hero-worshipped the 'warrior sons' of Sparta, whilst he himself, as Solon Michaelides notes, 'was greatly admired and honoured by the Spartans'. The Spartans recognised in Tyrtaeus's songs Tyrtaeus's recognition of themselves; the hero-musician is worshipped because he hero-worships the hero-worshippers.

Indeed, just as Tyrtaeus's heroic status was accorded to him by the hero-worship of the Spartans, the *violent* heroism of the Spartans was constituted by his *musical* hero-worship of them; by singing 'the need of beating back one's country's enemies', he turned the Spartans into heroes themselves – heroes who *could* beat back Sparta's enemies. As Michaelides observes, Tyrtaeus's 'embateria and war-songs ... inspired such enthusiasm [in] ... the Spartans that they beat the Messenians'.[14] In this sense, Tyrtaeus's form of heroism-as-hero-worship is almost democratic, since, by hero-worshipping his people, Tyrtaeus democratises heroism and makes everyone a hero. Despite his reputation for authoritarianism, Carlyle's creed of hero-worship *can* be seen in democratic terms: 'Hero-worship,' remarks Carlyle, is 'a recognition that there does dwell in that presence of our brother something divine; that every created man, as Novalis said, is a "revelation in the Flesh"' (*HHW*, 203). Unexpectedly, Carlyle seems to argue here for the democratisation of Christ and Christ's heroism; he implies that all 'brothers' are potentially 'heroes-as-divinities' given the recognition of hero-worship.

It is precisely in this way that the hero *serves* others – by hero-worshipping them and recognising in them 'something divine'. This is the case for all of the musical heroes Carlyle extols in his essay on opera, where the musician is 'the choicest benefactor to man' for 'serious nations' because music is an expression of 'whatsoever in them was divine'. For Carlyle, the musician reflects back whatever is divine in the nations to whom he sings: 'Aeschylus and Sophocles ... sang the *truest* (which was also the divinest) they had been privileged to discover here below ... [and] David, king of Judah, ... discerned the Godlike amid the Human [and so] struck tones that were an echo of the sphere-harmonies.' David *serves* his people by discerning, in his Psalms, the Godlike amid those people. It is in this sense that 'all noble poets were priests as well' (*O*, 398) – they '"sing the praise of God"' by discerning the 'Godlike amid the human'. For Carlyle, the musician-priest is he who 'presides over the worship of the people' (*HHW*, 115) in a dual sense: he facilitates their divine worship of God and of themselves.

Wagner would certainly have recognised himself in such a definition of the musician. Furness notes Wagner's oft-remarked 'insistence on the artist as priest' – and Wagner certainly theorises the role of artist-priest in a remarkably similar way to Carlyle. As a priest, the Wagnerian music-dramatist presides over a theatre which becomes, as Edward Dent remarks, 'a temple consecrated to the highest ideals of the German nation.... Wagner [believed] that a work of art should be a ... sublime act of *worship*'.[15] For Wagner, the artist-priest exists merely to express and reflect back the sublime hero-worship of the German people (the '*volk*' or '*folk*') to and for themselves. The artist-priest represents a point of mediation through which the *volk* expresses its self-worship. As he writes in *Opera and Drama* (1850–1),

> The Folk ... becomes in Mythos the creator of Art ... [an art] sprung from nothing but man's ... yearning to recognise in the object por-trayed ... himself and his own-est [*sic*] essence.... Art ... is nothing but the fulfilment of a longing to know oneself in the likeness of an object of one's love or adoration.... Thus did the Folk portray in Mythos to itself its ... *Hero*.

For Wagner, 'the only task of the poet [is] ... to expound ... this *mythos*',[16] to reflect back to the *volk* its ideal self in the 'hero'.

In this sense, Wagner's own music mastery is, at least theoretically, far closer to Carlyle's notion of the servant-master than that of Wagner's hero, Siegfried. Ideally, the Wagnerian artist-priest *serves* the *volk*, and he does so by expounding – and hence reconstituting in the present – what Goldman and Sprinchorn call the *volk*'s 'primordial unity'. For Wagner, this primordial unity *is* the hero. 'The Hellenic races,' he observes, 'solemnized the joint memorial celebration of their common descent ... in the glorification and adoration of the ... hero in whose being they felt themselves included as one common whole.'[17] In Siegfried, Wagner finds a similar locus of original unity for the German *volk*; as he writes of his 'discovery' of Siegfried in *A Communication to My Friends* (1851):

> In the ardour to discover *what* thing it was that drew me so resistlessly to the primal source of old home Sagas, I drove step by step in to the deeper regions of antiquity, where ... truly in the *utmost* reaches of old time [in the old Germanic Mythos] ... I was to light on the fair young form of *Man*, in all the freshness of his force.... What here I saw, was ... the real naked Man ... the type of the true *human being*.

Wagner finds in Siegfried a 'true' '[arche]type'[18] – he locates in the figure of Siegfried 'freshness', 'force', reality and truth; his dominant metaphors, that is, are those of presence and logocentricism. Indeed, according to Wagner, the truth of heroes like Siegfried is eternally and universally present for the German *volk* – as Wagner writes, 'the incomparable thing about the Mythos is that it is true for all time, and its content ... is inexhaustible throughout the ages'.[19]

Carlyle, on the other hand, qualifies such logocentricism in his description of these mythical heroes; 'in the *Nibelungen*', he observes,

> the persons ... are indeed brought vividly before us, yet not near and palpably present; it is rather as if we looked on that scene through an inverted telescope ... the life-large figures compressed into brilliant miniatures, so clear, so real, yet tiny, elf-like and beautified as well as lessened.[20]

Whilst Wagner emphasises tradition, archetype, presence and timeless truth in the heroes of the *Nibelungenlied*, Carlyle speaks of distance, ancientness and smallness. These miniature heroes are not timelessly and 'palpably present' like Wagner's Siegfried, but, like Odin in *Heroes and Hero-Worship*, are conceived in terms of immense historical distance and even *absence*. This is because the kind of heroism Volker and Siegfried represent is that of 'the hero as divinity' – heroism which is for-itself and does not involve the hero-worship of others. This is exactly the kind of heroism that is always already a 'a production ... of old ages; not to be repeated in the new'.

For this reason, Carlyle finds that the kind of musical heroism embodied in Volker is unreachably and impossibly distant, and the primordial unity of physical mastery with musical mastery is always already undone. Volker's musicianship is the same as his physical heroism – it serves his physical heroism and is entirely for-himself. As 'a vehicle for worship', Volker's music worships only Volker, so that he, like Odin, might 'have felt that perhaps *he* was divine'. As with Odin, though, such self-recognition is almost meaningless for Carlyle, forming as it does a vanishing origin of heroism. None of the music masters in his essay 'The Opera' are self-worshippers like Volker or Odin; none of these music masters unites in himself physical and musical heroism. Rather, they all embody the displaced heroism of musician-priest, a displaced unity that only implies the originary unity of musician-warrior. In other words, Aeschylus, Sophocles, David and even Tyrtaeus are musical heroes inasmuch as they worship the physical heroism of others in their music. For Carlyle, *musical* heroism is always already alienated from heroism-in-itself; it is only ever constituted as the worship of physical heroism-in-others.

Indeed, music mastery makes explicit what is implicit in *all* Carlylean heroism. Carlyle implies throughout his works that all heroism is *other* to the subject, all heroism is other to-itself, all heroism is self-less. When he defines hero-worship as 'the recognition that there does dwell in that presence of our brother something divine', he implies that divinity and heroism are *always* elsewhere, in 'our (br)*other*' rather than ourselves. This even applies to those 'heroes' who, unlike musician-priests, *are* violent in themselves: even Cromwell's and Napoleon's physical mastery is an expression of their own hero-worship of others. Unlike Siegfried, Cromwell and Napoleon are priestly hero-worshippers who worship God, Christ and their people through physical mastery. Napoleon's heroism, for instance, is dedicated to 'Democracy and ... to the French Revolution' – to, that is, his fellow countrymen. His countrymen reciprocate by recognising Napoleon as heroic: 'he rose naturally to be King,' according to Carlyle, because 'all men saw that he *was* such.... They went, and put him there; they and France at large [gave him] Chief-consulship, Emperorship, victory over Europe' (*HHW*, 240). Napoleon's 'democracy' is the ideal – if very peculiar – democracy of hero-worship; he is recognised by the people as King, because they see *him* recognising and worshipping *them* through his military mastery. At least as far as his early career is concerned, Napoleon is no hero-in-himself or for-himself; rather, his heroism is recognised by others, and is for-others.

According to Carlyle, it would seem that divinity and heroism are always absence in-themselves and only presence for-others. The transcendental hero-in-himself and for-himself is missing almost entirely from *Heroes and Hero-Worship*. Not only is the 'hero as divinity' a vanishing origin for Carlyle, but even Christ and God remain notably absent from the text. This makes *Heroes and Hero-Worship* a strangely godless text, and the system Carlyle expounds in it a strangely godless system; as he himself admits, 'the greatest of all Heroes is One – whom we do not name here!' (*HHW*, 11). Carlyle does not name Christ because, like Volker and Odin, he tends to disrupt Carlyle's scheme; if hero-worship is the recognition of divinity 'in that presence of our brother', transcendental heroes-in-themselves like Christ, Volker, Siegfried and Odin are an unnecessary irrelevance. Though Carlyle apparently retreats from the logical conclusion of his own creed, it seems clear that divinity-in-itself is an almost-absent irrelevance to a '*Hero*archy' in which it is always the *other* who is recognised as a hero by hero-worship. Divinity-in-itself is extraneous and extrinsic to Carlyle's ideal democratic society – a 'society [which is] ... founded on Hero-worship ... [and is] what we may call a *Hero*archy (Government of Heroes) ... [or] a graduated Worship of Heroes' (*HHW*, 12).

As a 'graduated Worship of Heroes', Carlyle's ideal *Hero*archical society and history are constituted as a chain of hero-worshippers who worship as heroes other hero-worshippers, who, in turn, worship as heroes other hero-worshippers, and so on. In 'The Opera', all the so-called heroes who Carlyle hero-worships are themselves hero-worshippers. Even the hero-worship that is the *Nibelungenlied* is itself a reconstruction of a reconstruction, and so on; as Carlyle observes,

> the fiction of the Nibelungen was at first a religious or philosophical Mythus; and only in later ages ... took the form of a story, or mere Narrative of earthly transactions; in which last form, moreover, our actual *Nibelungen Lied* is nowise the original Narrative, but the second, or even the third redaction of one much earlier.

The heroes of the *Nibelungenlied* are always receding and disappearing into the past, and this is why, no doubt, Carlyle emphasises their historical 'distance'. In his review of the poem, in fact, Carlyle is far more interested in worshipping their hero-worshipper, the poet of the *Nibelungenlied*: 'whoever he may be,' he remarks, 'let him have our gratitude, our love'.[21]

The difference, then, between Carlyle and the Wagner who wrote *Opera and Drama* and *Siegfried* is simple: whilst Carlyle's *Hero*archy is based on the hero-worship of hero-worshippers of hero-worshippers, Wagner hero-worships the godlike hero in and for-himself. It is certainly the case in *Siegfried*, for example, that Wagner hero-worships the *volk*'s heroism, not their hero-worship – he glorifies the 'hero in whose being they [feel] ... themselves included as one common whole'. Only in *Die Meistersinger von Nürnberg* (1861/7) does Wagner come close to Carlyle's standpoint. Like Carlyle's music masters, Wagner's *Mastersingers* reflect back not merely the *volk*'s heroism, but also the *volk*'s hero-*worship*: in Hans Sachs, the *volk* hero-worship the hero-worshipper. Here, Wagner portrays the same kind of chain of hero-worshippers of hero-worshippers that Carlyle implies in his essay 'The Nibelungen Lied'. In *Die Meistersinger*, Wagner argues, 'people may ... rediscover Hans Sachs, who in turn will point them further back and direct them to Walther, Wolfram, and the heroic lays'[22] – who in turn, presumably, direct them back still further. Wagner here comes close to

Carlyle in positing an ever-receding heroic origin; in this music-drama, Wagner displaces forever the origin that, in *Der Ring des Nibelung*, he locates so firmly in Siegfried.

Carlyle makes impossible such an origin for the musical hero when he argues that, though 'song ... is the primal element of us', it is, at the same time, 'a vehicle for worship'. The 'primal element' that is music is no simple origin, or presence, since hero-worship is necessarily for-others according to Carlyle: music, like hero-worship, is the recognition that presence is always elsewhere. It is never the listener or even musician who is a hero-in-himself – rather, according to Carlyle, music takes the listener and musician beyond the self to some kind of 'infinite'. For Carlyle, as for so many writers in the nineteenth century, music is the master-art which 'leads us to the edge of the Infinite, and lets us for moments gaze into that' (*HHW*, 83), but, whereas Wagner envisages this infinitude as the primal unity and presence of heroes like Siegfried, Carlyle sees it as the infinitely deferred presence of hero-worship. Whilst, for Wagner, the music master propounds the timeless, universal truth of the hero, for Carlyle, the music master ideally propounds the infinite and universal truth of hero-*worship*. This is the real emphasis of *Heroes and Hero-Worship*. 'To me,' Carlyle writes,

> 'Hero-worship' [is] ... a fact inexpressibly precious.... Had all traditions, arrangements, creeds, societies that men ever instituted, sunk away, this would remain.... Our faculty, our necessity to reverence Heroes ... it shines like a polestar.... Hero-worship exists for ever, and everywhere. (*HHW*, 202–3)

Heroes, hero-worshippers and revolutionaries

> Music is by no means (as are the other arts) the copy of the Ideas, but the *copy of the will* itself, whose objectivity the Ideas are. This is why the effect of music is so much more powerful and penetrating than that of the other arts, for they speak only of the shadow while music speaks of the essence. Music ... is in the highest degree a universal language which is related to the universality of concepts much as they are related to the particular things.
>
> (Arthur Schopenhauer, *The World as Will and Idea*)[23]

Whether it brings its listeners near the infinite 'polestar' that is hero-worship or takes them back to a 'hero in whose being they felt themselves included as one common whole', music for Carlyle and Wagner, as for Schopenhauer, must necessarily release its listeners from what Wagner calls the 'bounds of individuality'. For Wagner and Carlyle, as for many other writers in the nineteenth century, music ideally lifts listeners from the personal or empirical, taking them into the realm of the infinite or universal. In this respect, many writers and musicians appeal to a Romantic idealisation of music throughout the nineteenth century. Wagner, for instance, openly takes his lead from Schopenhauer when he argues that, in music,

> the *individual will* ... awakes ... as the *universal Will*.... We here have the will in the Individual ... imprisoned by the fancy ... of its difference from the essence of things outside ... whilst there, in the musician's case, the will feels *one* forthwith, above all bounds of individuality: for Hearing has opened it the gate through which the world thrusts home to it, it to the world.[24]

In George Eliot's novel *Daniel Deronda* (1876), Gwendolen Harleth seems to experience such a liberation from the 'bounds of individuality' when listening to the musician Klesmer's piano composition. Though she has just experienced a 'sinking of heart' in response to Klesmer's criticism of her own singing, she is willing to acknowledge that Klesmer's music possesses what he calls a '"sense of the universal"':

> He certainly ... [had] an imperious magic in his fingers that seemed to send a nerve-thrill through ivory key and wooden hammer.... Gwendolen, in spite of her wounded egoism, had fullness of nature enough to feel the power of this playing, and it gradually turned her inward sob of mortification into an excitement which lifted her for the moment into a desperate indifference about her own doings.[25]

As Beryl Gray writes, Gwendolen's own 'possession of a "sense of the universal" is reflected in her response to the music of others. It manifests itself immediately after Klesmer's attack on her song'.[26] 'Music,' writes Eliot, 'stirs all one's devout emotions [and] blends everything into harmony – makes one feel part of one whole, which one loves all alike, losing the sense of a separate self.'[27] Like Wagner, Carlyle and many others, Eliot believes that great music can relieve sympathetic listeners from slavery to the self – from the '*bounds* of individuality'.

By amplifying experience beyond the 'bounds of individuality', music also provides an escape route from slavery *to others*, as well as to the self. In *Daniel Deronda*, this is certainly the case on a personal level: as Susan Peck MacDonald notes, 'all that Deronda is associated with – *music*, religion, unselfishness – is a threat to Grandcourt's mastery [over] ... Gwendolen'.[28] It is also the case in a much wider sense. One example of this, as we have seen in Chapter 3, is the way American slaves used music to express dissatisfaction with and criticism of the institution of slavery. Paul Gilroy notes 'the [important] role of music and song within the abolitionist movement', and suggests that 'music ... [was] vital ... amidst the protracted battle between masters, mistresses and slaves'[29] in America. Eliot's novel gestures towards this (musical) battle when Deronda declares that 'he had always felt a little with Caliban, who naturally had his own point of view and could sing a good song' (*DD*, 279). Here, Eliot clearly equates the 'good song' of that archetypal slave, Caliban, with a certain amount of subversive independence on the part of the slave – with, that is, the slave's having 'his own point of view'. Caliban's slavery is subverted by his song because it makes Deronda feel for him 'beyond the bounds of [Deronda's] individuality' in a way that is incompatible with a master–slave relation based on absolute opposition. The (problematic) nature of this sympathy is discussed further in the 'Afterword'.

As regards music, however, *Daniel Deronda* is also concerned with songs that might pose a threat to a master–slave relation on a national level, as in the setting of Count Giacomo Leopardi's 'Ode to Italy' (1818) by a fictitious composer called Leo. The idea of music as a threat to mastery and slavery is encoded within the structure of this piece: the song's *recitative* is followed by 'a mournful melody' expressing Leopardi's 'plaint' for an Italy which, in 1818, 'sat like a disconsolate mother in chains' (*DD*, 414, 477). After this, the song breaks into 'a climax of devout triumph – passing from the subdued adoration of a happy Andante ... to the joyous outburst of an exultant Allegro' (*DD*, 414) which expresses worship for past Italian heroes. Of course, by extolling past heroes, the poet is exhorting his readers or listeners to reconstitute such heroism in the present and cast off Italy's 'chains'. Eliot would undoubtedly have been aware that the Italians' eventual escape from their Austrian masters was inextricably linked to music: 'Va, pensiero sull'ali dotate' from Giuseppe Verdi's opera *Nabucco* (1842) was sung throughout Italy during the *Risorgimento*. In this chorus, the Hebrew slaves lament their captivity in Babylon, but Verdi's audience found in this scenario an allegory of their own enslavement as a nation. Indeed, from 1842 onwards, Verdi was literally synonymous with Italian revolutionary nationalism, his name often being scrawled on walls and public monuments by the Italian revolutionaries as a mnemonic for 'Vittorio Emmanuele *Re D'*Italia'. (Victor Emmanuel was proclaimed King of Italy by the first, national Italian parliament in 1861.)

As is well known, the link between music and heroic nationalism was of fundamental importance in the nineteenth century. As Richard McGrady notes, 'by the middle of the nineteenth century ... musical nationalism began to have an increasing influence in the musical taste of the day'.[30] This nationalism, however, often assumes a peculiar form. In Carlyle's essay 'The Opera', Tyrtaeus's musicianship only reinforces the pre-existent mastery of Sparta over its enemies; by singing of 'the need of beating back one's country's enemies', Tyrtaeus upholds the hierarchical status quo of Sparta and its enemies. On the other hand, the music mastery of Verdi and the fictional Leo consists in breaking down the current Austria-Italy hierarchy. Modern musical heroes, it seems, are almost of necessity *revolutionaries*, in that they seek not to perpetuate but to resist established hierarchies. 'So many of our late Heroes,' remarks Carlyle, 'have worked ... as revolutionary men.' According to Carlyle, modern heroes are compelled to work as revolutionaries because the nineteenth century is a 'Valet-World ... governed by the Sham-Hero'. In this context, the reassertion of any genuine heroism *must* involve a revolution of the current order. Working within a society in which 'Ideals ... be not approximated to at all', the hero's reassertion of any kind of transcendental order must of necessity be revolutionary. As Carlyle writes,

> the history of all rebellions [is that] ... you have put the too *Un*able Man at the head of affairs! ... You have forgotten that there is any ... natural necessity whatever, of putting the Able Man there.... [Thus] the 'law of gravitation' acts ... [and] miserable millions burst-forth into Sansculottism [and] ... other madness. (*HHW*, 203, 217, 197–8)

Nevertheless, although he is there to overturn the corrupt 'Valet-World', the Carlylean hero is really part of the Sansculottist madness of revolution only in so far as he reasserts a kind of 'Ideal' master–slave hierarchy. As Carlyle suggests, 'While old false Formulas are getting trampled everywhere into destruction, new genuine Substances unexpectedly unfold themselves.... In rebellious ages, when Kingship ... seems dead ... Cromwell [and] Napoleon step-forth again as Kings' (*HHW*, 204). In the nineteenth century – which was, of course, a 'rebellious age' – musical revolutionaries such as Verdi and Leo 'step forth as

Kings' and replace one hierarchy with another: Austrian rule is to be replaced by the Italian rule of Vittorio Emmanuele. For Carlyle, even when the hero is involved in the 'madness' of rebellion, he is still 'the missionary of Order', though he 'seems an anarchist' (*HHW*, 203). Wagner, though, *is* an anarchist, and, as such, not interested in new 'Kings'. Unlike Carlyle, he wants to destroy *all* Kings and masters. For Wagner, revolution is not a means of producing new, greater masters, but is an end in itself. Certainly, Wagner and Carlyle share a contempt for contemporary hierarchies. As Goldman and Sprinchorn note, 'Like ... Carlyle ... Wagner saw his age sinking into a morass of philistinism as everywhere the burgher class triumphed over the decadent aristocracy and the fettered proletariat.'[31] Unlike Carlyle, however, Wagner looks forward to a future revolution in which these 'fettered proletariat' are 'delivered from every shackle' of bourgeois 'philistinism' and, indeed, from *all* mastery and slavery. This is clear from his essay 'The Revolution' (1849), where he sets out his aim as the destruction of mastery:

> From its root up will I destroy the order of things in which ye live.... Be his own will the lord of man, his own desire his only law, his strength his whole possession.... I will destroy the order of things that turns millions to slaves of a few.... In godlike ecstasy they leap from the ground ... [and] with the heaven-shaking cry *I am a Man!* the millions, the embodied Revolution, the God become Man, rush down to the valleys and plains.[32]

In part, this revolution is to be brought about by the musician: the revolutionary destruction of mastery is brought about by the music master, whose mastery, therefore, is presumably *self*-destructive. For Wagner, the connection between true art and revolutionary destruction is symbiotic, for not only does true Wagnerian art require a prior revolution, but the transcendental (anti-)mastery presupposed by the perfect artwork *is* a kind of revolution: 'Only the great Revolution of Mankind ... not slavish restoration,' he writes, 'can give us back that highest artwork.... The artwork of the future must embrace the spirit of a free mankind, delivered from every shackle.'[33] Wagner's own music is *Zukunftsmusik* – that is, 'Music of the Future' – because it is addressed not to a contemporary, bourgeois audience but to a revolutionary and masterless audience of the future. Wagner's music mastery seems to involve a symbolic negation or even destruction of his contemporary audience – or, to be more specific, of the bourgeois mastery represented by that audience. When Wagner describes the conflagration at the end of *Götterdämmerung* which destroys Valhalla and the old gods and heroes, he writes that *'the flames ... blaze up so that they fill the whole space in front of the hall, and appear to seize on the building itself.... The whole space of the stage seems filled with fire.'*[34]

The 'hall' referred to is the 'Hall of the Gibichungs', but could easily be misread as the hall of the theatre itself. At the end of *Götterdämmerung*, Wagner involves the theatre *and* its bourgeois audience in the gods' fate. Indeed, the climax of *Götterdämmerung* seems to foreshadow the 'terrible fire at the Ringtheater in Vienna on 8 December 1881', in which, as Dieter Borchmeyer notes,

> some four hundred members of the audience perished while waiting for a performance of Offenbach's *Tales of Hoffmann* to start.... When asked his opinion of the catastrophe [Wagner] ... replied: 'the most useless people frequented such an opera house; if poor workers are buried in a coal mine, that both moves and angers him, but a case like this scarcely affects him at all.'[35]

The event 'scarcely affects' Wagner because he has already symbolically set fire to the 'useless people' in his own audience in the *Zukunftsmusik* at the end of the *Ring*.

Since it is '"addressed to the ears of the future"' (*DD*, 87), Klesmer's music, it seems, is also *Zukunftsmusik*, and is thus also concerned with the dissolution, supersession and destruction of contemporary mastery and servitude – of, in particular, the bourgeois mastery of contemporary audiences. Bourgeois '"ears"', such as those of young Clintock, are unable to comprehend his artistry. Clintock tells Gwendolen that it is her singing '"which is the style of music for me. I never can make anything of this tip-top playing"' (*DD*, 40). Klesmer is also in accordance with Wagner's revolutionism in so far as '"he looks *forward* to a fusion of the races"' (*DD*, 206: my emphasis). After various discussions with Wagner on his plans to create an opera on *Siegfried's Death* (later *Götterdämmerung*), the impresario Eduard Devrient wrote in 1848: 'Now a united Germany is no longer enough for him. He wants a united Europe in which a united mankind will be free.'[36] Wagner and Klesmer share a 'sense of the universal' – a sense that *dreams*, in Wagner's own words, of a 'free mankind, delivered from every shackle of hampering nationality'.[37]

The fundamental divergence, however, between Wagner and Klesmer consists in their differing attitudes towards precisely *how* mankind will be freed and united. Whilst Wagner is propounding a future which presupposes the revolutionary destruction of the bourgeois present, Klesmer appeals to a discourse which seeks to elide the possibility of revolution. Though the politician, Mr Bult, considers Klesmer to be 'something of ... [the] fermenting sort', the latter's '"cosmopolitan ideas"' are presented in political and reformist, rather than revolutionary, terms. When Bult considers 'Klesmer [to be] ... hardly ... a serious human being who ought to have a vote', the statement reflects Bult's obsolescence – in view of the Reform Acts of 1832 and 1867, it is really the case that Bult's opinions that are becoming obsolete, rather than Klesmer's being in any way ultra-progressive, let alone revolutionary. Far from destroying contemporary politics in the name of a utopian future, Klesmer argues that musicians should ideally '"help to rule the nations ... as much as any other public men"' – help, that is, perpetuate the mastery of the bourgeoisie, however suspicious they may seem to politicians such as Bult. According to Klesmer, musicians '"count ... [them]selves on level benches with legislators"' like Bult. Klesmer's radicalism seems, by comparison with Wagner's and even Carlyle's, limited: he merely seeks to raise a servant-musician to the same status as a prominent member of the bourgeoisie. To put this another way, Klesmer's music mastery is only '"of the future"' in so far as it looks forward to the extension of bourgeois, political power to include, for instance, musicians and '"cosmopolitans"'. It looks forward to the completion of something that was already happening in the Reform Acts of 1832 and 1867. In this sense, Klesmer and his music are really very Victorian, very contemporary, his hopes for the future being based on a Victorian, bourgeois doctrine of ameliorative 'progress' and political reform. By contrast, Wagner saw his mission as in no way comparable to that of reformist legislators: he did not want to '"make the age ... as ... other public men"' (*DD*, 206), but rather sought to destroy the age, and thus envisage a *future* one beyond bourgeois rule.

Put another way, rather than appealing to a revolutionary code of heroism outside bourgeois mastery like Wagner, Klesmer operates from within the bourgeois order as its paid servant. As Eliot remarks, Klesmer's position in the Arrowpoint household is defined by 'the large cheque that Mr. Arrowpoint was to draw in ... [his] name' (*DD*, 203). Klesmer is not really the Arrowpoints' 'music *master*' but rather their music servant, in the literal, rather than Carlylean, meaning of that term – Klesmer's position is compared to that of a 'footman' (*DD*, 203).

The same can be said of all of the musicians portrayed in *Daniel Deronda*. At one point, Deronda feels that Mirah is merely 'an imported commodity disdainfully paid for by the fashionable public', just as his mother, the Princess, is perceived as one of those '"Jewish women ... thought of by the Christian world as a sort of ware to make public singers and actresses of"' (*DD*, 477, 541).

Something similar happens in 'The Opera', where Carlyle complains of the singer Coletti:

> O Coletti, you whose inborn melody, once of kindred ... to 'the Melodies Eternal,' might have ... made a bit of God's Creation more melodious, – they have purchased you away from that; chained you to the wheel of Prince Mahogany's chariot. (O, 402)

Like Klesmer and the Princess, Coletti has been bought by the ruling class to provide a 'mere accompaniment' to their 'amusements' (O, 401); and, just as the music master is reduced to a paid servant, so music is transformed into a servant art which, rather than expressing 'a sense of the universal' or the 'Infinite, is 'chained' in slavery to bourgeois mastery and the cash payment that constitutes that mastery. Music, like the music master, is merely 'a bonfire [used] to illuminate an hour's flirtation'; the Muses 'Euterpe and Melpomene,' Carlyle writes, 'sent-for regardless of expense ... were but the vehicle of a kind of *service* which I judged to be Paphian rather. Young beauties of both sexes used their opera-glasses ... not entirely for looking at the stage' (O, 401: my emphasis). This is why music is generally an 'ideot [*sic*] Harlot',[38] as Carlyle remarks in a letter of 1842. 'Sent-for regardless of expense', music merely serves the sexual urges of 'young beauties of both sexes' as a kind of procuress. What underlies the bourgeoisie's treatment of music as its paid servant is prostitution and procuration.

This also applies to the musician and music master. Catherine Gallagher argues that 'prostitution and art become, in ... *Daniel Deronda*, interchangeable activities',[39] and it is certainly fear of *male* prostitution that is implicit in Deronda's horror at being asked, as a boy, if he is going to be '"a great singer ... adored by the world ... like Mario and Tamberlik"'. In 'spite of his musical gift', comments Eliot, 'he set himself bitterly against the notion of being dressed up to sing before all those fine people who would not care about him except as a wonderful toy' (*DD*, 142–3).

For Deronda, the adoration accorded by 'fine people' to singers is similar to that accorded to the prostitute. Like the prostitute, the great singer is 'dressed up', paid and 'adored' like a 'wonderful toy' or a '"sort of ware"' or an '"imported commodity"'. Klesmer, of course, would not agree, for he attempts to draw a distinction between '"the real artist"' who has '"the dignity of a high purpose"' and the

'young lady [who relies] on … her beauty as a passport. She may desire to exhibit herself to an admiration which dispenses with skill. This goes a certain way on the stage … [where] beauty is taken when there is nothing more commanding to be had…. The woman who takes up this career is … usually one who thinks of entering on a luxurious life … – *perhaps* by marriage.' (*DD*, 220–1: my emphasis)

Klesmer attempts to distinguish here between the musician and the actress, the '"real artist"' and the pseudo-prostitute who desires a '"luxurious life"'. The novel, however, shows how these oppositions are unsustainable in the figure of the Princess Halm-Eberstein, for she is at once '"a great singer *and* actress"', '"a queen"' and '"a sort of ware"' for the '"Christian world"' (*DD*, 544: my emphasis). The Princess is at once music master and music *mistress*. Indeed, even Mirah's acting and singing slip easily into a form of prostitution, when the Count, encouraged by Mirah's father, asks her '"to visit him at his beautiful place, where [she] … might be queen of everything"' (*DD*, 186). The female singer seems to represent a peculiar point of ambiguity between artist and prostitute, musician and actress, '"queen"' and wage-slave, adored mistress and sexual toy.

In fact, the opposition between '"real artist"' and pseudo-prostitute is deconstructed at the very moment Klesmer attempts to establish it, since the male artist also provides a point of ambiguity between roles which are, supposedly, diametrically opposed to one another. Klesmer describes with 'scorn' (*DD*, 221) the career of the actress who merely desires to '"exhibit herself to an admiration which dispenses with skill"' for the sake of securing a '"luxurious life … [and] marriage"'. Immediately afterwards, however, he reveals that he himself is just about to secure a luxurious life by marriage to the rich heiress Catherine Arrowpoint: '"in relation to practical matters"', he declares to Gwendolen, '"I am expecting an event which would make it easy for me to exert myself on your behalf…. The event I mean is my marriage … with Miss Arrowpoint"' (*DD*, 222). Klesmer, in fact, is a kind of *male* prostitute, who gains a '"luxurious life"' not through his talents as a musician, but by 'interesting … Miss Arrowpoint … as a possible lover' (*DD*, 205). Klesmer is just another capitalist master who gains independent mastery not through his music, but through a form of prostitution. It seems that the greatest ambition for a musician such as Klesmer

is to become 'a [Franz] Liszt ... adored by ladies of all European countries with the exception of Lapland' (*DD*, 203). As Eliot notes in her
essay 'Liszt, Wagner and Weimar' (1855), Liszt was often described as
'the Napoleon of the *salon*, carrying devastation into the hearts of
countesses'[40] – countesses who, presumably, can turn musicians into
wealthy masters.

In this way, the nineteenth century's ruling classes replace the transcendental and, indeed, Napoleonic mastery of Carlyle's heroic poets
and musicians with various forms of prostitution. As Marx writes, 'the
bourgeoisie has stripped of its halo every occupation hitherto honoured and looked up to with reverent awe. It has converted the physician, the lawyer, the priest, the poet, the man of science into its paid
wage labourers.'[41] Even the heroic musician is not exempt from this:
for Carlyle, the musician *must* lose his 'halo' if, like Coletti, he 'sings
the praise of Chaos' (*O*, 398), of a profane hierarchy based on cash
payment, and not a divine one based on hero-worship. Rather than
expressing the 'Infinite' or 'universal' truth of hero-worship, Coletti is
'chained' to the bourgeois, capitalist particular. The music master, at
the Haymarket Opera House, possesses no '"sense of the universal"'
and releases neither himself nor his listeners from any kind of slavery;
rather, he is bought by capitalist mastery merely to 'sing the praises' of
capitalist mastery – or, as Carlyle personifies it, 'Mahogany'. According
to Carlyle, Coletti is 'the Cleopatra's pearl that [is] ... flung into
Mahogany's claret-cup' (*O*, 402); Coletti does not '"sing the praise of
God"' but only of that sham-master, 'Mahogany'.

For Carlyle, the ever-increasing secularisation of music under capitalism transforms the 'genius' Coletti into a 'wretched spiritual Nigger
... with mere appetite for pumpkin' (*O*, 402). The word 'Nigger' suggests, of course, a slippage between servitude and slavery, as if servitude to cash payment is, for the potentially heroic musician, a
disguised form of spiritual slavery. It is no accident, in this respect,
that Klesmer's description as part-'Sclave' (*DD*, 37) could easily be
misread as 'slave'. Around this time, slavery would have been associated particularly with the system in the American South, which was
not abolished until 1863. In his essay 'The Nigger Question' (1849),
however, Carlyle argues that it is the *capitalist* servant or labourer –
she/he who endures '*nomadic* servitude, proceeding by month's
warning, and free supply-and-demand' – who is the real, abject slave,
whilst the servant who is 'hired for life, or by a contract for a long
period, and not easily dissoluble' is saved, in fact, from slavery. '*Except*
by Mastership and Servantship,' he writes, 'there is no conceivable

deliverance from Tyranny and Slavery.'[42] In describing Coletti as a 'spiritual Nigger', Carlyle is referring to his essay on 'The Nigger Question' and implying that Coletti's slavery should be equated with that of the *emancipated* blacks in the West Indies rather than that of the slaves of the American South. 'In the West Indies,' he declares, 'you ... abolish Slavery to Men, and in return establish Slavery to the Devil.... To save men's bodies, and fill them with pumpkins ... is a poor task for human benevolence, if you have to kill their soul.' Coletti's soul, it would seem, has been killed by his capitalist slavery to what Carlyle calls 'the merely pumpkinish and grossly terrene'[43] when he could have been, like Aeschylus, Sophocles, David and Tyrtaeus, the servant of God and his community.

Carlyle was probably not aware that, in the early nineteenth century, there was one professional musician in England who was literally a 'nigger' and a slave – namely, Joseph Emidy (*c.*1775–1835). According to James Silk Buckingham, a contemporary writer, Emidy was

> born ... on the West Coast of Africa, sold into slavery to some Portuguese traders, taken by them to Brazil when quite a boy, and ultimately came to Lisbon with his ... master.... Here he manifested such a love for music, that he was supplied with a violin and a teacher; and in the course of three or four years he became sufficiently proficient to be admitted as one of the second violins in the orchestra of the opera.... While thus employed, it happened that ... the frigate *The Indefatigable*, visited the Tagus.... They had long wanted for the frigate a good violin player ... [so they] conceived the idea ... to kidnap him, violin and all, and take him off to the ship.... [Subsequently] he was never permitted to set foot on shore for seven long years! ... [Eventually] he was released ... [and] permitted to leave in the harbour of Falmouth, where ... he remained ... till the period of his death.[44]

In Falmouth, Emidy quickly became established as a music teacher or 'master'. Richard McGrady notes that 'teaching ... became a prominent feature of Emidy's work fairly quickly and it probably provided the basis of his livelihood'.[45] Emidy also worked as a composer and a performer in Falmouth and elsewhere in Cornwall. Buckingham writes that 'Emidee [*sic*] had composed many instrumental pieces, [such] as quartetts, quintetts, and symphonies' and that his violin playing in these and other works exhibited 'a degree of perfection never before heard in Cornwall'.[46]

Had Carlyle been aware of it, Emidy's musical mastery would, of course, have been problematic. As with so many writers of the nineteenth century, Carlyle considers blacks to form a servant-race because they are naturally 'more foolish' than whites: 'my obscure Black friends,' he declares, 'decidedly you have to be servants to those that are born *wiser* than you, that are born lords of you; servants to the Whites, if they *are* (and what mortal can doubt they are?) born wiser than you.'[47] For Buckingham, Emidy's music mastery *is* this doubt; Emidy's music mastery undermines Carlyle's racial hierarchy of merit. Buckingham argues that Emidy's mastery offers conclusive 'proof of the utter groundlessness of the fallacy which supposes the negro intellect to be incapable of ... arriving at an equal degree of excellence with that of the whites.... This man might have become a ... Beethoven.'[48]

Indeed, as a 'nigger' who is a also potential Beethoven, a professional wage-labourer who is also, according to his gravestone, a 'genius',[49] and a servant-teacher who is also a music master, Emidy upsets and subverts all Carlyle's oppositions. Emidy at once represents everything Carlyle detests in modern musicians *and* everything he applauds in past masters. As well as being representative of the new class of freelance, professional musicians, Emidy conforms to the definition of a true Carlylean hero. Like Tyrtaeus in Sparta, Emidy *served* the sailors on *The Indefatigable* in the war with France: 'to furnish music,' writes Buckingham, 'for the sailors' dancing ... [was] a recreation highly favourable to the preservation of their good spirits'.[50] Likewise, after arriving in Falmouth, Emidy's music mastery consisted in his serving a particular community – that is, Cornwall – and he gained recognition of his musical mastery both in the local press and on his gravestone, which reads: 'His talent soar'd and genius marked his flight. / In harmony he lived in peace with all.'[51] The figure and life of Emidy somehow seems to encode and combine feudal slavery, capitalist, professional mastery, Carlylean servant-mastery, hero-worshipping heroism and martial music mastery.

*

Many of Eliot's musicians also undermine any kind of neat schematisation, albeit in a very different way, being at once capitalist, freelance professionals and pseudo-feudal masters. At first glance, Eliot's Klesmer and Liszt certainly seem to conform to the image of the nineteenth century's emergent class of professional music masters. 'During the early nineteenth century,' William Weber observes, 'musicians underwent that critical change which sociologists have called "professional-isation".' At this time, he argues,

> individualism and self-interest ... emerged as guiding principles within the new corporate structure of human life.... We can see them most explicitly in the development of the musical profession. By 1848 ... public concerts were the undisputed province of professionals.... Self-interest in terms of musical performance was thus expressed ... [as] the economic gain of the professional.

Weber lays a great deal of emphasis on the role of self-interest within 'the new ... structure of human life.'[52] According to Eliot, however, Klesmer and Liszt express this self-interest and desire for economic gain not in terms of freelance independence, but as a form of parasitic prostitution with women of the master-classes. Liszt does not gain financial security on his own, but by 'carrying devastation into the hearts of *countesses*', by uniting his capitalist music mastery with the aristocracy. Whereas Beethoven tears up the title page of the *Eroica* Symphony in disgust at Napoleon's post-revolutionary reinstatement of feudal and 'imperial' forms of mastery, Eliot sees Liszt's success as based on an accommodation – sexual, musical and financial – with that post-revolutionary mastery.

Klesmer's mastery is still more complex. He unites himself with a member of the *nouveau-riche* master-class, but this master-class is in the process of accommodating itself with the aristocracy and appropriating aristocratic forms – again, by marriage. Although Catherine's '"grandfather gained the [Arrowpoints'] property in trade"' and not '"blood"', Catherine is expected to 'marry a needy nobleman' who is '"connected with the institutions of this country"' (*DD*, 210, 349, 203). As Catherine exclaims, '"Why is it to be expected of an heiress that she should carry the property gained in trade into the hands of a certain class? That seems to me a ridiculous mish-mash of superannuated customs and false ambition"' (*DD*, 211). This is the context that makes Klesmer's engagement to Catherine an 'insurrection against the established order of things' (*DD*, 202), an insurrection against the prevailing '"custom"' of the assimilation of '"property gained in trade"' by the nobility and aristocracy. The engagement would appear to be an insurrection against the accommodation between the rising capitalist classes and the aristocracy.

The engagement is, though, *only* an insurrection, *not* a revolution; it is against the aristocracy only in so far as it is *for* capitalist and bourgeois hierarchies and 'property gained in trade'. Klesmer's rise from servitude to mastery is emphatically *not* that of Carlyle's revolutionary heroes: though Catherine's mother argues otherwise, the marriage is not the '"poisoning and strangling"' (*DD*, 209) of the Arrowpoints. Rather, Klesmer's subsequent mastery is precisely the same as that of the Arrowpoints – he operates, that is, *within* the capitalist, bourgeois hierarchy and does not overturn it. In a sense, he turns into his employers, the Arrowpoints: just as Mrs Arrowpoint has previously enjoyed seeing 'Klesmer ... in the light of a patronized musician' (*DD*, 209), so Klesmer can himself subsequently offer to patronise Gwendolen and Mirah. Though he is at first viewed with 'a little disgust' by the 'exclusive society' at the Archery Meeting, he eventually becomes, through his insurrection, the *same* as that exclusive society, to the extent that, at one point, he is even mistaken for '"The Prime Minister"' (*DD*, 412). Rather than being a Napoleon, Cromwell, Beethoven or Wagner, he is a Coletti or a Liszt, since his insurrection confers on him a mastery that is political, bourgeois and capitalist, not revolutionary or heroic. In this way, he is both a '"mountebank or ... charlatan"' master and a '"mountebank or ... charlatan"' (*DD*, 211) servant; he is neither genuine, heroic, revolutionary music master nor obedient music servant. Just as his insurrection invalidates his servitude, the mastery he gains by that insurrection is, presumably, only 'that supreme, world-wide celebrity which makes an artist great to the most ordinary people by their knowledge of his great expensiveness' (*DD*, 86).

Klesmer's insurrection and subsequent capitalist mastery is made possible by the social mobility promoted by capitalism – what Carlyle calls the 'nomadic'[53] nature of modern social relations between masters and servants. Indeed, it is this nomadism that, conversely, also renders Mr. Arrowpoint's *laissez-faire*, capitalist mastery unstable. For Mr Arrowpoint, 'the large cheque that [he] ... was to draw in Klesmer's name seemed to make [Klesmer] ... [a] safe ...inmate' (*DD*, 203). But this safety is wholly illusory. Carlyle notes that, for 'the flower of *nomadic* servitude ... mutiny [is] ... in his heart', since, 'in the long-run, it is not possible to buy *obedience* with money'.[54] Such capitalist, nomadic mutiny as Eliot attributes to Klesmer, however, is not revolutionary or heroic in the Napoleonic sense, since it is contained within the Victorian drawing room. Klesmer is, like Liszt, only 'the Napoleon of the *salon*'. The real hero, Napoleon, 'rises' from the ranks to become 'King' by triumphing in 'Wagrams and Austerlitzes'; that is, he rises in spaces which really do 'obey the law of all or nothing' – heroic, anarchic spaces which are, in a sense, *outside* mastery, *outside* the feudal, aristocratic order which, in part, they destroy. Klesmer, on the other hand, exceeds his role as 'footman' within what is a peculiarly domestic and feminised space – he operates within, not outside, the realm of bourgeois mastery.

He does so by recourse to the very same techniques of mastery that Michel Foucault finds in Jeremy Bentham's Panopticon and bourgeois society in general – techniques which, by definition, are unheroic, *un*-Napoleonic, *un*-revolutionary, *un*-Hegelian, non-violent, non-confrontational and non-dialectical. Just as power within the Panopticon is based on a principle of 'surveillance ... and ... a certain concerted distribution of ... gazes',[55] Klesmer's insurgent mastery in the Panoptic drawing room consists in the fact that '"he has magic spectacles and sees everything through them"' (*DD*, 417). Klesmer's mastery is constituted by the 'magic' power of his gaze. In their first meeting, Klesmer's 'assertion of superiority' over Gwendolen is precisely his comment that '"it is always acceptable to *see* you sing"' (*DD*, 38: my emphasis). By this remark, Klesmer turns Gwendolen into the object of a gaze, and, in fact, the kind of prostitute-singer who exhibits '"herself to an admiration which dispenses with skill"'.

If Klesmer's mastery over Gwendolen is a sexualising gaze, it is also a mesmeric gaze. Klesmer is also Mesmer. Mesmerism is not only the '"*magic*"' in his '"spectacles"', it is also the 'imperious *magic* in his fingers', given the fact that mesmerism often depended on both the eyes and fingers of the mesmerist. Mesmerism works magically precisely because it is a strange kind of mastery that does not exist in any sense of physical 'might'. The various forms of mastery attributed to Tyrtaeus, the Spartans, Volker, Siegfried and Napoleon are, first and foremost, exhibitions of physical force. Klesmer's mesmerism is 'magic' because, though powerful in the sphere of the *salon*, it is based on an absolute absence of physical mastery, and, as in Bentham's Panopticon, 'a *real* subjection is born ... from a *fictitious* relation'.[56] Mesmeric power is utterly unheroic, un-Napoleonic and un-Hegelian despite its fictitious relation to such mastery – despite its appropriation of heroic, or Hegelian language and analogy. Klesmer's assertion of superiority over Gwendolen is compared to 'the late Teutonic conquests' (*DD*, 39), but the military mastery of Bismarck is very obviously lacking from his mesmeric mastery. Rather, Klesmer's mastery is, once again, more like that 'Napoleon of the salon', Liszt. As Walter Beckett observes, 'Liszt ... modelled [himself] on ... Paganini in that he strove ... to attain the ... mesmeric power over an audience wielded by the great devilish violinist', but this mesmeric power is ultimately empty from a Carlylean or Hegelian perspective; as Beckett continues,

> There was at one time a move to give ... [Liszt] letters of nobility by the Hungarian aristocracy.... Instead he was given a sword of honour, set with precious stones, that was for a long time a standing joke and provoked the following verse:
>
> > Liszt alone, of all warriors, is without reproach
> > For in spite of his big sword, we know that this
> > Has vanquished only semi-quavers
> > And slain only pianos.[57]

For the nineteenth-century music master, the 'big sword' is only ornamental and the military or violent element of Tyrtaeus's music mastery has become mere mystification. Similarly, although the mesmerist and subject were often seen to be engaged in what Alison Winter calls a 'mesmeric duel',[58] this duel evidently lacks the physical confrontation described in Hegel's 'Master–Slave Dialectic'.

Rather, mesmeric mastery and slavery are a power relation in which master and slave are predefined, in which the roles of mesmerist and subject have, more often than not, been allotted even before the supposed 'duel'. Instead of being a real, confrontational 'duel', the mesmeric encounter is expressive of pre-existing inequalities and hierarchies of various kinds. There is, for instance, a gender divide at work of which the Victorians would have been acutely aware: as Winter notes, 'most mesmerists were men' and 'subjects were ... commonly women'. However, since there were also 'often pronounced class ... differences between mesmerist and subject', the mesmerist becomes what Winter calls a 'potent class challenger'.[59] In a society emphasising social and gender differences, the confrontation between mesmerist and subject had the potential to be dangerously subversive, the 'potent' mesmerist from a servant-class asserting himself over the female mistress who, though nominally part of the master-class, has little real power. The confrontation between mesmerist and subject represents, therefore, the same moment of hierarchical instability as the relation between Klesmer and Catherine.

The analogy between music and mesmerism is, of course, long established. As Winter points out, Victorian mesmerists often used a musical discourse, and music critics employed the discourse of mesmerism:

> When Victorians spoke of musical or mental power, they often retooled an ancient analogy between the organisation of the mind

and the design of a musical instrument.... Mesmerists commonly portrayed the phrenological organs as a keyboard.... [and] equivalent analogies were put to use in explaining what the conductor did to the orchestra.[60]

The most famous fictional mesmerist-conductor is, no doubt, Svengali in George Du Maurier's *Trilby* (1894) – a character foreshadowed by Eliot's Klesmer. Indeed, all the forms that Svengali's music mastery assumes – conductor, pianist and 'singing-*master*'[61] – coalesce in the character of mesmerist. It is through mesmerism that the sounds of his orchestra become a kind of 'strange seduction ... as well as enchantment' (*T*, 209), in the same way that Klesmer's music is both seduction for Catherine and 'magic' for Gwendolen; and it is through mesmerism that Trilby is made a great singer:

'With one wave of his hand over her – with one look of his eye – ... Svengali could turn her into ... *his* Trilby.... She [could] suddenly ... produce wonderful sounds – just the sounds he wanted ... – and think his thoughts and wish his wishes.' (*T*, 298–9)

This '"*other* Trilby"' is, in a sense, a feminised version of Svengali himself – after all, her stage name is '*La* Svengali'. As Winter writes,

In the famous scenes of the novel, Svengali not only 'conducted' the heroine, Trilby, in her extraordinary singing performances ... but actually erased her....The sinister role of the conductor-mesmerist as a malevolent demagogue in *Trilby* here involved a far more frightening image of mental control and the destruction of individual identity than had ever appeared earlier in the century.[62]

Nevertheless, Svengali only makes explicit the fears that are *implied* earlier in the century by the more benign figure of Klesmer: Svengali's destruction of Trilby's individual identity is surely anticipated by Klesmer's ability to 'lift' Gwendolen out of her restrictive egoism. It would seem, though, that music only takes the listener from the self to *another* ego – that of the music master. Again, this is made explicit in *Trilby*: Du Maurier writes that, during La Svengali's performance at Le Cirque des Bashibazoucks, 'it was as if she said' to her audience '"I am *Svengali*, and you shall hear nothing, see nothing, think of nothing, but *Svengali, Svengali, Svengali!*"' (*T*, 213); through mesmerism, Trilby not only becomes Svengali, but also communicates Svengali's mesmerism to her listeners, turning everyone into Svengalis. As Wagner writes, 'the spellbound listener ... [falls] into a state essentially akin to that of hypnotic clairvoyance [and] ... it is in this state ... that we belong immediately to the *musician's* world'.[63]

Though describing here the hypnotic effect of music in positive terms, Wagner unwittingly foreshadows the problem with musical mesmerism which Svengali later reveals; by freeing the subject from what Wagner calls the 'bounds of individuality', the musical mesmerist may merely be imposing his own, more masterful individuality on that subject. As Michael Tanner points out, Nietzsche's main criticism of Wagner is that he 'turns his listeners/spectators into accomplices. Becoming a Wagnerian is, at least incipiently, becoming like Wagner.'[64] The loss of 'the sense of a separate self' in the mesmeric subject, or musical listener is here close to the selflessness attributed by Hegel to slavery; according to Hegel's definition of slavery, 'the slave sets aside its own being-for-self ... [so that] it ... has the lord for its essential reality'.[65] Whilst, for Eliot and many others, music ideally frees the listener from slavery to both the self and to others, the suspicion remains that music might be more like mesmerism, merely replacing one 'subjective consciousness' with the ego of the music master himself – merely replacing, that is, one form of slavery with another.

To put this another way, if, as Wagner and so many others argue, music is revolutionary, in the sense that it frees the self from slavery to the self, the anxiety must be that this 'revolution', or 'insurrection', might do no more than change one kind of individual slavery for another. This is clearly the case in *Trilby*. Svengali's mesmeric music mastery *is* revolutionary in that it utterly undermines the aristocratic and bourgeois mastery of his audience, but this revolution merely transfers their mastery to him. Early in the novel, Svengali tells Trilby that, at some time in the future,

> 'Svengali will go to London.... and hundreds of beautiful Englanderinnen will see and hear and go mad with love for him – Prinzessen, Comtessen, Serene English Altessen. They will soon lose their Serenity and their Highness when they hear Svengali! They will invite him to their palaces, and pay him a thousand francs to play for them; and after, he will loll in the best armchair, and they will sit all round him on footstools.' (*T*, 74)

Later, he partly realises these aims through his mesmeric powers over Trilby. As 'Herr Kreutzer, the famous composer' remarks, '"I heard her [La Svengali] in St Betersburg.... Ze vomen all vent mat, and pulled off zeir bearls and tiamonts and kave zem to her – vent town on zeir knees and gried and gissed her hants."' Again, the 'young Lord Witlow' says that, after La Svengali sang in Warsaw, '"All the fellows went mad and gave her their watches and diamond studs and gold scarf-pins.... I gave her a little German-silver vinaigrette"' (*T*, 170–1). Just as Klesmer wins Catherine's fortune, so here the master-class are mesmerised into surrendering the symbols of their power – their diamonds, silver and 'gold scarf-pins'. This 'revolution', or 'insurrection', however, merely transfers capitalist mastery to the enriched Svengali – it does not radically alter the nature, or diminish the fact, of that mastery. Mastery is still defined by its 'great expensiveness'. The revolution against mastery supposedly threatened in different ways by the end of Wagner's *Ring*, by Klesmer's music, by Leo's song, by Verdi's operas – the revolution brought about, in a sense, by Svengali's mesmerism – slips all too easily into a new kind of mastery: the mastery of the music master's ego.

Whilst, for Carlyle, music ideally expresses the universal truth of hero-worship, what concerns many writers like Du Maurier is that modern music is the antithesis and negation of any kind of heroworship. Whilst, for Carlyle, society is ideally a kind of democratic 'heroarchy' in which everyone hero-worships everyone else, Svengali's and Klesmer's forms of music mastery suggest an all too familiar democracy based on capitalism, self-worship and self-interest, whereby music can communicate only the musician's 'love of himself as a master of his art – *the* master' (*T*, 41). It is *this* kind of (musical) democracy that I will discuss in the final section of this chapter.

Heroes, hero-worshippers and Jews

> When the two are ... in psychical *rapport*, the selfless individual ... has for his subjective consciousness the consciousness of *the other*.
>
> (Hegel, *Philosophy of Mind*)[66]

It would *seem*, then, that, rather than releasing listeners from the 'bounds of individuality', or inducing in listeners a loss of 'the sense of separate self', the nineteenth-century music master merely imposes different individualistic bounds and a different egocentric tyranny – that of the music master himself. It would *appear* that the '"sense of the universal"', or 'Infinite', which Eliot, Carlyle, Schopenhauer, Wagner and many others demand from music, must necessarily be wholly absent from Svengali's mesmeric music mastery. Strangely, though, the music of Svengali and La Svengali is, at times, described by Du Maurier in exactly the same Schopenhauerian terms it would seem to invalidate. This is evident, for instance, in his description of the effect of Svengali's performance on the 'penny whistle' on Little Billee: 'He had ... never dreamed such music was possible.... While it lasted ... he saw deeper into the beauty, the sadness of things, the very heart of them ... – even into eternity itself, beyond the veil – a vague cosmic vision' (*T*, 23–4). Something similar takes place when La Svengali's music comes to express 'a ... *universal* motherhood' (*T*, 212: my emphasis). On both occasions, Du Maurier appropriates the discourse of Romanticism to describe Svengali's 'cosmic' music mastery, but, throughout *Trilby*, he also expresses a Victorian, or *post*-Romantic, suspicion of this pseudo-religious idealisation. Svengali's music is portrayed as at once a 'cosmic vision', a '"*bel canto* ... dream"' *and* a dangerous, egocentric form of mastery. After he has finished playing his penny whistle, Svengali's mastery is such that he can 'leer ... on his dumb-struck audience', declaring to them, '"it was lost, the *bel canto* – but I found it, in a dream – I, and nobody else – I – Svengali – I – I – *I!*"' (*T*, 24). Svengali's music is somehow a simultaneous expression of both a universal 'cosmic vision', or 'dream', and absolute an 'I'.

Music, it seems, often induces in its listeners a 'loss of the sense of separate self' only to replace that self with an *other* self which is somehow both absolutely egocentric *and* absolutely universal. If, as Winter writes, the musical mesmerist has the power of '"making ... many people into one"'[67] self, this is the universal and universalising 'self' of the mob; by being '*dumb*-struck', Svengali's audience is turned into what Carlyle calls 'the big, *dumb, universal* genius of Chaos'.[68] In the later nineteenth century, music is expressive of the relationship of the demagogue with the mob – a very different variant of the relationship between hero and hero-worshippers to which Carlyle appeals.

In *Nietzsche Contra Wagner* (1888), Nietzsche's criticism of Wagner accords with this pattern: he accuses Wagner of pandering to the mob when he asks, 'on *whom* are your effects achieved? On those whom a *noble* artist should never impress: on the mass, on the immature, on the blasé, on the sick, on the idiots, on *Wagnerians!*'[69] Likewise, Winter argues that the modern figure of the conductor – one of the most famous of whom was Wagner himself – was a particularly suspicious figure in this respect. Indeed, she asserts that 'the resemblance ... conductors bore to problematic figures such as the Napoleonic demagogue and the mesmerist suggests one reason ... [why] Britain was slow to accept such an obviously useful technique.'[70]

The association of the musical demagogue with Napoleon is part of a bourgeois, Victorian agenda, which attempts to *other* the mob leader. In so many ways, though, the mastery of both the conductor and, indeed, Svengali is *not* foreign to Victorian Britain, but is actually a summation of modern, bourgeois rule. Indeed, in Carlylean terms, it is the mesmeric master who is identified with the spread of *modern* democracy, whilst 'the Napoleonic demagogue' would seem to be a contradiction in terms. It is the Napoleonic *hero* who is foreign to democratic mastery – for Carlyle, the demagogue is neither Napoleonic nor alien to democracy. In 'Shooting Niagara' (1867), Carlyle cites the *un*-Napoleonic Benjamin Disraeli as an example of the democratic demagogue, describing him as 'a superlative Hebrew Conjuror, [who is] spell-binding all the great Lords, great Parties, great Interests of England ... [and] leading them by the nose, like helpless mesmerised somnambulant cattle' towards what Carlyle calls 'the Niagara Rapids'[71] of the Second Reform Act (1867). Carlyle's description here is strikingly reminiscent of the ways in which Herr Kreutzer, Lord Witlow and Svengali himself portray the mesmeric effect of Svengali's music on the ruling classes, who, as has been seen, so willingly surrender '"their Serenity and their Highness"' after they have heard his 'wife' sing.

Undoubtedly, there is a connection between Svengali and Disraeli; Daniel Pick points out that it is possible 'to detect in the "i" that ends Svengali, direct echoes of ... Disraeli', who provided 'the most conspicuous instance of ... entwined racial and mesmeric imagery ... before Svengali'.[72] To this should be added democratic imagery: just as Disraeli's Reform Act threatens to destroy the mastery of the 'great Lords, great Parties, great Interests of England', Svengali's mesmeric musicianship undermines the pseudo-aristocratic power of those who hear it. Both Disraeli and Svengali, that is, use their mesmeric powers to 'democratise', equalise and homogenise everyone alike. They use their mesmeric powers to bring about the kind of equalisation Carlyle derides in democracy when he writes that, 'certainly, by any ballot-box, Jesus Christ goes just as far as Judas Iscariot'.[73] Indeed, in this respect, both are reminiscent of Wagner as seen by Nietzsche. In the same way that Disraeli turns the old masters into 'mesmerised somnambulant cattle', Nietzsche's Wagner transforms his individual listeners into 'voting cattle': 'one leaves oneself at home when one goes to Bayreuth ... In the theatre one becomes people, herd female, pharisee, voting cattle, patron, idiot, *Wagnerian*.'[74]

For Nietzsche, Carlyle and Du Maurier, the loss of mastery and self-hood implied by music and mesmerism is equated with democracy and democratic mob-mastery, and such music expresses a very different kind of idealised 'universality' to that which Schopenhauer has mind. 'This *universal* big black Democracy,' writes Carlyle, '[involves a] multitudinous efflux of oratory and psalmody from the *universal* foolish human throat; drowning for the moment all reflection whatsoever.' The psalmody of democracy is, according to Carlyle, 'monstrous, loud, blatant, inarticulate as the voice of Chaos'.[75]

In this way, the music of democracy anticipates the 'emancipation of the dissonance',[76] to use the famous phrase coined in the twentieth century by Arnold Schoenberg (1874–1951). As Charles Rosen writes: 'It was Schoenberg's genius to have recognised ... the dispossession of the principal means of musical expression [the consonance] by the new force of what had been a subordinate and contributing element [the dissonance].' The dissonance – previously a 'subordinate' or servile element of music – is emancipated by Schoenberg, and what Rosen calls the traditional 'tonal hierarchy'[77] is thereby overthrown. Schoenberg's musical 'Serialism' presupposes the absolute equalisation and 'democratisation' of the twelve notes used.

The emancipation of the dissonance is also, symbolically, the emancipation of the Jew. After all, Schoenberg was a Jew. Du Maurier certainly describes Svengali's voice in terms of dissonance – '[it] was,' he remarks, 'very thin and mean and harsh, and often broke into a disagreeable falsetto' (*T*, 11). In a notorious essay entitled 'Judaism in Music' (1850), Wagner describes Jewish speech and music in a similar way:

> We are repelled ... by the ... aural aspect of Jewish speech.... The shrill, sibilant buzzing of [the Jew's] ... voice falls strangely and unpleasantly on our ears.... [Similarly,] however sublime we may care to imagine [the] ... musical religious service [of the Jew] ... who has not had feelings of repulsion, horror and amusement on hearing that nonsensical gurgling, yodelling and cackling?[78]

What seems to concern Wagner most, however, is the dissonance of the emancipated and assimilated Jew, whom he calls the 'cultured Jew'. For Wagner, the cultured Jew's contribution to Western music is just as cacophonous as the Hebraic 'musical religious service': 'the Jews' ... creations necessarily appear to us strange, cold, peculiar, listless, unnatural and distorted. Thus the works of Jewish music often produce in us the kind of effect we would derive from hearing a poem by Goethe translated into the Jewish jargon we know as Yiddish.'[79] Wagner's assertions depend on an opposition between genuinely Western musical 'language' – the music of the German *volk*, for example – and its appropriation by the 'cultured Jew'. Likewise, in her essay 'The Modern Hep! Hep! Hep!' (1879), Eliot discusses the 'danger' posed by the 'premature fusion [of the English] with immigrants of alien blood' in terms of its adverse effect on Western – in this case English – language and music:

> To one who loves his [*sic*] native language, who would delight to keep our rich and *harmonious* English undefiled by foreign accent ... it is an affliction ... to hear our beloved English with its words clipped, its vowels stretched and twisted, its phrases ... delivered always in the wrong tones, *like ill-rendered melodies*.[80]

One such 'ill-rendered melody' is Klesmer's 'fantasia' in *Daniel Deronda*, which seems to Gwendolen to be 'an extensive commentary on some melodic ideas not too grossly evident' (*DD*, 39) – and, significantly enough, Klesmer is, of course, part-Jewish. As Wagner writes,

> The fact that the Jew speaks modern European languages only as learnt and not as a native, makes it impossible for him ever to speak colloquially, authoritatively or from the depths of his being.... It is ... in song ... that [this] ... offensive peculiarity of the Jewish nature reaches its peak.[81]

Music, it seems, necessarily exposes the Jew's 'offensive peculiarity', or *other*-ness to his 'adopted culture'.

Gustav Mahler – a Jew who, like Klesmer, was born in Bohemia – points up the opposition between Jewish music and the music of the German *volk* in his First Symphony (1885–8). The third movement alternates a canonic funeral march based on the German folk-tune 'Brother Martin' (also known as 'Frère Jacques') with grotesque episodes, which include references to Jewish popular music. Mahler, that is, pits German music against its supposed opposite, a Jewish *Klezmer* band. The D minor tonality of the 'Brother Martin' theme is firmly established, whilst the irregular, 'Jewish' interruptions are highly dissonant and exhibit a considerable degree of chromaticism. Nevertheless, the two themes are gradually superimposed on each other and thereby combined during the movement – like Eliot's musician Klesmer, who is partly a 'combination of the German ... and the Semite', Mahler's stylised *Klezmer* band is at once both alien to the

German *volk* and the same. The music master encodes in himself and his music the emancipation and intertwining of the Semitic into the German. Indeed, the opposition between the Germanic and the Semitic which Wagner seeks to uphold is always being deconstructed: Wagner's own father may have been Jewish. As Goldman and Sprinchorn note, 'His putative father ... died shortly after Wagner's birth. Soon afterward his mother married ... Ludwig Geyer, an assimilated Jew.... Wagner ... concluded ... that Geyer was his natural father.'[82] Ironically, Wagner's attempt to *other* the Jew is also an act of 'Jewish self-hatred', to use Theodor Lessing's famous concept,[83] and, indeed, his attack on Jewish music and Judaism in music is also an attack on his own. After all, if Schoenberg's 'emancipation of the dissonance' extends Mahler's erosion of tonality to its logical conclusion, Mahler is, in turn, merely utilising and extending the extreme chromaticism of such works as *Tristan and Isolde* (1854–5). As Rosen suggests,

> simple tonal explanations of certain sections of the later works of Wagner often break down.... The new ability, through chromaticism and dissonance, to suspend the clear sense of key ... was eroding the lucid *hierarchical* structure of the triads.[84]

The loss of this hierarchical structure is also the loss of what is often called a *'home'* key, or triad in music; atonal music has no sense of absolute resolution, no return home. In this sense, atonal and even heavily chromatic music functions as a metaphor for the Jewish Diaspora: the 'homelessness' of certain parts of Wagner's and Mahler's music is also the homelessness of the Jewish people in the nineteenth century. Eliot's Klesmer is himself subject to this homelessness; at one point, he denies any nationality and proclaims himself '"the Wandering Jew"' (*DD*, 206), the figure who, according to Schopenhauer, is 'nothing but the personification of the whole Jewish race'.[85] As the *Encyclopaedia Judaica* observes, the 'Wandering Jew [is a] figure in Christian legend condemned to wander by Jesus until his second coming for having rebuffed or struck him on his way to the crucifixion'; and various versions of the legend portray the Wandering Jew 'as a fully-fledged personification of the Jewish people'.[86]

The musical significance of this figure is seen in the fact that it is not only Klesmer who calls himself 'the Wandering Jew', but also Mahler: 'I am,' he proclaimed, 'thrice homeless, as a native of Bohemia in Austria, as an Austrian amongst Germans, as a Jew throughout the world. Always an intruder, never welcomed.'[87] As modern 'homeless' musicians, Klesmer and Mahler are in agreement with Nietzsche who, as Borchmeyer notes, thought that 'all artists were Wandering Jews'.[88] Nietzsche implies that the modern artist is always marked by homelessness and Jewishness, and, indeed, in spite of his anti-Semitism, it is Wagner who, in the figures of Kundry in *Parsifal* (1882) and *The Flying Dutchman* (1843), arguably portrays the Wandering Jew's movement – or wandering – between the status of victim or villain to modern archetype, or even artist-hero. In *A Communication to My Friends*, Wagner writes:

> [In] the figure of the 'Flying Dutchman' ... a *primal* trait of human nature speaks out.... This trait, in its most *universal* meaning, is the longing after rest from amid the storms of life.... The Christian ... embodied this trait in the figure of the 'Wandering Jew': for that wanderer, *forever* doomed to a long-since outlived life, without an aim, without a joy, there bloomed no earthly ransom.[89]

If the modern music master is the Wandering Jew, she/he certainly expresses a *version* of the primal, the universal, the eternal. '"The Melodies Eternal"' which Carlyle and so many others demand from music *are* encoded within the Wandering Jew, but as eternal *damnation*, not salvation. It is the Wandering Jew who, 'behind [the Opera-house] stalks [as] the shadow of *Eternal* Death'. Again, it is the Wandering Jew's music that stares 'too truly down towards Falsity, Vacuity, and the dwelling-place of *Everlasting* Despair' (O, 402: my emphasis). Damnation is the other, negative or tragic infinitude, universality and eternity which beset the modern music master, and the Wandering Jew's eternal damnation, or inability to find salvation, can be equated with the lack of tonal homecoming in modern music. It follows that, by inducing in Gwendolen a loss of 'the sense of a separate self', Klesmer's music is turning her into a Wandering Jew as well. What underlies the portrayal of music in texts such as *Daniel Deronda* and *Trilby* is the anxiety that, by releasing the self from the 'bounds of individuality', modern music might be turning its listeners into Wandering Jews.

This anxiety is most obvious in Deronda's first experience of the synagogue. Deronda hears in this music the possibility of a 'Day of Reconciliation' (*DD*, 311) between religions and races, but this day would surely imply the transformation of everyone into a Wandering Jew, as would, in a sense, Mordecai's belief in '"the ultimate unity of mankind"' (*DD*, 628), and even Wagner's affirmation of a future in which a 'free mankind [is] delivered from every shackle of hampering nationality'. For Eliot, the anxiety implied by the future unity of nations is that it might slip all too easily into what she calls elsewhere 'a spirit of universal alienism (euphemistically called cosmopolitanism)',[90] where there is no local, religious or national identity, or home, just an alienated multitude of Wandering Jews. Likewise, Klesmer's musical dream of '"a fusion of the races"' is, in truth, born of Klesmer's own homelessness: his music possesses a '"sense of the universal"' only because he is a Wandering Jew himself. The universality of Klesmer's music is that of a 'universal alienism' or 'cosmopolitanism' which has reference to no local, or national, 'home' precisely because *he* has no local, or national, home. The converse of this is Vincenzo Bellini's music, which Klesmer derides as '"the passion and thought of people without any breadth of horizon"' (*DD*, 39). Bellini's music, that is, possesses a national and empirical identity that is unavailable to Klesmer. As Wagner writes, 'the Jew speaks the language of the country in which he has lived from generation to generation, but he always speaks it as a foreigner.... [in much the same way that] the Jewish musician fling[s] together the various forms and styles of all composers and eras.'[91] Magee seeks to rationalise Wagner's argument:

> The ghettos of Western Europe had only begun to be opened ... and their abolition was going on throughout the nineteenth century. The Jewish composers of Wagner's day were among the very first emancipated Jews, pastless in the society in which they were living.... So their art could not possibly be 'the conscious and proclaimed unconscious' [of the *volk*] which Wagner believed all great art to be.

During what Bryan Magee calls this 'transition period',[92] the Jewish music master is incapable of serving the *volk* because he is alienated from it. According to Magee and, by implication, Wagner, the nineteenth-century Jewish musician simply cannot conform to Carlyle's ideal of mastery, whereby the master serves others. The Jewish musician simply cannot serve his country or the *volk* of that country because he is not fully integrated into that country or the *volk*; he cannot be a Tyrtaeus, a music master whose singing *serves* his fellow countrymen.

From a Wagnerian perspective, rather, the Jewish music master is an emancipated servant who serves only him/herself. In this sense, the Wandering Jew is representative of the 'nomadic' form of servitude, which Carlyle finds in modern capitalism. The Wandering Jew becomes a model of the self-interested, masterless – and therefore *homeless* – capitalist servant. In 'The Nigger Question', Carlyle writes of London's 'thirty-thousand ... mutinous Serving-maids, who, instead of learning to work and to obey, learned to give warning', and, because of this, 'have tumbled from one stage of folly to the other stage; and at last are on the street'.[93] These 'mutinous Serving-maids' are made homeless by nomadic capitalism. For Carlyle, the kind of 'White Flunky' promoted by capitalism is 'disloyal, unheroic [and] ... inhuman in his character, and his work, and his position.... He is the flower of nomadic servitude, proceeding by month's warning, and free supply-and-demand.'[94] The wandering, nomadic, capitalist servant loses any potentially heroic signification because his attachment to an other, and thus to a *home*, is so subject to change; the nomadic servant's masterlessness means that his potential identity as hero, or even as human being, wanders aimlessly and endlessly.

This failure of capitalist 'nomadic' hierarchies to bestow meaning on servants is analogous to the Wandering Jew's inability to find salvation: both are caused by a repudiation of absolute, fixed mastery. For Carlyle, the Wandering Jew's denial of Jesus on the *Via Dolorosa* is paradigmatic of the denial of all true mastery in the nineteenth century. This is clear from the example of the 'mutinous Serving-maids', whom he describes as 'hapless enfranchised White Women, who took the "freedom" to serve the Devil with their faculties, instead of serving *God or man'.[95]*

Emancipation from fixed mastery is ultimately emancipation from God or Christ, and this, for Carlyle, is the subtext of modern, capitalist and democratic society. He posits a Jewish origin for democracy when he recycles, in *Latter-Day Pamphlets*, that oft-repeated accusation that the Jews committed deicide:

> A certain People, once on a time, clamorously voted by overwhelming majority, "Not *he*; Barabbas, not *he*!" ... Well, they got Barabbas; and they got ... such guidance as Barabbas and the like of him could give them; and ... they stumbled ever downwards and devilwards, in their truculent stiffnecked way; and – and ... after eighteen centuries of sad fortune, they prophetically sing 'Ou' clo'!' in all the cities of the world. Might the world ... understand their song a little![96]

Once again, the figure of the Wandering Jew is taken as a symbol of the whole Jewish race. In the same way that the legendary Ahasuerus is cursed for repudiating Christ on the *Via Dolorosa*, all Jews, according to

Carlyle, are cursed to be wanderers, stumbling 'ever downwards and devilwards', because of the 'vote' in which they first condemned Christ to be crucified. Indeed, Carlyle believes that, ever since, this 'vote' has continually been replayed in the '*song*' of the Wandering Jewish race, which therefore constitutes a recurrent reassertion of 'prosperous Semblances' ('old clothes') over 'the Supreme Fact'[97] of Jesus Christ. For Carlyle, the Jews wander and stumble 'downwards and devilwards', endlessly re-echoing the song-vote with which they first repudiated Jesus's mastery in a kind of hopeless and godless repetition-compulsion. In this way, the 'song' of the Jewish music master is always a negation of meaning and Supreme Fact. The song of the Jewish music master is merely a hopeless repetition of that first act of 'deicide', or master-cide of Christ by the Jewish people.

When Nietzsche argues that all modern artists are Wandering Jews, this is because *all* artists are somehow implicated in the accusation that the Jews had committed deicide; modern art merely repeats the song of the Jewish people over and over again. Indeed, in Carlylean terms, the (capitalist and democratic) self-interest of the artist, like that of the 'mutinous Serving-maids', *is* a kind of deicide or master-cide. This conceit is encoded and problematised in the artists in *Daniel Deronda*, where the Princess Halm-Eberstein's singing career depends on her '"escaping from bondage"' to her father by '"a contrivance which would bend ... all to the satisfaction of self"' (*DD*, 541, 568). Her status as a self-interested, capitalist artist is founded on her renunciation of her father's mastery. The Princess's career is based on an act of displaced patricide, or master-cide – after all, it is only after her father has died that, she says, '"I had my way"' (*DD*, 543). Likewise, once in London, Mirah proclaims to Deronda, '"I want to do something to get money"'–a capitalist aspiration made possible by her running away from Prague, where, she says, '"my heart [had] turned against my father"' (*DD*, 315, 187). By renouncing their fathers' mastery, both the Princess and Mirah become capitalist nomads, or Wandering Jews – this is surely the nature of the paternal '"curse"' under which the Princess labours as her singing career takes her '"from one country to another"' (*DD*, 540, 537). Similarly, after leaving her father, Mirah says that everything '"seemed all a weary wandering.... I thought of my People, how they had been driven from land to land and been afflicted, and multitudes had died of misery in their wandering"' (*DD*, 189). What *is* different, though, about these artists is that their status as Wandering Jews is constituted not by renouncing Christ or Christianity, but by renouncing the patriarchal mastery of traditional

Judaism. In *Daniel Deronda*, it is the cultured, Westernised Jew who is Ahasuerus. Though she is baptised into Christianity, it is ironically the Princess, not Mordecai, who is the epitome of capitalism's patricidal-cum-deicidal nomadism. This is not, of course, to claim that Eliot unproblematically condemns the Princess's renunciation of an oppressive patriarchy, but rather that the Princess's almost total egocentrism is the ultimate expression of the nomadism which Carlyle finds in capitalist, democratic emancipation. Carlyle argues that '"emancipation" ... [is] the cutting asunder of human relations',[98] and the Princess declares to Deronda, '"when your father died, I resolved that I would have no more ties, but such as I could free myself from"' (*DD*, 543). Again, Carlyle finds capitalist nomadism 'in every human relation, from that of husband and wife down to that of master and servant',[99] and the Princess represents a point of intersection between all of these forms of nomadic relations. The Princess embodies in the text the consummation of capitalist, democratic, pseudo-deicidal and master-cidal emancipation, resisting and rebuffing as she does not only patriarchal mastery, but Christian mastery, Jewish mastery and European racial mastery.

It is, then, ironically the female, cosmopolitan Wandering Jew who is a paradigmatic figure of modern democratic capitalism. Borchmeyer notes that, for the nineteenth century, 'Ahasuerus [was] one of the great symbolic figures of the age'. Admittedly, Borchmeyer's emphasis is on the *male* Ahasuerus, despite the obvious traces of the legend in Wagner's Kundry,[100] but it seems clear that the Jewish artist, whether female or male, is not just marginal to Western society, as Wagner suggests in his essay 'Judaism in Music', but also subversively fundamental and central to it. This doubleness is presumably due to the Jew's ambivalent position in European culture. As Bryan Cheyette observes, 'Jews were, simultaneously, at the centre of European metropolitan society and ... banished from its privileged sphere by a semitic discourse.'[101] Indeed, though Wagner attempts to banish the Jewish from the German, he too undermines such distinctions by simultaneously portraying the Jew as a central figure of 'European metropolitan society'. He argues that, 'as the world is constituted today, the Jew is more than emancipated, he is the ruler. And he will continue to rule as long as money remains the power to which all our activities are subjugated.'[102] In artistic *and* in general terms, it would seem that, for Wagner, the Jew is the master of 'the world [as it] is constituted today'.

Mikhail Bakunin, an anarcho-communist who greatly influenced Wagner, echoes many of his contemporaries by associating bourgeois mastery with Jewish hegemony: 'the Jews,' he declares, 'are the exploiters *par excellence* of all other peoples' labours'.[103] The Jews, according to Bakunin, are the *echt*-bourgeoisie, *echt*-capitalists and *echt*-democratic masters. In her essay, 'The Modern Hep! Hep! Hep!', even Eliot comes *close* to the anti-Semites in this suspicion of the Jewishness of modern mastery:

> At this moment [1879], the leader of the Liberal party in Germany is a Jew, the leader of the Republican party in France is a Jew, and the head of the Conservative ministry in England is a Jew.... 'The Jews', it is felt, 'have a dangerous tendency to get the uppermost places not only in commerce but in political life'.... There is truth in these views of Jewish social and political relations.[104]

This 'truth' is encoded in both Du Maurier's Svengali and Eliot's Klesmer: both embody a fear that the modern artist, democrat, capitalist, liberal, demagogue and bourgeois master are all in some way necessarily 'Jewish'; that, in fact, democracy and capitalism are Jewish conspiracies.

According to Carlyle, the Jewish race is always repeating its vote for Barrabas over the 'Supreme Fact' of Jesus Christ, just as democracy and capitalism are always repeating the act of deicide and reasserting masterlessness, or the sham-mastery of the 'Jew'. For Carlyle, continual deicide and sham-mastery form the 'origin, [and] the fatal necessity, of modern Democracy everywhere'.[105] In this way, democracy is a continual, ever-repeating pseudo-apocalypse, a continual crucifixion of true mastery. Carlyle believes that it is total equality and democratic 'emancipation' that allow the sham, Jewish master to gain control of a society, since democracy removes from mastery his ideals of 'might and right'. In a democratic context, right is merely defined by number of votes and physical might is all but irrelevant. As he writes,

> Let no man in particular be put at the top; let all men be accounted equally wise and worthy ... and then ... decide by count of heads, the vote of a Demerara Nigger [being] equal ... to that of a Chancellor Bacon: this, I perceive, will ... give the *minimum* of wisdom in your proceedings.... Folly in such million-fold majority, at length ... supreme in this earth.... Rushing ... in wild *stampede* (the Devil being in them) ... fast and ever faster ... to the sea of Tiberias, and the bottomless cloacas of Nature: quenched there.[106]

What Carlyle elsewhere calls the *'universal* cry of Liberty and Equality' (*HHW*, 203: my emphasis) is, here, the universalism of the apocalypse. The sense of the universal in La Svengali's singing, which so reduces the aristocracy to slavery and destroys all true mastery, is the apocalyptic universalism, which Carlyle finds in absolute equality, in absolute masterlessness. This is the real universalism and infinitude of modern music. After all, in *Daniel Deronda*, Mirah Lapidoth is described as a 'nightingale', whilst, in *Trilby*, La Svengali is called the 'queen of the nightingales' (*DD*, 305, *T*, 270), and it is the song of the nightingale that, in Mahler's Second Symphony, ushers in the Day of Judgement when 'none is great, none small', and all nomadically wander the earth together 'in *endless* procession'.[107]

5
Stump Orators, Phantasm Captains and Mutual Recognition: Popular Masters and Masterlessness in Dickens' *Hard Times* and Thomas Carlyle's 'Stump-Orator'

> Self-consciousness exists in and for itself when, and by the fact that, it so exists for another; that is, it exists only in being acknowledged.... [The subjects] *recognise* themselves as *mutually recognising* one another.
>
> (G.W.F. Hegel, *Phenomenology of Spirit*)[1]

> For Hegel ... liberal society is a reciprocal and equal agreement among citizens to mutually recognise each other.... 'Liberalism' can be seen as the pursuit of rational recognition, that is, recognition on a universal basis in which the dignity of each person as a free and autonomous human being is recognised by all.... Life in a liberal democracy ... shows us the way to the completely non-material end of recognition of our freedom.... The liberal state ... creates a classless society based on the abolition of the distinction between masters and slaves.
>
> (Francis Fukayama, *The End of History and the Last Man*)[2]

> We talk and think on the surface.
>
> (James Anthony Froude, 'Party Politics')[3]

For Hegel, 'mutual recognition' represents an absolute end to the relation of master and slave. In the *Phenomenology of Spirit* (1807), he posits this ideal state of equality and reciprocity as the end-point of the 'Master–Slave Dialectic'. As 'conclusions', both this chapter and the

Afterword are concerned with supposed end-points of mastery and slavery. Whilst the Afterword is a short analysis of a crucial moment of British imperialism, the current chapter leads on from the discussions of democracy in Chapters 3 and 4 to show how, for Carlyle and others, democratic discourses at once appropriate and complicate Hegel's notion of mutual recognition; how democracy is at once the negation of mastery and slavery and a means of perpetuating it in other forms; how, in fact, a pseudo-Hegelian state of democratic equality and mutual recognition is always haunted by past mastery and slavery, and mastery and slavery are always haunted by a possible future of democratic equality and recognition. If, as Sartre remarks, 'slavery is not a historical result capable of being surmounted',[4] this is also true of mutual recognition, which seems everywhere present in democratic discourse as a ghostly promise or, sometimes, as a threat.

According to Fukayama, 'popular self-government abolishes the distinction between masters and slaves; everyone is entitled to at least some share in the role of master [so] ... recognition becomes reciprocal when the state and the people recognise each other'.[5] Carlyle would *seem* to agree: in the *Latter-Day Pamphlets* (1850) he asserts, 'Priest, King, Home Office, all manner of establishments and offices among a people bear a striking resemblance to the people itself.'[6] Here, the modern state and the people do recognise each other and, indeed, are almost the same as each other, just as Fukayama claims. Nevertheless, unlike Fukayama, what really concerns Carlyle is not just the fact of such similarity, equality and mutual recognition in a democratic state, but the nature, modality and constitution of such reciprocity. Unlike Fukayama and, perhaps, Hegel himself, Carlyle refuses to affirm equality, reciprocity and recognition as progressive qualities in themselves. Instead, he argues in *Chartism* (1839) that the kind of reciprocity subsisting between popular masters and the people they master consists of 'Semblance recognising itself, and getting itself recognised, for Substance'.[7] This is pseudo-Hegelian language, but it is being used to define a rather different and more complex mode of recognition than that which Fukayama finds in modern democracy. For Carlyle, the relationship between the popular, democratic master and the masses is one of each mutually recognising as truth, or 'Substance' the insincerity, or 'Semblance' of the other. Writing of Chartism and other populist causes, Carlyle argues that 'sincere men, of never so limited an intellect, have an instinct for discriminating sincerity.... Masses of people capable of being led away by quacks are themselves of partially untrue spirit.'[8]

The peculiarity of this kind of mutuality lies in its ghostliness, whereby both quack-masters and the masses recognise as 'sincerity' the 'untrue *spirit*', or 'Semblance' of the other. Carlyle cannot bear such a meeting of ghostly Semblances, being philosophically wedded to the notion of Substance, to what Jacques Derrida calls 'the metaphysics of presence'.[9] For Carlyle, 'presence' (Substance) is almost always defined as heroic work or action, as opposed to the 'absence', which is mere speech, so, by recognising Semblance as Substance, the masses are mistaking the quacks' speech for true heroism. That is to say, Carlyle's argument with popular, democratic masters frequently depends on an opposition between the Semblance that is speech and the Substance that is heroic action. This can be clearly seen in 'Stump-Orator', one of the *Latter-Day Pamphlets*, where he asserts that, for the 'man [who possesses] ... wisdom, insight and heroic worth', speech is ideally 'but the tangible sign of [those] ... other faculties' (*LDP*, 178). By contrast, the popular leader who is the 'stump-orator' is a 'distracted phantasm' of 'Nature' (*LDP*, 175) because he and his speeches are really just ghostly signs for *unrealised* heroic action. As Carlyle writes, 'the eloquent man that delivers, in Parliament or elsewhere, a beautiful speech, and will perform nothing of it ... has enrolled himself among the *Ignes Fatui* and Children of the Wind' (*LDP*, 180).

Of course, what surely underlies and subverts such declarations is Carlyle's neurotic anxiety that he is himself one of these 'Children of the Wind'. Carlyle falls prey to his own opposition: if speaking and, by extension, writing are mere Semblance, then his work too is Semblance, not Substance. As Christine Persak notes, 'the contrast between language and action is central to Carlyle ... [but] this is obviously a dilemma for one who takes on himself the task of reforming society through writing'.[10] Carlyle was obviously, at some level, aware of this 'dilemma' – towards the end of 'Stump-Orator' he addresses a 'brave young British man', declaring that 'you are, *what I am not*, in the happy case to learn to *be* something and to *do* something, instead of eloquently talking about [it]!' (*LDP*, 213: my emphasis). Similarly, in a letter to John Stuart Mill of 1833, Carlyle admits that 'at some moments I have the sickliest misgivings about the vocation of Literary Men.... I dream of busting out into another sort of Activity.'[11] In *Heroes and Hero-Worship* (1840), he specifies what kind of 'Activity' this would ideally be: 'the Poet who could merely sit on a chair and compose stanzas,' he writes, 'would never make a stanza worth much. He could not sing the Heroic warrior, unless he himself were at least a Heroic warrior too.'[12] The question remains, how, according to this doctrine, it was possible for Carlyle to write *Heroes and Hero-Worship*, *Oliver Cromwell's Letters and Speeches* (1845) and *Frederick the Great* (1858–65), given his failure to become a 'Heroic warrior'. In fact, by asserting that 'the Poet ... could not sing the Heroic warrior, unless he himself were at least a Heroic warrior too', Carlyle suggests, perhaps unwittingly, that he is almost as heroic as the heroes he worships through his writing. As Branwen Pratt writes, 'What [Carlyle] ... says about Great Men describes his ideal image of himself.'[13] According to Carlyle's terms, though, this ideal *image* is only that: though he comes close to placing himself on the same plane as the heroes he writes about, his own heroism is mere unrealised potential, mere Semblance.

In this respect he is rather similar, oddly enough, to the stump-orator who appears in Charles Dickens' *Hard Times* (1854), a novel that is 'inscribed' to him.[14] Just as Carlyle seems to equate himself with the heroes he writes about, the popular orator and union leader, Slackbridge, implies his equality with the 'heroic' workers for whom he speaks. By addressing his '"fellow-sufferers, and fellow-workmen"', Slackbridge is obviously suggesting that he shares in their work. This 'ideal image' of himself is recognised as Substance by his audience in responses such as '"Good!" "Hear, hear, hear!" [and] "Hurrah!"' (*HT*, 170). Nevertheless, one worker, Stephen Blackpool, exposes Slackbridge's speech as the mere Semblance of equality when he declares to the latter, '" 'Tis this Delegate's trade for t' speak ... an he's paid for't.... Let him keep to't"' (*HT*, 173). Blackpool recognises that Slackbridge is not *really* equal to the workers, but, as Dickens himself suggests, is 'essentially below them' (*HT*, 170). Like Carlyle, Dickens denounces the popular leader and stump-orator, and does so by reference to the same hierarchical opposition between language and action, talking and doing, speaking and work: Dickens makes clear that Slackbridge is, morally speaking, 'below' his audience because he is just a speaker and not a 'Heroic Warrior', a 'Great Man' of action, or even a worker like those whom he addresses. Margaret Simpson points out that

> Slackbridge is based on one of the main agitators of the Preston [weavers'] strike [1853–4], a former weaver called Mortimer Grimshaw ... [who also figures as] Dickens' 'professional speaker,' Gruffshaw, in [his *Household Words* essay] 'On Strike'.... *Grimshaw was a full-time agitator who had no intention of returning to his trade.*[15]

As a 'professional speaker', Grimshaw/'Gruffshaw' is not a worker, despite the fact that, as Dickens writes in 'On Strike' (1854), he indicates equality with the workers by addressing them as 'O, my friends'.[16] As with his fictional counterpart, this is just the Semblance of equality.

In *Hard Times* and 'On Strike', then, the workers do not *seem* to resemble their demagogic leader and orator, Slackbridge, or reciprocate his dishonesty and 'quackery' in quite the way described by Carlyle when he talks of 'Semblance recognising itself, and getting itself recognised, for Substance'. When Carlyle writes that 'the impostor is false, but neither are his dupes altogether true',[17] his stress is on the similarity and equality of the masses with their popular 'quack' masters. Dickens' emphasis, however, is on the dissimilarity and disparity between Slackbridge and his audience of factory labourers, despite Slackbridge's own claims. Dickens remarks that, in comparison with his listeners, Slackbridge 'was not so honest ... not so manly ... not so good-humoured; he substituted cunning for their simplicity, and passion for their safe solid sense' (*HT*, 170). The 'crowd of earnest faces' have clearly chosen a 'leader' who is morally 'below them' (*HT*, 170) in the same way, as we saw in Chapter 3, that Major Pawkins is a political leader and 'man of the people' in the America of *Martin Chuzzlewit* (1843–4) precisely because he is worse than the people, being able to 'chew more tobacco, smoke more tobacco, drink more rum-toddy, mint-julep, gin-sling and cocktail, than any private gentleman of his acquaintance'.[18] In *Hard Times*, Dickens addresses this discrepancy between the 'man of the people' and the people themselves directly, expressing his own sense of the peculiarity of the relationship:

> Strange as it always is to consider any assembly in the act of submissively resigning itself to the dreariness of some complacent person, lord or commoner, whom three-fourths of it could ... raise out of the slough of inanity to their own intellectual level, it was particularly strange ... to see this crowd of earnest faces, whose honesty ... no competent observer free from bias could doubt, so agitated by such a leader. (*HT*, 170)

Nevertheless, though it seems to bring into question Carlyle's sense of the equality and reciprocity of 'quacks' with the 'masses', even the apparently unequal relationship here between dreary 'leader' and honest 'crowd' can be understood in terms of 'Semblance recognising itself, and getting itself recognised, for Substance'. The fact that the 'crowd of earnest faces' is 'so agitated by such a leader' *can* be explained by reference to Carlyle's peculiar formulation of (dishonest) recognition, reciprocity and equality. To be specific, just as the workers mistake Slackbridge's oratory for heroism and true leadership in their 'cheering', Slackbridge elicits this by his reciprocal recognition of their 'delusions' (*HT*, 175, 174): each recognises as Substance the Semblance, or 'untrue spirit', of the other. In other words, whereas Blackpool, 'knew ... [the workers] far below their *surface* weaknesses and misconceptions, as no one but their fellow-labourer could' (*HT*, 174: my emphasis), Slackbridge is not a fellow labourer, so can only float on this 'surface' of weaknesses, misconceptions and delusions. The paradigm of Hegelian recognition is reduced here to a meeting of surfaces, Semblances, misconceptions and delusions. This can be made clearer by reference to the *Latter-Day Pamphlets*, where Carlyle perceives the relation between popular, demagogic orator and audience in precisely these terms. Writing in particular of 'parliamentary eloquences', he comments,

> the dog that was drowned last summer, and that floats up and down the Thames with ebb and flood ever since – is it not dead? Alas, in the hot months, you meet here and there such a floating dog; and at length ... get to know him by sight. 'There he is again, still astir there in his quasi-stygian element!' you dejectedly exclaim ... and reflect ... on certain completed professors of parliamentary eloquence.... Dead long since, but *not* resting. (*LDP*, 200)

If the eloquent, parliamentary speaker here is the (un-)dead dog, it is surely not extrapolating too much from the passage to read '"his quasi-stygian element"' as an analogue for the speaker's environment – that is, his audience. The orator is seen merely to 'float' on his audience, owing all signs of animation to it, whilst simultaneously infecting that audience with his 'ooze' (*LDP*, 200). As this image implies, it seems that the populist speaker, whether as 'parliamentary eloquence' or as stump-orator, does not truly recognise or lead his hearers. Instead, he just talks 'as he fancies may suit the reporters and twenty-seven millions mostly fools' – just panders, that is, to the 'Fourth Estate [who in turn] look ... as if you had touched its lips with a staff dipped in honey' (*LDP*, 209, 200).

This particular form of equality and recognition is, according to Carlyle, symptomatic of democracy; it is, of course, because of democracy that the 'parliamentary eloquence' speaks as he believes will suit 'twenty-seven millions mostly fools'. In this way, Carlyle anticipates various critics of democracy who were writing later in the century, and particularly after the Reform Act of 1867. For a start, he predicts the increasing significance of speech for a political mastery which has come to be dependent on popular support; citing the writings of the contemporary political theorist Walter Bagehot as a point of reference, Alison Winter writes:

> A ... new style of leadership would be necessary to govern modern Britain, one emphasizing public oratory.... A landmark moment ... was Gladstone's speech at Greenwich in 1871, which was the first time a prime minister had ever addressed the public directly.... It was impossible to trace the 'fine lines of a national policy' before an audience of 25000. Gladstone's electrifying oratory was the result of carefully taking the measure of the masses ... [and thus] he consolidated his political power.[19]

'Political power', it seems, becomes increasingly dependent throughout the nineteenth century on popular oratory. For Carlyle, this is in the very nature of democracy; in another of the *Latter-Day Pamphlets*, 'The Present Time', he defines democracy as a 'multitudinous efflux of oratory and psalmody, from the universal foolish human throat', and it follows from this that, 'for the Englishman of the Nineteenth Century, ... Vox is the God of [the] ... Universe' (*LDP*, 10, 192). In other words, the democratic master is necessarily and inevitably the 'Chief of *Talkers*' as opposed to the 'Chief of *Doers*' (*LDP*, 195).

In so many ways, both Carlyle *and* Dickens were themselves just such democratic masters; both were, ironically enough, the same as the 'Chief of *Talkers*' they attack, gaining as they did immense popular support from the *demos*, and huge sales figures for their books, precisely for being such skilled orators. It is a commonplace of criticism that Carlyle and Dickens are rhetorical writers; Persak, for instance, notes Carlyle's 'rhetorical style', observing that he 'gained a large readership through his incisive social criticism'. As Persak observes, 'unlike Plato, who denounced discourse directed at a popular audience ... Carlyle's very endeavours as social critic demanded that the form of discourse he praised and used be aimed at a large segment of the public.'[20] There are a number of paradoxes here: in order for Carlyle's writings as a 'social critic' to have any salutary effect, they came to rely on as wide as possible an audience; in order to warn against popular, demagogic orators, Carlyle became himself a popular orator.

Likewise, Dickens similarly gained immense popularity with an overtly rhetorical style. His popularity was, of course, divisive even during his lifetime, often being cited as a fault in itself. In his novel

The Warden (1855), for instance, Anthony Trollope caricatures Dickens as 'Mr. Popular Sentiment'.[21] Pratt remarks that 'Boz's reputation equalled, if it did not surpass, Carlyle's. His followers, including as they did the uneducated masses, were more numerous. His power over his fellow men ... was greater in quantity.'[22] Such demagogic power and popularity are due, at least in part, to the rhetorical nature of his style. As John Schad remarks, 'one is well accustomed ... to treating the novels ... as primarily rhetorical events'[23] and what is important about this rhetoric, for Schad and other critics, is that it establishes a certain kind of relationship between Dickens and his readership. As he writes,

> that the novels of Dickens are peculiarly imbued with what Virginia Woolf called the 'sense of an audience' has invariably been a common observation .... Richard Altick, for instance, comments on Dickens' ... 'unique rapport ... [with] his readers'.[24]

The terms in which Schad defines this '"unique rapport"' or '"sense of an audience"' are strikingly reminiscent of the relationship which Dickens and Carlyle find between stump-orators and the masses. In the same way that the relationship between Slackbridge and his listeners is a meeting of surfaces, Schad argues that, in Dickens' novels, the 'reader is ... *resembled*, or *imitated*. Informed, that is, by Dickens' almost proverbial fascination with reflections [and] mimicry ... the novels effectively hold up a mirror to us who read.'[25] Dickens and his novels mirror the readers who, in turn, presumably mirror the novels.

This mode of sham-recognition, of pseudo-equality, of mimicry and reflection, obviously precludes genuine mastery or leadership as it is understood by Carlyle. For Carlyle, the

> right of the ignorant man to be guided by the wiser, to be, gently or forcibly, held in the true course by him, is the indisputablest.... The relation of the taught to their teacher, of the loyal subject to his guiding king, is, under one shape or another, the vital element of human Society.[26]

Such 'guidance' is simply not afforded by the stump-orator; if, for instance, Dickens merely reflects or mimics his readers and his readers' 'popular sentiments', he obviously does not, and cannot, teach them anything. Being nothing more than their uncanny double, he does not and cannot 'lead' them anywhere.

He certainly cannot lead them round Cape Horn. As a 'distracted phantasm' of Nature, the stump-orator is one of the representatives *par excellence* of what Carlyle calls the 'Phantasm Captains' of democratic society – those captains who, though aided by ballot-boxes and mass popularity, cannot 'double Cape Horn'. As Carlyle writes,

> Unanimity of voting, – that will do nothing for us.... Your ship ... may vote this and that ... in the most harmonious exquisitely constitutional manner: the ship, to get round Cape Horn, will find a set of conditions already ... fixed with adamantine rigour by the ancient Elemental Powers, who are entirely careless how you vote.... If you can ... valiantly conform to [these conditions] ... you will get round the Cape: if you cannot, – the ruffian Winds will blow you ever back again ... you will be flung half-frozen on the Patagonian cliffs, or ... sent sheer down to Davy Jones.... Ships accordingly do not use the ballot-box at all; and they reject the Phantasm species of Captains. (*LDP*, 15–16)

The Phantasm Captain of democracy is evidently the 'Flying Dutchman.' According to Dieter Borchmeyer,

> the vow sworn by ... the [Flying] Dutchman ... to sail round the Cape at any cost was transformed by popular tradition into a symbol of that hubristic spirit ... which transgressed the boundaries of knowledge ... laid down by the Bible and by the Church.[27]

For Carlyle, however, this transgression is doomed to absolute failure by 'the ancient Elemental Powers' – the *democratic* Flying Dutchman is condemned to eternal wreck by a divine order, by God, and by a transcendentalised, pantheistic Nature, who 'are [all] entirely careless how you vote'. Whilst the ideal Captain 'conforms' to the 'set of conditions already ... fixed with adamantine rigour' by these Elemental Powers, the democratic Captain is rendered a Phantasm by his alienation from them. Since 'the Universe itself is a Monarchy and Hierarchy ... with Eternal Justice to preside over it, ... enforced by Almighty Power' (*LDP*, 21–2), democratic rule is obviously *against* nature according to Carlyle. In this sense, the Flying Dutchman's 'vow' to round Cape Horn is merely another species of hollow oratory which has no reference to the Elemental Powers. Carlyle implicitly reduces the Dutchman to the status of a Slackbridge, suggesting that he is no more than an 'excellent stump-orator ... [who] from the Universe of Fact ... has turned himself away [and] ... is gone into partnership with the Universe of Phantasm' (*LDP*, 206).

Carlyle's analogy between the Flying Dutchman and the democratic master does not quite work, however, in that the Dutchman could quite as easily be seen in terms of a Romantic or Carlylean hero. Borchmeyer's description of the Dutchman as 'a symbol of that hubristic spirit ... which transgressed the boundaries of knowledge ... laid down by the Bible and by the Church' is similar to many critics' descriptions of the heroes in *Heroes and Hero-Worship*. William Thompson, for instance, points out that Carlyle's 'heroes all offend against magistrate, priest, or law'.[28] His heroes, that is, offend the very Elemental Powers he seems to uphold in the *Latter-Day Pamphlets*. This is most obviously true of Voltaire who, although 'a kind of Hero ... [who] spent his life in ... unmasking hypocrites in high places', is also labelled 'a kind of Antichrist'[29] by Carlyle. Evidently, the hero who unmasks 'hypocrites in high places' is dangerously close to the anarchist, the atheistic iconoclast, the revolutionary regicide, and, as Carlyle actually suggests, the Antichrist or deicide. Indeed, Jonathan Arac notes that Carlyle also saw *himself* as 'an ambiguous and satanic figure',[30] and he was frequently viewed in these terms by others. As Bentley observes,

> Nietzsche said that ... [Carlyle's] spluttering anger, his *chronic need of noise* are evidence that he did not believe what he pretended, even to himself, to believe. Carlyle overstressed religion in order to hide the shocking fact that he did not believe.... When Carlyle transmuted his dyspepsia into a moral adulation of the Hero, the theory put on a religious dress. This was the crowning hypocrisy.[31]

Ironically, Carlylean stump-oratory here becomes a disguise for atheism. Carlyle's vehement profession of faith is just 'noise', just Semblance standing in for Substance.

According to Carlyle, however, it is not he but other democratic masters and, in particular, popular speakers who use the noise, or 'musical wind-utterances' (*LDP*, 176), of stump-oratory as a means of covering up godlessness. As he writes,

> Alas, our noble men of genius [are] ... assiduously trained ... to ... speak *words* ... instead of doing real kingly *work* to be approved of by the gods! [In this way] our 'Government' [is] ... responsible to no God that I can hear of but to the twenty-seven million *gods* of the shilling gallery. (*LDP*, 29)

Carlyle attributes this godlessness to all careers available 'to the gifted soul that is born in England', including that of the Church itself. 'At the gates of [the] ... Church just now', he declares,

> hard bonds are offered you to sign ... a solemn engagement to constitute yourself an impostor before ever entering ... [and] to take Chaos for Cosmos, and Satan for the Lord of things.... If you ... enter, the condition is well known: 'Talk; who can talk best here?' (*LDP*, 184, 189)

If such talk and noise are *really* dedicated to 'Satan' and a godless 'Chaos', it depends for its effect on being taken for Substance, true faith, genuine wisdom. Though the orator is really 'a mouthpiece of Chaos ... poor benighted mortals ... lend ear to him as to a voice from Cosmos' (*LDP*, 176). Though oratory is mere surface, mere Semblance 'without wisdom, without veracity, without conviction *more than skin-deep*' (*LDP*, 212: my emphasis), this Semblance depends on being taken by others as Substance, wisdom, veracity, conviction. In other words, the mastery that is stump-oratory is *necessarily* democratic because, being only Semblance and empty noise, it relies absolutely on being (mis)recognised by its audience in order to signify at all.

This *mis*recognition, however, is itself only noise, disguising the masses' own godlessness and masterlessness under democratic rule. As 'a mouthpiece of Chaos', the democratic orator is merely echoing back to the masses their own noise – a noise that is also 'the voice of Chaos' because of the godless and masterless nature of democracy and popular rule. In the revolutions of 1848, Carlyle argues,

> everywhere ... Democracy rose monstrous, loud, blatant, inarticulate as the voice of Chaos ... [as] everywhere the people ... take their own government on themselves; and open "kinglessness," what we call *anarchy* ... is everywhere the order of the day. (*LDP*, 5–6)

Being 'responsible ... [only] to the twenty-seven million *gods* of the shilling gallery' instead of any truly divine hierarchy, British Parliamentary Eloquences and other democratic leaders necessarily lend their voices to this 'loud, blatant ... Chaos', rather than speaking against it. 'Authentic *Chaos* [has] come up into this sunny Cosmos again,' Carlyle writes, 'and *all* men [are] singing *Gloria in excelsis* to it' (*LDP*, 29). All men, whether Parliamentary Eloquences, stump-orators or just voters, sing a *Gloria in excelsis* to Chaos, *mis*taking democracy for Cosmos.

For Carlyle, the only sacred song left in the world is this godless act of self-worship on the part of the 'twenty-seven million *gods* of the shilling gallery'. In his essay 'The Opera' (1852), he argues that music ideally exists 'to "sing the praise of God"',[32] but the democratic *Gloria in excelsis* is sung both *by* the masses (or their mouthpieces) *to* the masses. Instead of a music that is expressive of divine hierarchy, or those 'Sphere Harmonies and Eternal Melodies ... [of] Nature's monitions' (*LDP*, 185), musical noise is here expressive of a masterless, godless Chaos.

Furthermore, though this democratic, chaotic, self-reflexive *Gloria* is still perceived as harmonious Cosmos by the masses who sing or hear it, this kind of harmony is not modelled on 'Sphere Harmonies' or some divinely ordained hierarchical structure, but is based on the non-hierarchical harmony of unanimity. According to Charles Rosen, harmony in the West is traditionally based on a 'lucid *hierarchical* structure of ... triads'. As he writes,

> tonality is ... a system with ... a central perfect triad: all the other triads ... are arranged around the central one in a hierarchical order. The central triad, called the tonic, determines the key of the ... music.... A tonal work must begin by implying the central position of the tonic, and it must end with it.[33]

For Rosen, the tonic functions as a master reference point within a secure tonal hierarchy; but the modern harmony of democracy is constructed according to a non-hierarchical, masterless system of unisonal unanimity. In 'The Present Time', for instance, Carlyle argues that the Phantasm Captain gains power 'in the most *harmonious* exquisitely constitutional manner ... with *unanimous* votings' (*LDP*, 16: my emphasis). When, in Dickens' essay 'On Strike', the chairman of the democratic delegates' meeting declares that 'what we want is 'armony ... and con-cord', this harmony is defined as an absence of 'differences'[34] among the workers. Such an absence of differences, though, is obviously not the same as traditional harmony, despite how it seems to the workers. Traditional tonal harmony depends on a hierarchical scheme of differentiation, not on unisonal or unanimous equalisation.

Carlyle repeatedly criticises democracy's propensity for exalting a masterless unanimous harmony as a truth in or for-itself. As he writes, 'Phantasm Captains with *unanimous* votings ... [are] considered to be all the law and all the prophets at present', but this does not mean the Phantasm Captain's ship can 'double Cape Horn': 'the ship's crew may be very unanimous ... but if the tack they unanimously steer on is guiding them into the belly of the Abyss, it will not profit them much!' (*LDP*, 16: my emphasis). It is, Carlyle argues, 'needless to vote a false image true; vote it, revote it by ... jubilant unanimities and universalities ... it helps not a whit' (*LDP*, 203).

Despite Carlyle's remonstrances, however, the workers in *Hard Times* firmly believe in harmonious and 'jubilant unanimities' as truths in themselves, and it is this belief that causes them to go 'astray'. Playing on the fact that his listeners all 'felt [that] his only hope [was] ... in his allying himself to the comrades by whom he was surrounded', Slackbridge calls the workers his '"friends and fellow-sufferers, and fellow-workmen, and fellow-men"' and demands that they '"rally round one another as One united power"' (*HT*, 171, 170). He calls for '"a noble and majestic *unanimity*"', which demands that every individual member of the United Aggregate Tribunal '"abide by the injunctions issued by that body for your benefit, *whatever they may be*"' (*HT*, 171: my emphasis). This belief in unanimity for its own sake explains why, though the workers are all individually 'a little conscience-stricken' over the treatment of Blackpool, they still leave the assembly 'cheering'. They do so because they feel that 'private feeling must yield to the common cause' (*HT*, 175). This utilitarian, socialist and, in particular, *democratic* platitude tellingly reveals what Carlyle sees as the self-perpetuating fault in democracy – that if 'the common cause' must always override private feeling, then common causes create their own 'commonness'. Put another way, common causes become popular precisely because of their perceived popularity. This explains why Carlyle generally envisages democracy in terms of 'unanimities' rather than in the more traditional, oppositional language of majorities and minorities. If a cause is true because of its popularity, majorities must inevitably slip into unanimities. In a democratic context, private feeling must always be wrong because it is in the minority, so it will always be superseded by public and thus unanimous opinion. As we saw in Chapter 3, the tyranny of unanimity is the logical outcome of Alexis de Tocqueville's concept of the 'tyranny of the majority', as expressed in his near-contemporary treatise on *Democracy in America* (1835).[35]

Indeed, for Carlyle, democracy *is* unanimity precisely because of the unanimity of belief in it. By giving the impression of universalising power, universal suffrage must obviously be universally popular; over and above their divergent opinions on individual issues, 'all men' who vote within a democracy are voting *for* that democracy. As Carlyle writes, 'democracy ... [is] what is called "Self-government" of the multitude by the multitude, [and] is in words the thing everywhere passionately clamoured for at present'.[36] This 'clamour' is also a kind of music – just as '*all* men [are] singing *Gloria in excelsis*' to the 'authentic *Chaos* [which has] come up into this sunny Cosmos again', democracy is greeted in Europe in 1848 by the idle multitude [who] lift-up their voices ... celebrating ... that now the ... long-expected Year One of Perfect Human Felicity has come.... One of the inevitablest private miseries ... is this multitudinous efflux of oratory and psalmody, from the universal foolish human throat. (*LDP*, 10)

All men, that is, sing a universal and unanimous psalmody and *Gloria* within democracy – a psalmody and *Gloria* sung *to* that democracy.

It is by conducting and harmonising this music that Slackbridge gains mastery – he is a master because he plays on his listeners' absolute faith in democracy and unanimous harmony: he is described as a 'fugleman' who 'gave the time' to his listeners – and 'the multitude of doubtful faces (a little conscience-stricken) brightened at the sound, and took it up' (*HT*, 175). Slackbridge acts, that is, as what Winter calls 'a central harmonising influence';[37] he is able to conduct and 'harmonise' those in front of him precisely because his listeners are so desirous of such "armony' and unanimity. In this way, de Tocqueville's 'tyranny of the majority' is also Slackbridge's tyranny of unanimous harmony. After the expulsion of Stephen Blackpool, the workers overcome their 'conscience' and return to unanimous harmony under Slackbridge's mastery because they believe in it as an absolute truth in and for-itself. When the men unanimously yield to the 'common cause' at the end of Slackbridge's speech, the 'common cause' can be *mis*read as a return to the 'common *chord*' – as a unanimous return to simple harmony for its own sake. De Tocqueville's 'tyranny of the majority' is also Slackbridge's tyranny of the common chord.

As Winter notes, the analogy between popular master and conductor was frequently invoked in the nineteenth century:

In 1820 ... Louis Spohr brought conducting to London.... The newly unified body [the orchestra], inspired by its potential for harmoniously coordinated action, 'over-ruled all further opposition' [from its official directors].... [In this way] Spohr assembled the players in a collectivity and then provoked an insurrection.... [This partly explains] the resemblance that he and future conductors bore to problematic figures such as the Napoleonic demagogue.[38]

Despite these associations, Winter suggests that the harmonising role of conductor is generally represented in the mid-nineteenth century as one of the more 'healthy forms of [social] incorporation'. 'In the orchestra,' Winter writes, 'players consented to the leadership of the conductor and were aware of how they were being led', whereas, in the French Revolution, 'the rule of the masses was actually the rule of the demagogues [because the] ... people [who] were united into a single body ... lost their power of independent   judgement [and] ... became ... vulnerable to illegitimate political leaders'.[39] This Victorian distinction between types of 'healthy' and 'unhealthy' incorporation is based on the conscious consent or otherwise of those incorporated – conducting serves as a healthy and truly *democratic* model of mastery because of the independent consent of those being led. The problem is that Slackbridge's 'conducting' evidently refutes this belief. It is apparent in their 'cheering' that Dickens' workers *do* consent to their collectivisation and harmonisation under Slackbridge's unhealthy leadership, just as, in 'The Present Time', the Phantasm Captain's crew consents to his sham-mastery by voting 'in the most *harmonious* ... constitutional manner'. For Dickens and Carlyle, the demagogue and the unhealthy social incorporation he represents are aligned *with* and not against popular consent. Both writers thus express suspicions that Winter finds more prevalent later in the century – suspicions of the unhealthy social coordination and harmony *within* democracy.

In the *Latter-Day Pamphlets*, Carlyle envisages this unhealthy coordination in terms of the 'beautifulest marching music' to which 'the whole world, with one accord, are marching' (*LDP*, 182); it is, presumably, this kind of marching music which democratic masters like Slackbridge conduct. After all, the march form represents in itself a mode of social coordination – by its very nature, it is meant to coordinate a group of people marching together. For all its revolutionary and proletarian associations, the march form symbolises not social disintegration but social coordination; it represents musically the belief that 'private feeling must yield to the common cause'. Indeed, marching music also represents the way in which the common cause shades into the common chord, since the popular march form is conventionally heavily dependent for its effect on a constant return to the common chord.

Over and above this incessant return to simple harmony, Carlyle wonders where the march of democracy is *ultimately* heading, and, in fact, he posits a destination that *seems* at odds with a constant reaffirmation of the common chord. 'How many men,' he asks,

> have gone [the] ... road [of the stump-orator] escorted by the beautifulest marching music from all the 'public organs;' and have found at last that it ended – where? It is the *broad* road, that leads direct to Limbo and the Kingdom of the Inane.... The whole world, with one

accord, are marching thither, in melodious triumph, all the drums and hautboys giving out their cheerfulest *Ça-ira*. (*LDP*, 182)

A march that 'leads direct to Limbo' is a rather direction*less* direct march, and this, of course, is the point of the passage: the melodious march towards universal suffrage is a march to nowhere, and, presumably, it is towards this democratic 'Limbo' that Slackbridge leads his audience when he acts as its 'fugleman'. After all, this fugleman only leads his audience to 'disperse' (*HT*, 175) – not towards the battle his speech implies. As Carlyle writes in *Chartism*,

> Towards democracy, and that only, the progress of things is everywhere tending as to the final goal and winning-post. So think, so clamour the multitudes everywhere. And yet ... in democracy can lie no finality ... with the completest winning of democracy there is nothing yet won, – except emptiness, and the free chance to win! Democracy is, by the nature of it, a self-cancelling business; and gives in the long-run a net result of *zero*.[40]

The multitudes mistake democracy – and, by extension, the democratic master – for a 'goal' in itself; in the 1840s, one of the Chartists' aims was, of course, the demand for universal male suffrage. Carlyle argues, however, that democracy is meaningless as a goal in itself, and can really only ever be 'a swift transition towards something other and farther' because it yields nothing and achieves nothing by itself. The 'something other and farther', for Carlyle, is the goal of true, *un*democratic mastery: 'the right of the ignorant man to be guided by the wiser, to be, gently or forcibly, held in the true course by him,' he writes, is the true goal 'which 'Society [always] struggles towards ... by enforcing and accomplishing ... more and more.'[41] *Within* democracy, however, this 'winning-post' can never be reached and the goal of genuine mastery becomes an ever-receding horizon – vanishing, that is, with every increase in suffrage. This is why 'with the completest winning of democracy there is nothing yet won, – except ... the free chance to win!' In other words, a society marching towards the false goal of universal suffrage is only marching towards a masterless, endless Limbo.

In this march, recourse to a common chord or cause can only ever be a provisional solution: the march towards universal suffrage is never-ending and so precludes the absolute closure of a conclusive return to the tonic or 'home chord'. Only transitory and illusory returns are possible. To put this another way, the music of democracy always appears to be marching towards tonal resolution, but never quite reaches it. In this respect, democracy's music mimics the real thing in the nineteenth century, for, as Rosen writes,

> It was the inspiration of the ... nineteenth century to extend and expand [the] ... moment of [tonal] ambiguity.... By the end of the century, the final appearance of the tonic chord in many works of [Richard] Strauss, [Max] Reger ... sounded like a polite bow in the direction of academic theory; the rest of the music has often proceeded as if it made no difference with what triad it ended.... There is no longer any [real] sense of [tonal] direction.... Even clear sections of stable tonality sometimes have no specific relation to a total scheme. The degree of stability has become only a localized effect, never a generalized one.[42]

As Schoenberg writes in 'Opinion or Insight?' (1926), 'the tonic' is no longer really 'in command' in such music:

> Many modern composers believe they are writing tonally if they occasionally introduce a major or minor triad, or a cadence-like turn of phrase, into a series of harmonies that lack ... any terms of reference.... [They] are acting like believers who buy an indulgence. They betray their God, but remain on good terms with those who call themselves His attorneys.[43]

In other words, late nineteenth- and early twentieth-century music implicitly asserts the godlessness and masterlessness of atonality, whilst appearing to adhere to the tonal hierarchy.

It is in this context that the obvious inconsistency of Carlyle's frequent use of musical analogies for democracy and democratic masterlessness should be located and understood. In the *Latter-Day Pamphlets*, he describes the phenomenon of democracy in terms of consonance and, as was seen in the previous chapter, dissonance as well. As well as being a 'harmonious' process with its 'unanimous votings', democracy is also described as 'monstrous, loud, blatant, inarticulate as the voice of Chaos' (*LDP*, 5). Similarly, the stump-orator's speech is at once seen in terms of music and 'melody' and as 'unmelodious ... and ghastly and bodeful, as the speech of sheeted spectres in the streets at midnight!' (*LDP*, 173, 212). The point is surely that, for Carlyle, the *implicit* truth of the harmony of democracy is absolute *a*-harmony: the harmony of democracy is haunted by the 'sheeted spectres' of a future atonality. The unanimity Carlyle finds in democracy is only the superficial, 'skin-deep' Semblance of harmony; the frequent return to a common chord (and cause) has become meaningless in its non-tonal and non-hierarchical context. In this, Carlyle's writings anticipate the views of Schoenberg in the twentieth century. As Rosen notes, it was 'Schoenberg [who recognised] ... the irrelevance of this occasional and *superficial* return to the formal clarity of tonal harmony ... in 1909'.[44] Schoenberg's recognition took the form of what he called the 'emancipation of the dissonance'.[45] He realised the abolition of any tonal hierarchy through the absolute equalisation and democratisation of the twelve notes of the chromatic scale, an equalisation and democratisation that were going on throughout the nineteenth century. Schoenberg made conscious the unconscious atonality underlying nineteenth-century music's increasingly 'superficial' harmonic hierarchisation. As he writes, '"The emancipation of the dissonance"' meant that the dissonance 'came to be placed on an equal footing with the sounds regarded as consonances ... [through] an unconscious process'.[46] In other words, it is towards the 'Limbo' of twentieth-century atonality that the 'beautifulest marching music' is heading. The Limbo of atonality is the implicit truth beneath the 'skin-deep' harmony of democracy, and, in retrospect, this is the historical context in which Carlyle's seemingly incongruous musical metaphors for democracy can be understood. The constant reaffirmation of a unisonal, unanimous harmony does not uphold the 'hierarchical structure of the triads' on which tonal music depends. Since, as has been seen, unanimity is based on an absence of hierarchical 'differences', unanimous harmony inevitably marches towards the absolute equalisation of notes presupposed by twentieth-century atonality.

*

Schoenberg's method of 'Twelve-Note Composition' – which depends on the equalisation of tones – has frequently been criticised, as Rosen notes, for 'substituting a purely *artificial* system for one that had been handed down to be used along with the laws of physics'.[47] Accordingly, in his essay 'Heart and Brain in Music' (1946), Schoenberg remarks that his music 'has earned me the title of constructionist [and] engineer'.[48] In the twentieth century, the music master is an engineer who necessarily produces machinic music. Indeed, the 'Music of Machines' was an important movement in 1920s music, being associated particularly with Communist composers like

Alexander Mossolov, whose orchestral piece of the same name (1926) is dominated by the machinic sounds of an 'Iron Foundry'.

Carlyle implies, however, that the 'Music of Machines' is already haunting nineteenth-century political and industrial life. The 'musical wind-utterances' of parliamentary eloquence and stump-orator are machinic, being compared to music produced by such mechanical instruments as the 'hurdy-gurdy' – as Persak notes, for Carlyle, 'rhetoric is "mechanical"'.[49] Indeed, it is clear that not only is musical rhetoric in some way machinic, but those masters who produce such music are themselves machines. Rather than being 'engineers' like Schoenberg, Carlyle sees democratic masters as machines or *engines*. He calls the parliamentary eloquence a 'dead ... bagpipe', and remarks that 'such parliamentary bagpipes I myself have heard play tunes, much to the satisfaction of the people. Every tune lies within their compass; and their mind (for they still call it *mind*) is ready as a hurdy-gurdy on turning of the handle' (*LDP*, 199). Popular speakers are seen in very similar ways by Dickens as well. In *Martin Chuzzlewit*, for instance, that great American stump-orator and 'master-mind', Elijah Pogram, is described as 'a clock-work figure that was just running down'.[50] Similarly, in *Hard Times*, the description of Slackbridge's actions invites comparison with a steam engine: 'The orator ... delivered himself of ... what ... froth and fume he had in him.... By dint of roaring at the top of his voice ... he had taken so much out of himself ... that he was brought to a stop and called for a glass of water' (*HT*, 170). Slackbridge calls the workers the '"slaves of an iron-handed and a grinding despotism"' and the victims of '"the iron foot of despotism"' (*HT*, 169, 267), but, as a kind of steam engine himself, he seems unwittingly to be referring to his own '"iron-handed"', machinic mastery as well.

Slackbridge's actions are machinic because of their automatic nature – when, for instance, he is 'wiping his hot forehead', it is 'always from left to right, and never the reverse way' (*HT*, 172). This uninterrupted and unvarying mode of 'wiping' is exactly the kind of automaticity associated with the steam engine. In this sense, he personifies what Timothy Clark calls 'the nightmare fascination of a world without interiority', where 'bodies take on the mode of being of objects [which are] ... clumsily *automatised*'.[51] For Clark, Dickens' automatised bodies are similar to the *corpses* described by Maurice Blanchot, so, in this respect, the popular master is merely the mechanically reanimated corpse of dead masters. In fact, one of these dead masters is the demagogue himself: the popular speaker is the reanimated corpse of the master he himself could have been. In Blanchot's words, the corpse 'resembles *himself.* The cadaver is its own image.... It is similarity and also nothing more.'[52] When he examines the careers open to the 'born genius' in modern England, Carlyle argues that Parliament transforms this potential master into the corpse of the mastery to which he might have aspired. The potential for mastery subsequently exists in the corpse only as 'an obscure possibility',[53] to use Blanchot's phrase. The career of parliamentary eloquence gradually kills off genuine mastery and genius and replaces it with the Semblance or reanimated corpse of such mastery. The 'moral life of [this] ... human creature,' writes Carlyle,

> is rapidly bleeding out of him.... By and by you will have a dead parliamentary bagpipe, and your living man fled away without return! ... A poor human creature and learned friend, once possessed of many fine gifts, possessed of intellect, veracity, and manful conviction on a variety of objects, has he now lost all that; – converted all that into a glistering phosphorescence which can show itself on the outside; while within, all is dead ... a painted sepulchre full of dead-men's bones! (*LDP*, 199–200)

The 'dead-men's bones' in this 'painted sepulchre' are also the bones of other masters, both past and present. Slackbridge refers explicitly to the workers' 'forefathers' and other past masters, such as 'the Roman Brutus' and 'the Spartan mothers' (*HT*, 175), and he does so to legitimise his own sham-mastery from the past. Indeed, his references to 'Brotherhood' and 'the God-created glorious rights of Humanity' (*HT*, 170) echo the language of the leaders of the French Revolution. In so doing, Slackbridge reproduces almost exactly the strategies of Louis Bonaparte's *coup d'état* of 1851, which, as Marx famously argues, was a grotesque and spectral parody of 1789. In the 1851 *coup*, Marx asserts, 'only the *ghost* of the old revolution walked about'.[54] The problem is that this reconstitution of past mastery in a contemporary, bourgeois, post-revolutionary present can never be wholly successful – it can only ever be a form of machinic reanimation. Following the revolutions of 1848, Carlyle argues,

> Some remounting, – very temporary remounting, – of *the old machine*, under new colours and altered forms, will probably ensue soon in most countries: the old histrionic Kings will be admitted back ... under 'Constitutions'.... But there is now no hope that such arrangements can ... be other than poor temporary makeshifts. (*LDP*, 8: my emphasis)

Past mastery haunts the present as a machinic ghost or ghostly machine – the ghostly machine that is uncanny reanimation. 'The old machine' of past mastery has become uncanny. Indeed, it is in terms of the *uncanniness of reanimation* that the apparently disparate images associated with Slackbridge's sham-mastery can be made to cohere. Slackbridge is at once both a Phantasm Captain, a ghost of such past masters as the Roman Brutus, *and* a machine; Slackbridge's mastery refers back to ancient history for legitimation, but is also associated with the very modern image of the steam engine. These images are not, however, incompatible. Sigmund Freud notes in his essay 'The Uncanny' (1919) that 'apparent death and the reanimation of the dead have been represented as most uncanny themes', and this kind of uncanniness is at once ghostly and machinic; 'a feeling of the uncanny', Freud observes, often arises from

> 'doubts whether an apparently animate being is really alive; or conversely, whether a lifeless object might not be in fact animate'.... [Examples] ... in this connection [include] ... the impression made by waxwork figures, ingeniously constructed dolls and automata, ... [and] the impression of automatic, mechanical processes at work behind the ordinary appearance of mental activity.[55]

Freud cites the doll Olympia in E.T.A. Hoffmann's tale 'The Sandman' as an instance of this kind of uncanny effect, but the description could equally well apply to Carlyle's and Dickens' popular masters.

Indeed, masters like Slackbridge are uncanny in a very strict sense, insofar as they represent 'something repressed which *recurs*',[56] to use Freud's phrase. Slackbridge embodies, in a returned and displaced form, the workers' unconscious desire for *genuine* masters. In *Past and Present* (1843), Carlyle describes the demands of the workers taking part in the Manchester Insurrection:

> these ... workers mean only, by [a] day's wages for [a] day's work, certain coins of money adequate to keep them living.... They as yet clamour for no more; the rest, still *inarticulate* ... only lies in them as a ... dumb, altogether *unconscious* want.[57]

This '*unconscious* want' is, according to Carlyle, really the demand for genuine masters and leadership; as he remarks in *Chartism*,

> all popular commotions and maddest bellowings, from Peterloo to the Place-de-Grève ... [are] bellowings, *in*articulate cries ... to the ear

of wisdom they are inarticulate prayers: 'Guide me, govern me! I am mad and miserable, and cannot guide myself!'[58]

The focus here is on the inarticulacy of popular commotions: the proletariat are unable to articulate properly their desire for true mastery. For this reason, the masters whom the masses themselves choose do not and cannot fulfil their unconscious want. Since the masses are 'inarticulate' and cannot 'guide' or 'govern' themselves – and since they are not even aware of their desire for genuine leadership – masters like Slackbridge, who are chosen by and from the masses, cannot provide the guidance the masses really need. Indeed, popular orators like Slackbridge respond to the mad 'bellowings' of the masses only with *more* empty bellowings, *more* 'roaring' (*HT*, 212) – bellowings which, despite their Semblance of articulacy, are actually as inarticulate as the proletariat for whom they seem to speak. As 'a mouthpiece of Chaos', Slackbridge is just as unable as the workers to articulate consciously what, according to Carlyle, the workers want *un*consciously. Instead of demanding or providing true mastery, Slackbridge can articulate the people's 'rage and pain' only in terms of *more* masterlessness – he can express only the workers' conscious wish to '"crumble into dust the oppressors that too long have battened on the plunder of our families"' (*HT*, 170). Just as the Chartists demanded universal suffrage, Slackbridge and the workers he seems to represent can express their masterlessness only in terms of more masterlessness, or, indeed, the overthrow of *all* mastery. Slackbridge seems to declare, along with Carlyle's French revolutionaries, '"Liberty and Equality;" no Authority needed any longer.... We have had such *forgeries*, we will now trust nothing'.[59] Like the French revolutionaries, Slackbridge is merely the conscious voice of an unconscious *lack* – a lack, that is, of true authority or mastery. He represents not Substance, but rather the returned and displaced embodiment of an unconscious *absence* of true mastery and hierarchy in nineteenth-century, industrial Britain. What the workers are actually unconsciously expressing through him is the desire to '"crumble into dust"' an absence of real leadership; what they really want to make absent is an absence. Indeed, since Slackbridge is himself representative of this absence, he is, ironically, another one of the symptoms the workers unconsciously want to crumble into dust.

This absence is the absence posited by the invisible, utilitarian, *laissez-faire* non-mastery of industrial capitalists like Josiah Bounderby. This is the masterlessness to which Blackpool refers when he says to Bounderby, '"Let thousands on thousands alone, aw leadin' the like lives and aw faw'en into the like muddle, and they will be as one, and yo will be as anoother, wi' a black unpassable world betwixt yo"' (*HT*, 182). Dickens certainly seems to be drawing directly here on Carlyle's critique of *laissez-faire* mastery, which he defined 'as good as an *abdication* on the part of governors; an admission that they are henceforth incompetent to govern.' Carlyle goes on to argue that this 'self-can-celling Donothingism and *Laissez-faire* should have got so ingrained into our Practice, is the source of all [our] ... miseries'.[60] He is right in that, as David Craig remarks, 'the economic system favoured by the Utilitarians – *laissez-faire* – [had a] ... tendency to produce uncontrolled slumps [which] might have been designed to turn able-bodied and industrious workmen into paupers'.[61] In 'The Present Time', Carlyle describes the effects of *laissez-faire* mastery thus:

> supply-and-demand, Leave-it-alone, Voluntary Principle, Time will mend it: – ... British industrial existence seems fast becoming one huge poison-swamp of reeking pestilence physical and moral; a hideous *living* Golgotha of souls and bodies buried alive. (*LDP*, 27)

For Carlyle, the huge problems posed by this masterless Golgotha can be solved only by a mastery that disavows *laissez-faire* principles. The answer, for Carlyle, is not to be found in working-class or popular masters, who can reassert only masterlessness, but rather in the very 'Captains of Industry' who have brought about the modern Golgotha. 'In England,' he asserts, 'one class ... of men, recognisable as the beginning of a new ... "Aristocracy," has already in some measure developed itself: the Captains of Industry; – happily the class who ... first of all, are wanted in this time' (*LDP*, 35). The problem is, of course, that 'Captains of Industry' like Dickens' Bounderby turn themselves into Phantasm Captains by abdicating and making invisible this new, aristocratic role through a policy of *laissez-faire* – and, subsequently, Bounderby's phantasmic absence comes to be represented by Slackbridge. As Blackpool remarks, some-what accusingly, to Bounderby, '"I'm as sooary as yo, sir, when the people's leaders is bad ... They taks such as offers. Haply 'tis na' the sma'est o' their misfortuns when they can get no better"' (*HT*, 178). Blackpool is implying here what Carlyle states – namely, that a '"better"' leader would presumably be a Bounderby who has dis-avowed his *laissez-faire* principles and become a real Captain of Industry. In his absence, the people have to take '"such as offers"', and Bounderby's absence is taken over by the absence that is

Slackbridge. In this sense, Slackbridge is a ghostly, uncanny, *returned* Bounderby, even though Bounderby cannot, of course, recognise him as such; that is to say, Slackbridge is the Phantasm Captain of a Phantasm Captain – a ghost of a ghost.

As a returned Bounderby, Slackbridge represents the conscious embodiment of the unconscious threat inherent in Bounderby's *laissez-faire* mastery – the threat posed by a masterless proletariat. In other words, when Slackbridge calls for the United Aggregate Tribunal to '"crumble into dust the [workers'] oppressors"', he is actually only making conscious the anarchic masterlessness which a *laissez-faire* policy unconsciously asserts. The anxiety inherent in *laissez-faire* mastery is that the workers must ultimately come to establish them-selves as a 'common cause', or indeed a unanimous, common chord. For Carlyle, the threat posed by the masterless working class is that posed by 'the wild horse [who] bounds homeless through the wilder-ness, [and who] is not led to stall and manger; but neither does he toil for you, but for himself only.' As he writes,

Laissez faire, laissez passer! The master of horses when the summer labour is done, has to feed his horses through the winter. If he said to his horses: 'Quadrupeds, I have no longer work for you.... Go and seek cartage, and good go with you!' ... [But] *they* can find no cartage. They gallop distracted along highways, all fenced in to the right and to the left: finally, under pains of hunger, they take to leaping fences; eating foreign property, and – we know the rest.[62]

Under the *laissez-faire* masterlessness of capitalism, the 'wild horse' of the working class gallops towards the anarchy that is Chartism, master-lessness, or even Communism. Just as the unanimous harmony espoused by nineteenth-century democracy is marching towards the Limbo of atonality, Bounderby's *laissez-faire* non-mastery is haunted by the Marxian 'spectre of Communism'[63] – and it is this spectre which Slackbridge represents. Addressing directly his bourgeois, capitalist reader, Carlyle declares that,

I do not suppose ... many persons in England ... have much faith in Fraternity, Equality and the Revolutionary Millenniums ... in this age: but there are many movements here too which tend inevitably in the like direction; and good men, who would stand aghast at a Red Republic and its adjuncts, seem to me travelling at full speed towards that or a similar goal! Certainly, the notion everywhere pre-

vails among us.... That the grand panacea for social woes is what we
call 'enfranchisement'. (*LDP*, 24)

For Carlyle, democratic enfranchisement, like capitalist utilitarianism,
is much the same as Communism; as the 'consummation of No-gov-
ernment and *Laissez-faire*', democracy marches inevitably towards a
'Red Republic'.[64]

Also heading this way, according to Carlyle, is British industrialism;
paradoxically, Communism is implicit in the *laissez-faire* of British capitalism, for not only does *laissez-faire* capitalism entail an abdication of
real mastery on the part of the ruling class, it clearly also combines,
homogenises and opposes the classes. This homogenisation and opposition poses a threat to masters like Bounderby, a threat which is con-
veyed by Blackpool's words when he declares to Bounderby that, '"Let
thousands on thousands alone ... and *they will be as one*, and yo will be
as anoother, wi' a black unpassable world betwixt yo"' (*HT*, 182: my
emphasis). Blackpool continues,

> 'Look how we [workers] live ... an in what numbers ... an wi' what
> sameness.... Look how ... yo are awlus right, and how we are awlus
> wrong.... Look how this ha growen and growen ... bigger and
> bigger, broader an broader ... fro generation unto generation.' (*HT*,
> 177, 180–1)

According to Marx, the threat posed by this working-class '"sameness"'
and unanimity is the '"bigger and bigger, broader an broader"' spectre of
that ultimate, unanimous combination, Communism. As Marx writes,

> With the development of industry, the proletariat ... becomes con-
> centrated in greater masses.... The various interests and conditions
> of life within the ranks of the proletariat are more and more
> equalised, in proportion as machinery obliterates all distinctions of
> labour.... Thereon, the workers begin to form combinations (Trades
> Unions).[65]

For Marx, the collectivisation and equalisation of the proletarian class
under capitalism prefigures the collectivisation of Communism; as he
notes, 'the advance of industry ... replaces the isolation of the labourers ... by their revolutionary combination.... What the bourgeoisie,
therefore, produces ... is its own grave-diggers. Its fall and the victory
of the proletariat are equally inevitable.'[66]

The problem for Dickens and Carlyle is that the mastery and 'victory
of the proletariat' is merely the victory of masterlessness, of an anarchy

which is merely the logical culmination of *laissez-faire, not* its ultimate negation. As Robin Gilmour points out, Marx aligns the proletariat with a teleological 'message of redemption through history',[67] but Dickens and Carlyle envisage no such teleology. Blackpool suggests no end or cure for such ever-increasing '"sameness"' or for what is '"growen and growen ... bigger and bigger, broader an broader ... fro generation unto generation"'. Rather, this is merely the 'progress' towards what Carlyle calls 'Limbo' and what Blackpool calls a '"muddle"' (*HT*, 180), a masterless muddle which finds in Communism not an end or cure but presumably its ultimate expression.

This is because the combination and collectivisation of which Communism is the extreme example is merely another kind of machine for Carlyle. Communism is just the (il)logical conclusion of the nineteenth century's masterless mastery of *machinic* collectivisation. When Carlyle argues in the 'Signs of the Times' (1829) that the nineteenth century is 'the Age of Machinery', he includes in this description the constant drive towards collective, rather than individual, activity:

> Has any man ... a piece of spiritual work to do, [he] ... must first call a public meeting, appoint committees ... eat a public dinner; in a word, construct or borrow machinery.... Men have lost faith in individual endeavour ... of any kind. Not for internal perfection, but ... for Mechanism of one sort or other, do they hope and struggle.[68]

As the ultimate expression of mechanical combination and equalisation, Communism – or the total democracy Carlyle equates with Communism – is merely a distilled form of the masterless mastery of machinery. Since, according to Marx, 'the proletarian movement is the self-conscious, independent movement of the immense majority, in the interest of the immense majority',[69] this collective movement comes to assert what Carlyle calls a 'blind No-God, of Necessity and Mechanism', which holds the people 'like a hideous World-*Steam-engine* ... imprisoned in its own *iron* belly'.[70] In this, Communism is itself haunted by the mechanical ghost of the French Revolution of 1789; based as it was on the precepts of '"Liberty and Equality"' and 'the faith that, wise great men being impossible, a level immensity of foolish small men would suffice', the French Revolution initially viewed 'Nature ... [as] a "Machine" ... [which] could not any longer produce Great Men'.[71]

Past and future revolutionary masterlessness is, it seems, both the ghost in the machine *and* the machine in the ghost of contemporary

184 *Mastery and Slavery in Victorian Writing*

mastery. Likewise, Communism represents both the ghost (or 'spectre') in the machine *and* the machine in the ghost (or 'Phantasm') of nine-teenth-century industrial, capitalist and democratic mastery and mas-terlessness. For Carlyle and Dickens, the future victory of the proletariat is the victory of masterless machines *and* Phantasm Captains – the victory, in other words, of 'all Slackbridges' (*HT*, 172) everywhere. Since the proletariat have been treated '"as if they was figures in a soom, or machines ... wi'out souls to weary and souls to hope"' (*HT*, 182), the victory promised by universal suffrage or Communism can only be the victory of a soulless, machinic workforce.

In *Mary Barton* (1848), Elizabeth Gaskell implies this when she likens the rise of the proletariat to the

> actions ... of Frankenstein, that monster ... ungifted with a soul....The people rise up to life; they irritate us, they terrify us, and we become their enemies.... Why have we made them what they are; a powerful monster, yet without the inner means for peace and happiness?[72]

For Gaskell, the proletariat mechanically 'rise up' to 'terrify' the very bourgeois masters who 'made them what they are' – who created such soulless, mechanical monsters. This, for bourgeois writers like Carlyle, Dickens and Gaskell, is the real nature of the rise of the proletariat, a rise that is not 'redemption' or resurrection but mechanical reanima-tion and, perhaps, a terrifying revenge.

Indeed, the anxiety as to what kind of redemption is offered by Communism is fundamental even to a text like Marx's *The Communist Manifesto*, which leaves unresolved a conflict between the promise of revolutionary redemption and the machinic nature of those who are to be redeemed. The proletariat, argues Marx, 'have a world to win', but elsewhere he asserts that the proletariat form merely 'an appendage of the machine'.[73] These irreconcilable images are of fundamental impor-tance: Marx's whole theory of the rise of the proletariat is based on a *machinic* view of historical inevitability that sits uneasily with his vision of the proletariat as an active and Christ-like agent. Gilmour notes Marx's insistence that 'the revolutionary transformation of society is ... something that *must* come because it is an inevitable outcome of the scientific development of the modern body politic'. At the same time, though, Gilmour suggests that, for Marx, the 'place of Jesus was [occupied by] a suffering proletariat', for whom, as has been pointed out, Communism represents a 'message of redemption through history'.[74] Of course, the depiction of the proletariat as a suffering Christ to be resurrected by revolution was almost a commonplace of nineteenth-century art and left-wing politics. For instance, one of the most famous of the Chartist poets, Ernest Jones, writes of the working class,

> We are dead, and we are buried!
> Revolution's soul is tame!
> They are merry o'er our ashes,
> And our tyrants rule the same!
> But the Resurrection's coming
> As the Resurrection came.[75]

Again, Slackbridge is obviously being portrayed as a kind of Christ when he holds 'out his right hand at arm's length ... to still the thundering sea'; indeed, by comparing Blackpool to '"Judas Iscariot"' (*HT*, 172), Slackbridge is aligning both himself and his audience with Christ. For writers like Dickens, Carlyle and Gaskell, however, this is a zombie-Christ who is mechanically *reanimated* by history rather than truly resurrected; this is a Christ who, like Frankenstein's Monster, is a mechanically reanimated corpse, not a resurrected master, hero or Saviour. This Christ is, in Carlyle's words, merely a soulless and 'glistering phosphorescence which can show itself on the outside; while within, all is dead, chaotic, dark; a painted sepulchre full of dead-men's bones!' (*LDP*, 200).

Afterword, After Slavery, After Shooting Niagara

> 'When I say a man of colour,' returned Mark, 'I mean that he's been one of them as there's picters of in the shops. A man and a brother, you know, sir,' said Mr. Tapley, favouring his master with a significant indication of the figure so often represented in tracts and cheap prints.
>
> 'A slave!' cried Martin, in a whisper.

(Charles Dickens, *Martin Chuzzlewit*)[1]

Mark Tapley is alluding here to the famous abolitionist emblem, designed around 1790 by Josiah Wedgwood, which, as Hugh Thomas notes, 'consisted of a picture of a chained Negro on bended knee with as legend the question: "Am I not a man and a brother?"' As Thomas suggests, 'this ... emblem ... was an inspired piece of propaganda',[2] and, by the time Dickens wrote *Martin Chuzzlewit* (1843–4), the image and slogan had become so ingrained in public consciousness that Dickens could assume that his reader will follow the link Martin makes between '"a man and a brother"' and a '"slave".' Undoubtedly, in the context of Dickens' novel the connection is heavily ironic – Mark goes on to enumerate the ways in which the '"man of colour"', Cicero, has certainly not been treated as a '"man and a brother"' whilst being a slave. Nevertheless, the connection also encodes certain Victorian attitudes towards the notions of equality and recognition that I want to explore further in this 'Afterword'.

By recognising Cicero as a '"slave"' merely from the description of him as a '"man and a brother"', Martin unwittingly equates slavery with equality and recognition; oddly enough, to be recognised here as a '"slave"' is also to be recognised as an equal, as a '"man and a brother"' – and vice versa. Though the original point of Wedgwood's image is to express the *dis*connection and *dis*similarity of the state of slavery with manhood and brotherhood, disconnection and dissimilarity have seemingly become connection and similarity through a process of popular association – to the point at which a slave can be recognised as such because he *is* 'a man and a brother.' Despite the heavy irony, the passage exposes an anomalous, problematic, yet prevalent tendency in the writings of both abolitionist *and* pro-slavery writers, whereby equal and mutual recognition is associated with the master–slave relation rather than with what succeeds that relation.

This departs from Hegel's model. For Hegel, as we have seen, freedom, equality and mutual recognition simply cannot be provided within the master–slave relation. Whilst remaining in slavery, Hegel's slave is certainly not recognised as '"a man and a brother"'. Hegel argues in the *Phenomenology of Spirit* (1807) that the only kind of recognition provided by the master–slave relation is 'one-sided and unequal', whereas the ideal, utopian and future state of mutual recognition is defined as one in which

> each [self-consciousness] sees the *other* do the same as it does.... Each is for the other the middle term, through which each mediates itself with itself and unites with itself.... They *recognise* themselves as *mutually recognising* one another.[3]

For Hegel, such mutual recognition, freedom and equality necessarily involve the total supersession of the master–slave phase; as he suggests in the *Elements of the Philosophy of Right* (1821), the 'free spirit consists ... in overcoming this formal phase of its being'.[4] Richard Norman points out that Hegel views 'the relationship of master and slave ... as a first step from the state of nature to social life ... subsequently giving way to a form of society in which all men are recognised as free'.[5]

As we saw in Chapter 3, however, many Victorian writers argue against, or at least complicate, Hegel's teleological view of mastery and slavery. Carlyle often appropriates Hegelian language in discussing mastery, slavery and recognition, whilst, at the same time, seeking to elide the subversive – and perhaps revolutionary – implications of Hegel's teleology. To put this another way, Carlyle simply does not agree with Hegel in positing mastery and slavery as 'a first step ... to social life'; rather, Carlyle insists over and over again that 'the relation of the taught to their teacher, of the loyal subject to his guiding king, is, under one shape or another, the vital element of human Society ...

indispensable to it, and perennial in it'.[6] He rejects Hegel's view that 'slavery ... contains ... only the starting point on the way to truth',[7] and posits the master–slave relation as an absolute and universal truth in itself. Consequently, Carlyle comes to identify those Hegelian 'truths' of freedom, equality and mutual recognition with the master–slave relation, rather than with its sublation and abolition –that is, he effectively theorises the casual connection made between slavery, manhood and brotherhood in Dickens' *Martin Chuzzlewit*. This is perhaps most obvious in his essay 'The Nigger Question' (1849), where, as we have seen, he writes that,

> a poor Negro overworked on the Cuba sugar-grounds ... is sad to look on; yet he inspires me with sacred pity, and a kind of human respect is not denied him; him, the hapless brother mortal, performing something useful in his day, and only suffering inhumanity, not doing it or being it.

Carlyle is able to recognise this 'poor Negro' as a 'brother mortal' and 'human' being precisely because slavery had not been abolished in Cuba at this time.[8] In contrast, he argues that, since emancipation in 1833, the typical West Indian black has become 'the dead soul of a man, – in a body which [only] ... pretends to be vigorously alive', and that the analogous 'free-labourer' or 'White Flunky' in Britain is 'disloyal, unheroic ... [and] *in*human in his character'.[9]

Ironically, emancipation here is seen in terms of the denial of human recognition: in becoming so-called free-labourers, both West Indian black and 'White Flunky' also become perceived as 'inhuman'. By contrast with Hegel, the end of slavery that is abolition for Carlyle represents the negation and antithesis of recognition, manhood, brotherhood, equality and freedom. And oddly enough, he is right to some extent, since emancipation in 1833 very obviously did *not* mean simple freedom and recognition for the slaves. Instead, from the 1840s onwards, abolitionist discourses of 'sacred pity' for slaves were gradually replaced by, and indeed transformed into, later imperialist discourses, which actively denied imperial subjects recognition as men and brothers or women and sisters. As Patrick Brantlinger notes, there was a 'period of relative sympathy in writing about Africa between 1790 and 1830', but Nancy Stepan suggests that 'just as the battle against slavery was being won by abolitionists, the war against racism was being lost. The Negro was legally freed [in] ... 1833, but in the

British mind he was still mentally, morally and physically a slave.'[10] As Robert Young writes,

> 'The same but different' was the trope of ... of humankind as a universal egalitarian category.... This ... universalism was set against [a] ... darker aphorism: 'different – and also, different, unequal.' The historian can detect a gradual shift from the dominance of the former to the latter view from the eighteenth to the nineteenth centuries.... In Britain, it can be plausibly argued that it was the conjunction of three historical events that dramatically altered the popular perceptions of race and racial difference and formed the basis of the widespread acceptance of the new ... claims of a permanent racial superiority: the ... 'Indian Mutiny' of 1857; ... the ... American Civil War (1861–6) ... [and] ... Governor Eyre's merciless suppression of the Jamaica Insurrection at Morant Bay in 1865.[11]

In this respect, one of the writers who best reflects and represents the change in 'popular perceptions of race' is Dickens, particularly if the Niger expedition of 1841 is added to Young's list of pivotal moments. As we saw in Chapter 3, Dickens moved from expressions of outrage against slavery in *American Notes* (1842) and *Martin Chuzzlewit*, to the conciliatory equivocations of the essay 'North American Slavery', to threats of vengeful genocide in response to the Indian Mutiny, to public support for Governor John Eyre, who, as Brahma Chaudhuri points out, had endorsed the 'killing [of] 439 blacks, flogging [of] 600 men and women, and burning [of] more than 1000 houses'[12] in response to the Jamaica Insurrection of 1865. In *Martin Chuzzlewit*, Dickens at least holds out the possibility of equal and mutual recognition when Martin first meets an American black face-to-face: 'Martin stared at him for a moment,' Dickens remarks, 'and [then] burst into a hearty laugh; to which the negro ... so heartily responded, that his teeth shone like a gleam of light. "You're the pleasantest fellow I have seen yet," said Martin, clapping him on the back.'[13] Despite the patronising tone, the scene momentarily holds out the possibility of individualised, face-to-face, mutual recognition between white and black, and it does so in precisely the terms defined by Hegel – that is, 'each [self-consciousness] sees the *other* do the same as it does.' By the time of the Jamaica uprising in 1865, however, the very idea of such recognition, of a particular black being singled out '"the pleasantest fellow"' by a white, has become inconceivable to Dickens, and he can now only express contempt for ideas of identification and equality. 'That platform-sympathy with the black,' he declares in a letter of 1865,

> makes me stark wild. Only the other day, here was a meeting of jaw-bones of asses at Manchester, to censure the Jamaica Governor for his manner of putting down the insurrection! So we are badgered about New Zealanders and Hottentots, as if they were identical with men in clean shirts at Camberwell.[14]

Like so many abolitionist writers of the nineteenth century, Dickens here conveniently forgets his own earlier 'platform-sympathy' with black slaves and emphasises the difference between 'New Zealanders and Hottentots' and the emergent middle classes of suburban Camberwell. In this sense, Carlyle's discussion of recognition in 'The Nigger Question' exposes, from a *pro*-slavery standpoint, the ideological trajectory of many *abolitionists* in nineteenth-century Britain, whereby writers who, earlier on in the century, expressed a certain degree of identification and recognition for slaves were often the same people who later espoused difference, otherness, scientific racialism, white supremacy and aggressive imperialism.

There are various explanations for this. First, it is apparent that expressions of 'platform-sympathy' and 'sacred pity' on the part of early nineteenth-century abolitionists are forms of recognition that simultaneously depend on the *in*equality of the master–slave relation, and hence cease with emancipation. Pity, after all, is possible only as a reaction to inequality; in the case of many early nineteenth-century abolitionists, pity represents a theoretical form of recognition which appeals to what Hegel calls the 'truth ... implicit in ... the bondsman'[15] – that is, freedom and equality, manhood and brotherhood – within a particular and explicit framework of inequality. Consequently, once this framework is abolished, the peculiar form of *equal/unequal* recognition it made possible is also done away with.

This is perhaps best demonstrated by reference to a much later, *post*-abolition, post-American Civil War text, George Eliot's *Daniel Deronda* (1876). Unusually for the later nineteenth century, Eliot's novel does *seem* to hold out the possibility of interracial sympathy, identification and recognition. At one point, Eliot stages a short debate on the rebellion in Jamaica in which 'Grandcourt held that the Jamaican negro was a beastly sort of baptist Caliban; [but] Deronda said he had always felt a little with Caliban, who naturally had his own point of view and could sing a good song'.[16] Deronda, it seems, sympathises, or 'feel[s] with' the 'Jamaican negro' in a way that Young and others find more characteristic of the eighteenth and earlier nineteenth centuries – in the same way, in fact, that Martin Chuzzlewit comes to identify with the American black he meets.

This, though, is precisely the point: Deronda's sympathy *is* characteristic of an earlier age; his mode of recognition is a peculiar flashback to that of the abolitionists, but is rendered meaningless and empty by his own post-emancipation, post-Civil War context. Deronda expresses sympathy for 'Caliban', a *slave* of the past,[17] but signally fails to recognise the modern subjects of imperialism, whether those subjects be the insurgent Jamaicans, their leader George William Gordon whom Grandcourt condemns as a 'baptist Caliban', or the 'half-breeds' whom Mr Torrington blames for colonial unrest. All Deronda can say in response to Torrington is that 'the whites had to thank themselves for the half-breeds'.[18] Deronda's sympathy is dependent on racial separation and slavery; he cannot and does not recognise the modern 'baptist Calibans' or 'half-breeds' as he does 'Caliban' himself because his sympathy, like that of the earlier abolitionists, is conceivable only within the framework of the master–slave relation's explicit racial inequality. The master–slave relation has changed since Caliban, however, and, in this sense, Deronda recognises and feels for a colonial subject who no longer exists, who is dead and gone. In a post-emancipation context, such sympathy is anachronistic, and cannot engage with the very different discourses which define so-called 'free-trade' imperialism and racial domination.

In fact, Deronda's sympathy for Caliban and slaves recalls that of the many British writers, propagandists, politicians and missionaries who, as Brantlinger notes, persisted in 'maintaining the crusade against slavery and the slave-trade even after Britain and the United States had ceased to engage in them' – a crusade against slavery which was by no means the same thing as a crusade against imperialism, and was often complicit with colonial conquest. As Brantlinger remarks,

> The Governor Eyre controversy showed [that] many Victorians sympathised with the poor at home but not with the exploited abroad.... Slavery, however, remained an important issue from the 1840s to the end of the century.... After 1865 slavery seemed to be largely confined to Africa.... [So] after abolishing slavery on their own ground, the British turned to the seemingly humane work of abolishing slavery – and all 'savage customs' – on African ground.

When Deronda feels for the slave Caliban, then, he is assuming a pro-imperialist stance, and this is part of the ironic and paradoxical nature of later imperialist ideology, whereby abolitionist sympathy was gradually appropriated as an excuse for further incursion into Africa and colonial domination. As Brantlinger remarks, 'the movement for the abolition of slavery was also a precursor to the European partitioning of Africa'.[19] Moreover, whilst the British appear to be recognising blacks as free by turning to the abolition of slavery 'on African ground', they are, by this very act, presumably transforming those freed 'slaves' into the 'exploited abroad' – the subjects of capitalistic and racialised colonialism – who are denied the recognition of Victorians' sympathy. Recognition is here made impossible at the very moment of its realisation. Terry Eagleton remarks in an essay on Eliot that 'sympathy doesn't get you anywhere',[20] and, in the case of British abolitionism, he would seem be right: the form of recognition that is sympathy for slaves has no teleology, no end-point. Abolitionist sympathy does not and cannot realise the equality and freedom it promises for slaves, but only achieves the reconstitution of hierarchies based on imperial exploitation in which *all* recognition is denied.

Deronda is like so many others, then, in expressing sympathy for the slave 'Caliban' yet backing away from any kind of identification or association with those modern, subversive, imperial subjects, the 'baptist Caliban', the 'half-breeds' and the blacks who are no longer 'manageable'. Indeed, Deronda's (in)famous creed of racial 'separateness with communication' encodes a whole Victorian discourse based on the desire for a geographically and racially discrete 'other', one who is absolutely marked out from white Europeans, and who is in no way mixed up with whites, whether religiously (like the 'baptist' Caliban) or sexually (the 'half-breeds'). Just as, by 1848, Dickens has decided that 'between the civilised European and the barbarous African there is a great gulf set',[21] Deronda argues for the geographical separation and segregation of races, particularly in the form of a future homeland for Jews. Like Dickens, his emphasis here is on separation, not communication. 'Eliot's ... last novel,' Susan Meyer writes, 'simply removes [the] ... racially alien figure ... from England .... [so it evinces] an *increase* in imperialist sentiment and an endorsement, by way of proto-Zionism, of racial separatism.'[22] Clearly, the geographical separation Deronda and Dickens invoke is also a racial separatism which, to use Young's terms, sees races not as '"the same but different"', part of 'humankind as a universal egalitarian category', but just as '"different – and also, different"'. In this sense, Deronda's proto-Zionist project is based on the same racial discourse which, after abolition, supported further colonial collaboration. Deronda's ethos reflects the later Victorians' stress on racial difference and retreat from notions of sameness, equality, identification, sympathy and association which characterise so much earlier abolitionist writing and thought.

To some extent, what underwrites this retreat from ideas of sameness and equality is the fear of interracial confrontation and violence. As Meyer observes of the Indian Rebellion,

> the events in India of 1857–8 caused a hardening of British racism and a more ruthless sense of the need to subjugate those of other races.... The maintenance of the British empire was beginning to feel like a grim and violent project, one attended with significant costs ... to the British.... The contact between races is [subsequently] represented as violent and destructive.[23]

This 'hardening of British racism' represents a decisive move away from abolitionist and Enlightenment notions of equality towards the kind of imperialist militarism and racial subjugation upheld by Carlyle in 'Shooting Niagara' (1867), where he asserts that the kind of 'Martial Law' used by Governor Eyre in Jamaica is 'of more validity than any other law whatever.'[24] Such responses, on the part of Carlyle and the British public in general, are surely constituted by the generally unspoken fear that, without the explicit inequality of the master–slave relation, implicit acknowledgement of sameness may be dangerous, and may lead to a *violent* actualisation, on the part of imperial subjects, of the equality seemingly promised by the Emancipation Act in 1833. The neurotic fear of many Victorians is that, without a fixed master–slave relation, any theoretical and sympathetic recognition of racial equality may provoke an attempt to realise in reality the abstract equality that has been posited by abolitionist propaganda. Once again, though writing from a pro-slavery standpoint, it is Carlyle who explains and makes conscious this generally unspoken and unconscious anxiety on the part of many apparently liberal, pro-abolitionist and pro-democratic thinkers of the later nineteenth century. As he writes in 'The Nigger Question',

> I have to complain that, in these days, the relation of master to servant, and of superior to inferior ... is fallen sadly out of joint.... No man reverences another; at the best, each man slaps the other good-humouredly on the shoulder, with, 'Hail, fellow; well met:' –

at the worst (which is sure enough to follow) ... clutches him by the throat, with, "Tyrannous son of perdition, shall I endure thee, then, and thy injustices forever?"[25]

What Carlyle spells out here is a (problematic) notion that was discussed at length in Chapter 3. In short, this is the fear that, without a fixed master–slave relation, there is nothing to define the behaviour between masters and subjects – nothing to stop a friendly 'slap' on the back slipping into violence. This fear surely underpins the retreat Dickens made during his later career from that moment of recognition, reciprocity and equality in *Martin Chuzzlewit* when Martin is seen 'clapping ... on the back' the black he meets in America. In the light of the Jamaican rebellions of 1831 and 1865 and the Indian Mutiny, many Victorians like Dickens became concerned that 'good-humoured' expressions of egalitarianism might well be dangerous in the way Carlyle described, whereby a 'clap' leads to a 'slap', which leads to a 'clutch'.

Carlyle makes clear the Victorians' fearful realisation, in the aftermath of various colonial uprisings, that Hegel might be right – that the actualisation of true equality might not be merely a matter of a philosophical acknowledgement, as many Enlightenment figures claimed, or even an Act of Parliament, but might rather be a violent, confrontational, life-and-death struggle for recognition. This is the kind of struggle, in fact, that the sepoys at Meerut in India and that 'baptist Caliban', George William Gordon, attempted to bring about, and by which twentieth-century colonial history was indelibly marked. After all, Hegel defines mutual recognition as a state in which 'each [self-consciousness] sees the *other* do the same as it does', so post-emancipation imperialists must always be afraid that colonial subjects will start mirroring and returning the violence done to them by colonial rule. In this sense, Hegel foreshadows a Victorian fear that racial equality might only be constituted by violent struggle, and this fear in turn foreshadows Frantz Fanon's claims in the twentieth century that

> decolonisation is the meeting of two forces, opposed to each other by their very nature.... Their first encounter was marked by violence, and their existence together ... was carried on by dint of a great array of bayonets and cannon.... Decolonisation ... will [similarly] only come to pass after a murderous ... struggle between the two protagonists.[26]

Notes

Introduction

1. Georg Wilhelm Friedrich Hegel, *The Philosophical Propaedeutic*, ed. Michael George and Andrew Vincent, trans. A.V. Miller (Oxford: Basil Blackwell, 1986), 62.
2. Georg Wilhelm Friedrich Hegel, *Phenomenology of Spirit*, trans. A.V. Miller (Oxford: Oxford University Press, 1977), 58, 67, 79
3. Ibid., 109.
4. Peter Singer, *Hegel* (Oxford: Oxford University Press, 1983), 57.
5. Hegel, *Phenomenology of Spirit*, 111–14.
6. Raymond Plant, *Hegel* (London: George Allen and Unwin, 1972), 151.
7. Hegel, *Phenomenology of Spirit*, 111.
8. Ibid., 114.
9. Plant, *Hegel*, 151.
10. Hegel, *Phenomenology of Spirit*, 115.
11. Singer, *Hegel*, 61.
12. Hegel, *Phenomenology of Spirit*, 116–17.
13. J. N. Findlay, 'Foreword', in Georg Wilhelm Friedrich Hegel, *Phenomenology of Spirit*, trans. A.V. Miller (Oxford: Oxford University Press, 1977), xvii.
14. Hegel, *Phenomenology of Spirit*, 117–19.
15. Richard Norman, *Hegel's Phenomenology: A Philosophical Introduction* (New Jersey: Humanities Press, 1981), 50.
16. Georg Wilhelm Friedrich Hegel, *The Philosophy of History*, trans. J. Sibree (New York: Dover, 1956), 111.
17. Singer, *Hegel*, 62.
18. Hegel, *The Philosophy of History*, 99.
19. Ibid., 112–13.
20. Georg Wilhelm Friedrich Hegel, *Lectures on the History of Philosophy*, trans. E.S. Haldane and Frances H. Simson, 3 vols (London: Routledge and Kegan Paul, 1968), I. 96.
21. Ibid., 99.
22. Hegel, *The Philosophy of History*, 99.
23. Jean-Paul Sartre, *Being and Nothingness: An Essay on Phenomenological Ontology*, trans. Hazel E. Barnes (London: Methuen, 1957), 267–8.
24. Georg Wilhelm Friedrich Hegel, *Elements of the Philosophy of Right*, ed. Allen W. Wood, trans. H.B. Nisbet (Cambridge: Cambridge University Press, 1991), 88, 279.
25. Ibid., 97–8.
26. Wilkie Collins, *My Miscellanies* (Farnborough: Gregg International, 1971), 226.
27. Patrick Brantlinger, *Rule of Darkness: British Literature and Imperialism, 1830–1914* (Ithaca and London: Cornell University Press, 1988), 174.
28. Francis Fukayama, *The End of History and the Last Man* (Harmondsworth: Penguin, 1992), 200.

29. Jacques Lacan, *Écrits: A Selection*, trans. Alan Sheridan (London: Tavistock, 1977), 308.
30. Ibid., 307.
31. Hegel, *Phenomenology of Spirit*, 113–14.
32. Lacan, *Écrits*, 308.
33. William Lloyd Garrison, 'Preface', in Frederick Douglass, *Narrative of the Life of Frederick Douglass, An American Slave, Written by Himself*, ed. William L. Andrews and William S. McFeely (New York and London: W. W. Norton, 1997), 8.
34. Karl Marx and Friedrich Engels, *The Communist Manifesto*, ed. A.J.P. Taylor (Harmondsworth: Penguin, 1967, 1985), 79: my emphasis.
35. Ibid., 92.
36. Ibid.
37. Leon Trotsky, *The Permanent Revolution*, cited in C. Wright Mills, *The Marxists* (Harmondsworth: Penguin, 1963), 268.
38. Ibid., 282.
39. Josif Stalin, *Leninism*, quoted in ibid., 285.
40. Thomas Carlyle, *On Heroes, Hero-Worship and the Heroic in History*, in *The Works of Thomas Carlyle*, 30 vols (London: Chapman and Hall, 1904), V. 240–2.
41. Wilkie Collins, *The Woman in White*, ed. John Sutherland (Oxford: Oxford University Press, 1996), 610.
42. Marx and Engels, *The Communist Manifesto*, 82, 89.
43. Bruce Robbins, *The Servant's Hand: English Fiction From Below* (Durham, NC and London: Duke University Press, 1993), 81.
44. Carlyle, *Heroes and Hero-Worship*, 243, 242.
45. Thomas Carlyle, *Latter-Day Pamphlets*, in *The Works of Thomas Carlyle*, 30 vols (Chapman and Hall, 1898), XX. 8.
46. Charles Dickens, *Our Mutual Friend*, ed. Stephen Gill (Harmondsworth: Penguin, 1985), 48.
47. Carlyle, *Heroes and Hero-Worship*, 240, 204.
48. Ibid., 240, 203.
49. Ibid., 203.
50. Thomas Carlyle, 'The Nigger Question', in *Critical and Miscellaneous Essays, IV*, in *The Works of Thomas Carlyle*, 30 vols (London: Chapman and Hall, 1899), XXIX. 363; Carlyle, *Heroes and Hero-Worship*, 217.
51. Ibid., 241.
52. Carlyle's ambivalent attitude towards German philosophy is apparent in his essay 'Characteristics' (1831) where he writes that, though it is a kind of 'vortex', in 'Hegelism ... [and] the higher Literature of Germany, there ... lies ... the beginning of a new revelation of the Godlike' (Thomas Carlyle, 'Characteristics', in *Critical and Miscellaneous Essays, III*, in *The Works of Thomas Carlyle*, 30 vols (London: Chapman and Hall, 1899), XXVIII. 41).
53. Georg Wilhelm Friedrich Hegel, *System of Ethical Life* and *First Philosophy of Spirit*, ed. and trans. H.S. Harris and T.M. Knox (Albany: University of New York Press, 1979), 128.
54. Thomas Carlyle, *Chartism*, in *Critical and Miscellaneous Essays, IV*, in *The Works of Thomas Carlyle*, 30 vols (London: Chapman and Hall, 1899), XXIX. 147.
55. Ibid.

56. Thomas Carlyle, *Past and Present*, in *The Works of Thomas Carlyle*, 30 vols (London: Chapman and Hall, 1899), XXX. 89.
57. Carlyle, *Heroes and Hero-Worship*, 209, 218.
58. Ibid., 226.
59. Carlyle, *Latter-Day Pamphlets*, 21–2.
60. Carlyle, *Heroes and Hero-Worship*, 211, 213, 216.
61. Thomas Carlyle, 'Last Words of Thomas Carlyle: On Trades-Unions, Promoterism and the Signs of the Times', in D.J. Trela, 'Thomas Carlyle "On Trades-Unions, Promoterism and the Signs of the Times"': An Unknown and Nearly Unpublished Manuscript', *Victorian Institute Journal*, 25 (1997), 240.
62. Lacan, *Écrits*, 308.
63. Eric Bentley, *A Century of Hero-Worship* (Boston: Beacon Hill, 1957), 71.
64. Carlyle, *Heroes and Hero-Worship*, 340.
65. Ibid., 1.
66. Norman, *Hegel's Phenomenology*, 51.

Chapter 1

1. Georg Wilhelm Friedrich Hegel, *Philosophy of Mind*, trans. William Wallace and A. V. Miller (Oxford: Clarendon Press, 1971), 172. The quotation is taken from Hegel's notes which, as Richard Norman points out, were 'compiled from Hegel's own and from those of students who attended his lectures' (Norman, *Hegel's Phenomenology*, 50).
2. Sartre, *Being and Nothingness*, 267–8.
3. Hegel, *Phenomenology of Spirit*, 114.
4. Norman, *Hegel's Phenomenology*, 51–2.
5. Collins, *The Woman in White*, 13. All further references to this novel in Chapter 1 appear parenthetically in the text.
6. Lacan, *Écrits*, 308.
7. Karl Marx, *Capital: A Critique of Political Economy*, trans. Ben Fowkes (Harmondsworth: Penguin, 1976), I. 1054.
8. Marx and Engels, *The Communist Manifesto*, 82.
9. Ibid., 82.
10. Kathleen Tillotson, 'Introduction: The Lighter Reading of the Eighteen-Sixties', in Wilkie Collins, *The Woman in White*, ed. Anthea Trodd (Boston: Houghton Mifflin, 1969), ix.
11. Robbins, *The Servant's Hand*, 7–13.
12. Ibid., 11; he is quoting from Theresa McBride, *The Domestic Revolution: The Modernisation of Household Service in England and France, 1820–1920* (London: Croom Helm, 1976), 11.
13. Carlyle, *Chartism*, 167, 162. Carlyle provides an important point of intersection between Collins, Marx and Hegel: both Collins and Marx had read a great deal of his work, and Carlyle had at least some acquaintance with Hegel's philosophy.
14. Hegel, *Phenomenology of Spirit*, 113–14.
15. Carlyle, *Chartism*, 131.
16. Thomas Carlyle, 'Signs of the Times', in *Critical and Miscellaneous Essays, II*, in *The Works of Thomas Carlyle*, 30 vols (London: Chapman and Hall, 1899), XXVII. 67.
17. Collins, *My Miscellanies*, 226, 228.

18. Lacan, *Écrits*, 308.
19. Hegel, *Phenomenology of Spirit*, 113.
20. Tamar Heller, *Dead Secrets: Wilkie Collins and the Female Gothic* (New Haven and London: Yale University Press, 1992), 129.
21. D. A. Miller, *The Novel and the Police* (Berkeley: University of California Press, 1988), 162.
22. Hélène Cixous, 'Sorties: Out and Out: Attacks/Ways Out/Forays', trans. Betsy Wing, in *The Hélène Cixous Reader*, ed. Susan Sellers (London: Routledge, 1994), 38.
23. Carlyle, *Heroes and Hero-Worship*, 218.
24. German extracts taken from Georg Wilhelm Friedrich Hegel, *Phenomenology of Spirit: A Selection*, ed. and trans. Howard P. Kainz (Pennsylvania: Pennsylvania State University Press, 1994), 62.
25. Hegel, *Phenomenology of Spirit*, 117.
26. Ibid., 115.
27. Cyndy Hendershot, 'A Sensation Novel's Appropriation of the Terror-Gothic: Wilkie Collins' *The Woman in White*', *Clues*, 13 (1992), 129.
28. Miller, *The Novel and the Police*, 177–8.
29. Hendershot, 'A Sensation Novel's Appropriation of the Terror-Gothic', 129.
30. Heller, *Dead Secrets*, 117.
31. Hegel, *Phenomenology of Spirit*, 116.
32. Michel Foucault, *Discipline and Punish: The Birth of the Prison*, trans. Alan Sheridan (Harmondsworth: Penguin, 1991), 202–3.
33. Friedrich Nietzsche, *On the Genealogy of Morals: A Polemic*, trans. Douglas Smith (Oxford: Oxford University Press, 1998), 30.
34. Ibid., 26–8.
35. Ibid., 19.
36. Miller, *The Novel and the Police*, 176.
37. Hegel, *Phenomenology of Spirit*, 116.
38. Ferdinand de Saussure, *Course in General Linguistics*, ed. Charles Bally and Albert Sechehaye, trans. Roy Harris (London: Duckworth, 1983), 67.
39. Hegel, *Phenomenology of Spirit*, 114.
40. Carlyle, *Heroes and Hero-Worship*, 217, 222–3.
41. Karl Marx, *The Eighteenth Brumaire of Louis Bonaparte*, in *Selected Writings*, ed. David McLellan (Oxford: Oxford University Press, 1977), 324.
42. Ibid., 310.
43. Carlyle, *Heroes and Hero-Worship*, 243.
44. Ibid., 217.
45. Marx, *The Eighteenth Brumaire of Louis Bonaparte*, 301.
46. Carlyle, *Heroes and Hero-Worship*, 237, 242.
47. Marx, *The Eighteenth Brumaire of Louis Bonaparte*, 301.
48. Maurice Blanchot, *The Space of Literature*, trans. Ann Smock (Lincoln and London: University of Nebraska Press, 1982), 258.
49. Hegel, *Phenomenology of Spirit*, 114.

Chapter 2

1. George Eliot, 'Servants' Logic', in *Essays of George Eliot*, ed. Thomas Pinney (London: Routledge and Kegan Paul, 1963), 392. All further references to

this essay in Chapter 2 appear parenthetically in the text, prefixed with the abbreviation 'SL'.

2. Basil Bernstein, 'Social Class, Language, and Socialization'. in *Language and Social Context*, ed. Pier Paolo Giglioli (Harmondsworth: Penguin, 1972), 164. Bruce Robbins points out the similarity between the discourse that Eliot attributes to domestic servants and the 'context-bound' language Bernstein attributes to the working class in general; see Robbins, *The Servant's Hand*, 89.

3. E.S. Turner, *What the Butler Saw: Two Hundred and Fifty Years of the Servant Problem* (London: Michael Joseph, 1962), 101.

4. It is also the unspoken text of Bernstein's paper.

5. Dorothy Marshall, *The English Domestic Servant in History* (London: The Historical Association, 1949), 24.

6. Foucault, *Discipline and Punish*, 11, 8.

7. N.N. Feltes, '"The Greatest Plague of Life": Dickens, Masters and Servants', *Literature and History*, 8 (1978), 204.

8. Ibid., 204.

9. Marshall, *The English Domestic Servant in History*, 12.

10. Robbins, *The Servant's Hand*, 77.

11. Immanuel Kant, *Critique of Pure Reason*, ed. Vasilis Politis, trans. J.M.D. Meiklejohn (London: J. M. Dent, 1993), 31.

12. Wendell V. Harris, *The Omnipresent Debate: Empiricism and Transcendentalism in Nineteenth-Century English Prose* (DeKalb: Northern Illinois University, 1981), 7.

13. George Eliot, 'The Future of German Philosophy', in *Essays of George Eliot*, ed. Thomas Pinney (London: Routledge and Kegan Paul, 1963), 153.

14. Harris, *The Omnipresent Debate*, 12.

15. Plato, *Republic*, trans. Robin Waterfield (Oxford: Oxford University Press, 1998), 193.

16. Sylviane Agacinski, 'We are not Sublime: Love and Sacrifice, Abraham and Ourselves', in *Kierkegaard: A Critical Reader*, ed. Jonathan Rée and James Chamberlain (Oxford: Blackwell, 1997), 140–2, 136.

17. Ibid., 136.

18. Immanuel Kant, *Religion Within the Limits of Reason Alone*, trans. Theodore M. Greene and Hoyt H. Hudson (New York: Harper and Row, 1960), 11.

19. Agacinski, 'We are not Sublime', 142.

20. Eliot, 'The Future of German Philosophy,' 151.

21. Ibid., 150.

22. Kant, *Critique of Pure Reason*, 32.

23. Ibid., 32.

24. Hegel, *System of Ethical Life*, 114. Eliot was aware of Hegel's work through her partner, G.H. Lewes.

25. A.D. Lindsay, 'Introduction,' in Immanuel Kant, *Critique of Pure Reason*, trans. J.M.D. Meiklejohn (London: J. M. Dent and Sons, 1934), xx.

26. Oliver Lodge, 'Science in the '"Sixties"', in *The Eighteen-Sixties: Essays by Fellows of the Royal Society of Literature*, ed. John Drinkwater (Cambridge: Cambridge University Press, 1932), 251.

27. Robin Gilmour, *The Victorian Period: The Intellectual and Cultural Context of English Literature, 1830–1890* (Harlow: Longman, 1993), 138. He is quoting from Maxwell's essay 'Molecules' (1873).

28. Lodge, 'Science in the "Sixties"', 262.
29. Ibid., 262–3.
30. Thomas Carlyle, *Sartor Resartus*, *The Works of Thomas Carlyle*, 30 vols (London: Chapman and Hall, 1899), I. 54.
31. Michael Cotsell, *The Companion to 'Our Mutual Friend'* (London: Allen and Unwin, 1986), 26.
32. Dickens, *Our Mutual Friend*, 51. All further references to this novel in Chapter 2 appear parenthetically in the text, prefixed with the abbreviation '*OMF*'.
33. Deborah A. Thomas, 'Dickens and Indigestion: The Deadly Dinners of the Rich', *Dickens Studies Newsletter*, 14:1 (1983), 8.
34. Ibid., 7.
35. Carlyle, *Chartism*, 168, 155–6, 129–30.
36. Turner, *What the Butler Saw*, 100–1.
37. Ibid., 158.
38. Robbins, *The Servant's Hand*, 81.
39. Quoted in Feltes, '"The Greatest Plague of Life"', 205.
40. Timothy Clark, 'Dickens through Blanchot: The Nightmare Fascination of a World without Interiority', in *Dickens Refigured: Bodies, Desires and Other Histories*, ed. John Schad (Manchester: Manchester University Press, 1996), 23.
41. Blanchot, *The Space of Literature*, 258.
42. George Eliot, 'The Natural History of German Life', in *Essays of George Eliot*, ed. Thomas Pinney (London: Routledge and Kegan Paul, 1963), 271.
43. Quoted in Herbert Sussman, 'Cyberpunk Meets Charles Babbage: *The Difference Engine* as Alternative Victorian History', *Victorian Studies*, 38:1 (1995), 4.
44. William Gibson and Bruce Sterling, *The Difference Engine* (New York: Bantam, 1991), 422.
45. Sussman, 'Cyberpunk Meets Charles Babbage', 17.
46. Quoted in ibid., 17–18.
47. Marx and Engels, *The Communist Manifesto*, 87.
48. Turner, *What the Butler Saw*, 100.
49. Feltes, '"The Greatest Plague of Life"', 202.
50. Pamela Horn, *The Rise and Fall of the Victorian Servant* (Stroud: Sutton, 1995), 25.
51. Marshall, *The English Domestic Servant in History*, 4–5.
52. Charles Dickens, 'Old and New Servants', in *All the Year Round: A Weekly Journal*, ed. Charles Dickens (London: Chapman and Hall, 1867), XVII. 80.
53. G.K. Chesterton, *Criticisms and Appreciations of the Works of Charles Dickens* (London: J.M. Dent and Sons, 1992), 213.
54. Agacinski, 'We Are Not Sublime', 141–2.
55. Thomas Thomson, *The History of Chemistry* (New York: Arno Press, 1975), 190.
56. Charles Dickens, *Dombey and Son*, ed. Peter Fairclough (Harmondsworth: Penguin, 1985), 253.
57. Turner, *What the Butler Saw*, 163–4.
58. Horn, *The Rise and Fall of the Victorian Servant*, 93.
59. Robbins, *The Servant's Hand*, 81.
60. Cotsell, *The Companion to 'Our Mutual Friend'*, 26.
61. Or Mme du Barry.

62. Gilmour, *The Victorian Period*, 134–5.
63. Quoted in ibid., 135.
64. Beatrice Webb, *My Apprenticeship* (Cambridge: Cambridge University Press, 1979), 130.
65. Charles-Albert Reichen, *A History of Chemistry* (London: Leisure Arts, 1964), 20.
66. Gilmour, *The Victorian Period*, 134.
67. George Henry Lewes, *The Biographical History of Philosophy: From its Origins in Greece Down to the Present Day* (London: John W. Parker and Son, 1857), 654.
68. Kant, *Critique of Pure Reason*, 31.
69. Gilmour, *The Victorian Period*, 113.
70. Reichen, *A History of Chemistry*, 26.
71. Marx and Engels, *The Communist Manifesto*, 85–6.

Chapter 3

1. Lacan, *Écrits*, 308.
2. Charles Dickens, *Martin Chuzzlewit*, ed. Margaret Cardwell (Oxford: Clarendon Press, 1982), 267. All further references to this work in Chapter 3 appear parenthetically in the text, prefixed with the abbreviation 'MC'.
3. Hugh Thomas, *The Slave Trade: The History of the Atlantic Slave Trade, 1440–1870* (London: Picador, 1997), 469.
4. Charles Dickens and Henry Morley, 'North American Slavery', in *The Uncollected Writings of Charles Dickens: Household Words 1850–1859*, 2 vols, ed. Harry Stone (London: Allen Lane The Penguin Press, 1969), II. 434.
5. Hegel, *Phenomenology of Spirit*, 114.
6. Carlyle, *Chartism*, 147.
7. Charles Dickens, *American Notes for General Circulation* and *Pictures From Italy*, ed. F.S. Schwarzbach and Leonée Ormond (London: J.M. Dent, 1997), 243. All further references to this work in Chapter 3 appear parenthetically in the text, prefixed with the abbreviation 'AN'.
8. Frederick Douglass, *Narrative of the Life of Frederick Douglass, An American Slave, Written by Himself*, ed. William L. Andrews and William S. McFeely (New York and London: W.W. Norton, 1997), 40. All further references to this work in Chapter 3 appear parenthetically in the text, prefixed with the abbreviation 'NFD'.
9. Thad Ziolowski, 'Antitheses: The Dialectic of Violence and Literacy in Frederick Douglass's Narrative of 1845', in *Frederick Douglass: New Literary and Historical Essays*, ed. Eric J. Sundquist (Cambridge: Cambridge University Press, 1990), 149.
10. Stanley M. Elkins, *Slavery: A Problem in American Institutional and Intellectual Life* (Chicago: University of Chicago Press, 1968), 38.
11. Ibid., 216.
12. Arthur A. Adrian, 'Dickens on American Slavery: A Carlylean Slant', *PMLA*, 67:4 (1952), 328; Brahma Chaudhuri, 'Dickens and the Question of Slavery', *Dickens Quarterly*, 6:1 (1989), 4.
13. Jon Roper, *Democracy and Its Critics: Anglo-American Democratic Thought in the Nineteenth Century* (London: Unwin Hyman, 1989), 174.

14. Georg Wilhelm Friedrich Hegel, Letter to Niethammer, 13 October 1806, in *Hegel: The Letters*, ed. and trans. C. Butler and C. Seiler (Indianapolis: University of Indiana Press, 1984), 114.
15. Carlyle, *Heroes and Hero-Worship*, 240.
16. Ziolowski, 'Antitheses', 149.
17. Carlyle, *Heroes and Hero-Worship*, 217, 243.
18. Marx, *The Eighteenth Brumaire of Louis Bonaparte*, 301.
19. Carlyle, *Latter-Day Pamphlets*, 22.
20. Dickens and Morley, 'North American Slavery', 436.
21. Peter J. Parish, *Slavery: The Many Faces of a Southern Institution* (Durham: British Association for American Studies, 1979), 12.
22. Dickens and Morley, 'North American Slavery', 436.
23. Thomas, *The Slave Trade*, 469.
24. Hegel, *Phenomenology of Spirit*, 115.
25. Carlyle, *Chartism*, 163.
26. Ibid., 157: my emphasis.
27. John W. Blassingame, *The Slave Community: Plantation Life in the Antebellum South* (New York and Oxford: Oxford University Press, 1979), 6; Thomas, *The Slave-Trade*, 793.
28. Hegel, *The Philosophy of History*, 99.
29. Jacques Derrida, *Glas*, trans. John P. Leavey Jr. and Richard Rand (Lincoln and London: University of Nebraska Press, 1986), 207.
30. Hegel, *The Philosophy of History*, 30–1.
31. Judith N. Shklar, *Freedom and Independence: A Study of the Political Ideas of Hegel's 'Phenomenology of Mind'* (Cambridge: Cambridge University Press, 1976), 59.
32. Thomas, *The Slave Trade*, 795.
33. See Genesis 9.18–29.
34. Charles Dickens, Letter to John Forster, 15 April 1842, in *The Letters of Charles Dickens*, 12 vols, ed. Madeline House, Graham Storey and Kathleen Tillotson (Oxford: Clarendon Press, 1974), III. 197; see also *AN*, 231.
35. Abraham Lincoln, 'Address to the Young Men's Lyceum of Springfield, Illinois: The Perpetuation of Our Political Institutions', in *The Portable Abraham Lincoln*, ed. Andrew Delbanco (Harmondsworth: Penguin, 1993), 21–2.
36. Cited in Dickens, *The Letters of Charles Dickens*, III. 197.
37. Theodore D. Weld, *American Slavery As It Is: Testimony of a Thousand Witnesses* (New York: Arno Press, 1968), 157.
38. Garrison, 'Preface', 9. Since it forms part of Douglass's *Narrative*, all further references to this preface in Chapter 3 appear parenthetically in the text, prefixed with the abbreviation '*NFD*'.
39. Lincoln, 'Address to the Young Men's Lyceum of Springfield, Illinois', 22–3.
40. Carlyle, *Latter-Day Pamphlets*, 20.
41. Lincoln, 'Address to the Young Men's Lyceum of Springfield, Illinois', 18.
42. Weld, *American Slavery As It Is*, 144; John Hope Franklin and Alfred A. Moss Jr., *From Slavery to Freedom: A History of Negro Americans* (New York: McGraw-Hill, 1988), 114–15.
43. Elkins, *Slavery*, 55.

44. Ibid., 55.
45. James Walvin, *Questioning Slavery* (London: Routledge, 1996), 53; Elkins, *Slavery*, 101.
46. Parish, *Slavery*, 11.
47. Marian E. Musgrave, 'Patterns of Violence and Non-Violence in Pro-Slavery and Anti-Slavery Fiction', *CLA*, 16 (1973), 431.
48. Hegel, *The Philosophy of History*, 98–9.
49. Roper, *Democracy and Its Critics*, 42.
50. Blassingame, *The Slave Community*, 151, 315.
51. Eugene D. Genovese, *The World the Slaveholders Made: Two Essays in Interpretation* (London: Allen Lane The Penguin Press, 1970), 158.
52. Quoted in N. N. Feltes, '"The Greatest Plague of Life"', 200.
53. Genovese, *The World the Slaveholders Made*, 159.
54. Parish, *Slavery*, 6; Eugene D. Genovese, *The Political Economy of Slavery: Studies in the Economy and Society of the Slave South* (London: MacGibbon and Kee, 1966), 3; Elkins, *Slavery*, 141.
55. Parish, *Slavery*, 7.
56. Carlyle, Letter to N. Beverley Tucker, October 1 1850, quoted in Elkins, *Slavery*, 217.
57. Carlyle, 'The Nigger Question', 371. All further references to this essay in Chapter 3 appear parenthetically in the text, prefixed with the abbreviation 'NQ'.
58. Carlyle, *Chartism*, 162.
59. Thomas Carlyle, 'Shooting Niagara', in *Critical and Miscellaneous Essays, V*, in *The Works of Thomas Carlyle*, 30 vols (London: Chapman and Hall, 1899), XXX. 6. All further references to this essay in Chapter 3 appear parenthetically in the text, prefixed with the abbreviation 'SN'.
60. Hegel, *Phenomenology of Spirit*, 117–18.
61. Abraham Lincoln, 'Final Emancipation Proclamation', in *The Portable Abraham Lincoln*, ed. Andrew Delbanco (Harmondsworth: Penguin, 1993), 272.
62. John Stuart Mill, *Considerations on Representative Government*, in *On Liberty and Other Essays*, ed. John Gray (Oxford: Oxford University Press, 1998), 232–4: my emphasis.
63. Hegel, *Phenomenology of Spirit*, 118.
64. Carlyle, *Chartism*, 135.
65. Marx and Engels, *The Communist Manifesto*, 87.
66. Dickens and Morley, 'North American Slavery', 438.
67. Franklin and Moss, *From Slavery to Freedom*, 214.
68. Lucinda H. MacKethan, 'Metaphors of Mastery in the Slave Narratives', in *The Art of Slave Narrative: Original Essays in Criticism and Theory*, ed. John Sekora and Darwin T. Turner (Illinois: Western Illinois University Press, 1982), 57.
69. Marx and Engels, *The Communist Manifesto*, 93.
70. Lacan, *Écrits*, 308.
71. Franklin and Moss, *From Slavery to Freedom*, 227, 237–8.
72. Charles Dickens, Letter to John Forster, 30 January 1868, in Charles Dickens, *Dickens on America and the Americans*, ed. Michael Slater (Hassocks: Harvester Press, 1979), 235.

73. Alexis de Tocqueville, *Democracy in America*, ed. Henry Steele Commager, trans. Henry Reeve (London: Oxford University Press, 1946), 231.
74. Marx and Engels, *The Communist Manifesto*, 120–1.
75. Musgrave, 'Patterns of Violence and Non-Violence in Pro-Slavery and Anti-Slavery Fiction', 431.
76. Marx and Engels, *The Communist Manifesto*, 89–90: my emphasis.
77. Hegel, *Elements of the Philosophy of Right*, 86–7.
78. Dickens and Morley, 'North American Slavery', 437.
79. Chaudhuri, 'Dickens and the Question of Slavery', 3.
80. Dickens and Morley, 'North American Slavery', 435, 437.
81. Hegel, *Phenomenology of Spirit*, 117.
82. Franklin and Moss, *From Slavery to Freedom*, 132.
83. Dickens and Morley, 'North American Slavery', 437.
84. Quoted in H. Bruce Franklin, 'Animal Farm Unbound', in *Modern Critical Interpretations: Frederick Douglass's 'Narrative of the Life of Frederick Douglass'*, ed. Harold Bloom (New York: Chelsea House, 1988), 29.
85. Henry-Louis Gates Jr., 'Binary Oppositions in Chapter One of Narrative of the Life of Frederick Douglass an America Slave Written by Himself', in *Afro-American Literature: The Reconstruction of Instruction*, ed. Dexter Fisher and Robert B. Stepto (New York: The Modern Language Association of America, 1979), 224.
86. Shklar, *Freedom and Independence*, 59.
87. Alexandre Kojève, *Introduction to the Reading of Hegel: Lectures on the 'Phenomenology of Spirit'*, ed. Raymond Queneau and Alan Bloom, trans. James H. Nichols (New York and London: Basic Books, 1969), 16.
88. Foucault, *Discipline and Punish*, 27.
89. Dickens and Morley, 'North American Slavery', 437–8. Of course, it almost goes without saying that statistics like these are inherently problematic anyway.
90. Franklin and Moss, *From Slavery to Freedom*, 132, 130; Parish, *Slavery*, 5.
91. Lawrence W. Levine, *Black Culture and Black Consciousness: Afro-American Folk Thought from Slavery to Freedom* (New York: Oxford University Press, 1977), 132–3.
92. MacKethan, 'Metaphors of Mastery in the Slave Narratives', 61.
93. Ziolowski, 'Antitheses', 149.
94. Franklin and Moss, *From Slavery to Freedom*, 132.
95. Harriet Beecher Stowe, *Uncle Tom's Cabin; or, Life Among the Lowly*, ed. Ann Douglas (Harmondsworth: Penguin, 1986), 340. Douglass and Dickens had certainly read *Uncle Tom's Cabin*. Dickens' and Morley's article 'North American Slavery' is, in part, a review of the novel.
96. Franklin and Moss, *From Slavery to Freedom*, 226–7: my emphasis.
97. A.L. Le Quesne, *Carlyle* (Oxford: Oxford University Press, 1982), 33, 32.
98. Carlyle, *Chartism*, 285; Carlyle, *Latter-Day Pamphlets*, 425–6.
99. Hegel, *Philosophy of Mind*, 175.
100. Dickens and Morley, 'North American Slavery', 442.
101. Chaudhuri, 'Dickens and the Question of Slavery', 4.
102. Ibid., 8.

Notes 205

103. Quoted in ibid., 8.
104. Carlyle, *Latter-Day Pamphlets*, 26: my emphasis.
105. Charles Darwin, *The Origin of Species By Means of Natural Selection*, ed. J.W. Burrow (Harmondsworth: Penguin, 1968), 115, 116: my emphasis.
106. Gilmour, *The Victorian Period*, 129.
107. Franklin and Moss, *From Slavery to Freedom*, 197, 194–5.
108. Ibid., 197.
109. Marianne McLeod Gilchrist, 'The Shaw Family of Staten Island: Elizabeth Gaskell's American Friends', *The Gaskell Society Journal*, 9 (1995), 4–5.
110. Ibid., 5–7.
111. Theodor Adorno remarks, rather cryptically, that 'horses are the survivors of the age of heroes' (Theodor W. Adorno, *In Search of Wagner*, trans. Rodney Livingstone (London: NLB, 1981), 8), but here it would seem that heroes emerge from the age of horses.
112. Weld, *American Slavery As It Is*, 143.
113. Singer, *Hegel*, 13.
114. Stowe, *Uncle Tom's Cabin*, 340.
115. Roper, *Democracy and Its Critics*, 42; Weld, *American Slavery As It Is*, 143.
116. Franklin and Moss, *From Slavery to Freedom*, 197.
117. Dickens and Morley, 'North American Slavery', 437.
118. Stowe, *Uncle Tom's Cabin*, 343–4.
119. Carlyle, *Heroes and Hero-Worship*, 196.
120. Carlyle, *Chartism*, 159.
121. Leo Tolstoy, *War and Peace*, trans. Rosemary Edmonds (Harmondsworth: Penguin, 1982), 1411.
122. Carlyle, *Chartism*, 157.
123. Ibid., 158–9.
124. Carlyle, *Heroes and Hero-Worship*, 240.
125. Carlyle, *Chartism*, 158, 160.
126. Tocqueville, *Democracy in America*, 199.
127. Ian Shapiro, 'Three Fallacies Concerning Majorities, Minorities, and Democratic Politics', in *Majorities and Minorities*, ed. John W. Chapman and Alan Wertheimer (New York and London: New York University Press, 1990), 80.
128. Walvin, *Questioning Slavery*, 62.
129. Tocqueville, *Democracy in America*, 191–2.
130. Quoted in Roper, *Democracy and Its Critics*, 76.
131. Quoted in Jerome Meckier, *Innocent Abroad: Charles Dickens's American Engagements* (Lexington: University Press of Kentucky, 1990), 102.
132. Carlyle, *Latter-Day Pamphlets*, 33.
133. Stowe, *Uncle Tom's Cabin*, 584, 583.
134. Anne Aresty Naman, *The Jew in the Victorian Novel: Some Relationships Between Prejudice and Art* (New York: AMS Press, 1980), 20.
135. Carlyle, *Latter-Day Pamphlets*, 33–4, 22.
136. Howard M. Sachar, *A History of the Jews in America* (New York: Alfred A. Knopf, 1992), 26.
137. T. Peter Park, 'Thomas Carlyle and the Jews', *Journal of European Studies*, 20:1 (1990), 6; he is quoting Carlyle from Charles Gavan Duffy, *Conversations with Carlyle* (New York: Scribner, 1892), 117.

138. Quoted in Bryan Cheyette, 'White Skin, Black Masks: Jews and Jewishness in the Writings of George Eliot and Frantz Fanon', in *Cultural Readings of Imperialism: Edward Said and the Gravity of History*, ed. Keith Ansell-Pearson, Benita Parry and Judith Squires (London: Lawrence and Wishart, 1997), 116.
139. Ibid., 109.
140. Levine, *Black Culture and Black Consciousness*, 306.
141. Philip V. Allingham, 'The Names of Dickens's American Originals in *Martin Chuzzlewit*', *Dickens Quarterly*, 7:3 (1990), 329.
142. Carlyle, *Latter-Day Pamphlets*, 34, 33.
143. Bryan Cheyette, *Constructions of 'the Jew' in English Literature and Society: Racial Representations, 1875–1945* (Cambridge: Cambridge University Press, 1993), 9.
144. Carlyle, *Latter-Day Pamphlets*, 14, 182.
145. Meckier, *An Innocent Abroad*, 120.
146. Carlyle, *Heroes and Hero-Worship*, 226–7.
147. Allingham, 'The Names of Dickens's American Originals in *Martin Chuzzlewit*', 334.
148. John Stuart Mill, *On Liberty*, in *On Liberty and Other Essays*, ed. John Gray (Oxford: Oxford University Press, 1998), 232–4: my emphasis.
149. Carlyle, *Heroes and Hero-Worship*, 202.
150. Allingham, 'The Names of Dickens's American Originals in *Martin Chuzzlewit*', 334.
151. Significantly, the 'headlines' in *Martin Chuzzlewit* – of which 'Pogrammania' is one – were added by Dickens in 1867.
152. Robbins, *The Servant's Hand*, 171.

Chapter 4

1. Thomas Carlyle, 'The Opera', in *Critical and Miscellaneous Essays, IV*, in *The Works of Thomas Carlyle*, 30 vols (London: Chapman and Hall, 1899), XXIX. 397–8. All further references to this essay in Chapter 4 appear parenthetically in the text, prefixed with the abbreviation 'O'.
2. Carlyle, *Past and Present*, 89–91. Significantly enough, in their discussion of the etymology of the word 'master', M K. Flint and E.J. Dobson find that the term 'master' has been used in the past both in the sense of 'minister' (that is, servant) and in connection with 'instruments of music' (M.K. Flint, and E.J. Dobson, 'Weak Masters', *Review of English Studies*, 10 (1959), 58–9).
3. Carlyle, *Chartism*, 147.
4. J.C. Stobart, *The Glory That Was Greece*, ed. R.J. Hopper (London: Book Club Associates, 1972), 83.
5. Richard Wagner, *Beethoven*, in *Richard Wagner's Prose Works*, 8 vols, trans. William Ashton Ellis (London: Kegan Paul, 1896), V. 121.
6. Thomas Carlyle, 'The Nibelungen Lied', in *Critical and Miscellaneous Essays, II*, in *The Works of Thomas Carlyle*, 30 vols (London: Chapman and Hall, 1899), XXVII. 261–2.
7. Carlyle, *Heroes and Hero-Worship*, 106, 78–9. All further references to this work in Chapter 4 appear parenthetically in the text, prefixed with the abbreviation '*HHW*'.

8. Hegel, *Phenomenology of Spirit*, 114–15.
9. Richard Wagner, *The Ring of the Nibelung*, trans. Andrew Porter (London: Faber Music, 1970), 185; Charles Osborne, *The Complete Operas of Wagner: A Critical Guide* (London: Grange Books, 1995), 234. Wagner had certainly come across Carlyle's writings. As Dieter Borchmeyer points out, Wagner wished he could 'have been in touch with people like Carlyle and Schopenhauer' (Dieter Borchmeyer, *Richard Wagner: Theory and Theatre*, trans. Stewart Spencer (Oxford: Clarendon Press, 1991), xv).
10. Wagner, *The Ring of the Nibelung*, 207.
11. Ibid., 231.
12. Ibid., 109–10.
13. Cited in Stobart, *The Glory That Was Greece*, 83.
14. Solon Michaelides, *The Ancient Music of Greece: An Encyclopaedia* (London: Faber and Faber, 1978), 345–6.
15. Raymond Furness, *Wagner and Literature* (Manchester: Manchester University Press, 1982), 7; Edward J. Dent, *Opera* (Harmondsworth: Penguin, 1949), 74, 83: my emphasis.
16. Richard Wagner, *Opera and Drama*, in *Richard Wagner's Prose Works*, 8 vols, trans. William Ashton Ellis (New York: Broude Brothers, 1966), II. 155, 191.
17. Albert Goldman, and Evert Sprinchorn, 'Introduction', in *Wagner on Music and Drama: A Selection from Richard Wagner's Prose Works*, ed. Albert Goldman and Evert Sprinchorn, trans. William Ashton Ellis (London: Victor Gollancz, 1977), 26; Richard Wagner, *Wagner on Music and Drama: A Selection from Richard Wagner's Prose Works*, ed. Albert Goldman and Evert Sprinchorn, trans. William Ashton Ellis (London: Victor Gollancz, 1977), 81.
18. Richard Wagner, *A Communication to My Friends*, in *Richard Wagner's Prose Works*, 8 vols, trans. William Ashton Ellis (London: Kegan Paul, 1892), I. 357–8.
19. Wagner, *Opera and Drama*, 191.
20. Carlyle, 'The Nibelungen Lied', 236.
21. Ibid., 270.
22. Quoted in Borchmeyer, *Wagner*, 254. The quotation is taken from an early prose draft by Wagner of the drama's scenario (1845).
23. Arthur Schopenhauer, *The World as Will and Idea*, ed. David Berman, trans. Jill Berman (London: J. M. Dent, 1995), 164, 169.
24. Wagner, *Beethoven*, 72.
25. George Eliot, *Daniel Deronda*, ed. Graham Handley (Oxford: Oxford University Press, 1998), 39–40. All further references to this novel in Chapter 4 appear parenthetically in the text, prefixed with the abbreviation '*DD*'.
26. Beryl Gray, *George Eliot and Music* (Basingstoke: Macmillan, 1989), 103.
27. Quoted in ibid., x.
28. Susan Peck MacDonald, '*Middlemarch*, *Daniel Deronda*, and Hegel's "Master–Slave Relationship"', in *Courage and Tools: The Florence Howe Award for Feminist Scholarship, 1974–1989*, ed. Joanne Glasgow and Angela Ingram (New York: Modern Language Association of America, 1990), 64: my emphasis.
29. Paul Gilroy, *The Black Atlantic: Modernity and Double Consciousness* (London: Verso, 1993), 88, 74.

30. Richard McGrady, *Music and Musicians in Nineteenth Century Cornwall: The World of Joseph Emidy – Slave, Violinist and Composer* (Exeter: University of Exeter Press, 1991), 149.
31. Goldman and Sprinchorn, 'Introduction', 16.
32. Wagner, *Wagner on Music and Drama*, 72–4.
33. Ibid., 64–5.
34. Wagner, *The Ring of the Nibelung*, 328.
35. Borchmeyer, *Richard Wagner*, 89.
36. Quoted in Paul Lawrence Rose, *Wagner: Race and Revolution* (London: Faber and Faber, 1992), 67.
37. Wagner, *Wagner on Music and Drama*, 65.
38. Thomas Carlyle, Letter to William Charles Macready, 25 January, 1842, in *The Collected Letters of Thomas and Jane Welsh Carlyle*, 24 vols – in progress, ed. Charles Richard Sanders et al. (Durham, NC: Duke University Press, 1970–95), XIV. 22.
39. Catherine Gallagher, 'George Eliot and Daniel Deronda: The Prostitute and the Jewish Question', in *Sex, Politics and Science in the Nineteenth-Century Novel*, ed. Ruth Bernard Yeazell (Baltimore: Johns Hopkins University Press, 1986), 47.
40. George Eliot, 'Liszt, Wagner, and Weimar', in *Essays of George Eliot*, ed. Thomas Pinney (London: Routledge and Kegan Paul, 1963), 97. As Alison Byerly notes, 'many critics have proposed Franz Liszt as a model for Klesmer' (Alison Byerly, '"The Language of the Soul": George Eliot and Music', *Nineteenth-Century Literature*, 44:1 (1989), 11).
41. Marx and Engels, *The Communist Manifesto*, 82.
42. Carlyle, 'The Nigger Question', 364, 368, 362.
43. Ibid., 359–60, 373.
44. James Silk Buckingham, *Autobiography*, 2 vols (London: Longman, 1855), I. 167–9.
45. McGrady, *Music and Musicians in Nineteenth Century Cornwall*, 39.
46. Buckingham, *Autobiography*, 170, 169. All Emidy's compositions have been lost.
47. Carlyle, 'The Nigger Question', 378–9.
48. Buckingham, *Autobiography*, 171–2.
49. Quoted in McGrady, *Music and Musicians in Nineteenth Century Cornwall*, 1.
50. Buckingham, *Autobiography*, 167.
51. Quoted in McGrady, *Music and Musicians in Nineteenth Century Cornwall*, 1.
52. William Weber, *Music and the Middle Class: The Social Structure of Concert Life in London, Paris and Vienna* (London: Croom Helm, 1975), 11, 115.
53. Carlyle, 'The Nigger Question', 364.
54. Ibid., 367, 364–5.
55. Foucault, *Discipline and Punish*, 201–2.
56. Ibid., 202: my emphasis.
57. Walter Beckett, *Liszt* (London: J M. Dent and Sons, 1963), 24.
58. Alison Winter, *Mesmerized: Powers of Mind in Victorian Britain* (Chicago and London: University of Chicago Press, 1998), 1.
59. Ibid., 2, 4.
60. Ibid., 309.

61. George Du Maurier, *Trilby*, ed. Elaine Showalter (Oxford: Oxford University Press, 1998), 170. All further references to this novel in Chapter 4 appear parenthetically in the text, prefixed with the abbreviation '*T*.
62. Winter, *Mesmerized*, 339.
63. Wagner, *Beethoven*, 75: my emphasis.
64. Michael Tanner, *Wagner* (London: HarperCollins, 1996), 18.
65. Hegel, *Phenomenology of Spirit*, 116–17.
66. Hegel, *Philosophy of Mind*, 104: my emphasis.
67. Winter, *Mesmerized*, 342.
68. Carlyle, 'The Nigger Question', 361: my emphasis.
69. Friedrich Nietzsche, *Nietzsche Contra Wagner*, in *The Portable Nietzsche*, ed. and trans. Walter Kaufmann (London: Chatto and Windus, 1971), 667.
70. Winter, *Mesmerized*, 310.
71. Carlyle, 'Shooting Niagara', 11, 10.
72. Daniel Pick, *Svengali's Web: The Alien Enchanter in Modern Culture* (New Haven and London: Yale University Press, 2000), 73, 131.
73. Carlyle, 'The Nigger Question', 363.
74. Nietzsche, *Nietzsche Contra Wagner*, 665–6.
75. Carlyle, *Latter-Day Pamphlets*, 10, 5.
76. Arnold Schoenberg, 'Opinion or Insight?', in *Style and Idea: Selected Writings of Arnold Schoenberg*, ed. Leonard Stein, trans. Leo Black (London: Faber and Faber, 1984), 258.
77. Charles Rosen, *Schoenberg* (Glasgow: Fontana, 1976), 70, 80. It should be noted that Schoenberg himself rejected any political connotations of Serialist techniques; see Arnold Schoenberg, 'Is it Fair?', in *Style and Idea: Selected Writings of Arnold Schoenberg*, ed. Leonard Stein, trans. Leo Black (London: Faber and Faber, 1984), 249–50.
78. Richard Wagner, 'Judaism in Music', in *Richard Wagner: Stories and Essays*, ed. Charles Osborne (London: Peter Owen, 1973), 28–32.
79. Ibid., 33.
80. George Eliot, 'The Modern Hep! Hep! Hep!', in *Impressions of Theophrastus Such* (Edinburgh and London: Blackwood, 1879), 283–4: my emphasis.
81. Wagner, 'Judaism in Music', 33, 27–9.
82. Goldman and Sprinchorn, 'Introduction', 11–12.
83. Quoted in Furness, *Wagner and Literature*, 95.
84. Rosen, *Schoenberg*, 38–9: my emphasis.
85. Quoted in Borchmeyer, *Richard Wagner*, 204.
86. *Encyclopaedia Judaica*, 16 vols (Jerusalem: Keter Publishing, 1971), XVI. 259–61.
87. Quoted in Deryck Cooke, *Gustav Mahler: An Introduction to his Music* (London: Faber and Faber, 1980), 7.
88. Borchmeyer, *Richard Wagner*, 204.
89. Wagner, *A Communication to My Friends*, 307: my emphasis.
90. Eliot, 'The Modern Hep! Hep! Hep!', 281–2.
91. Wagner, 'Judaism in Music', 27, 33.
92. Bryan Magee, *Aspects of Wagner* (St. Albans: Granada, 1972), 38–9.
93. Carlyle, 'The Nigger Question', 366.
94. Ibid., 364.
95. Ibid., 366.

96. Carlyle, *Latter-Day Pamphlets*, 33–4.
97. Ibid., 33.
98. Ibid., 24.
99. Carlyle, 'The Nigger Question', 368.
100. Borchmeyer, *Richard Wagner*, 194.
101. Cheyette, *Constructions of 'the Jew' in English Literature and Society*, 12.
102. Wagner, 'Judaism in Music', 25.
103. Quoted in Rose, *Wagner*, 62.
104. Eliot, 'The Modern Hep! Hep! Hep!', 282.
105. Carlyle, *Latter-Day Pamphlets*, 22.
106. Carlyle, 'The Nigger Question', 362.
107. Quoted in Cooke, *Gustav Mahler*, 53–4: my emphasis.

Chapter 5

1. Hegel, *Phenomenology of Spirit*, 112.
2. Fukayama, *The End of History and the Last Man*, 200–2.
3. James Anthony Froude, 'Party Politics', in *Short Studies on Great Subjects*, 4 vols (London: Longmans, Green and Co., 1891), III. 453.
4. Sartre, *Being and Nothingness*, 267.
5. Fukayama, *The End of History and the Last Man*, 203.
6. Carlyle, *Latter-Day Pamphlets*, 163. All further references to the *Latter-Day Pamphlets* in Chapter 5 appear parenthetically in the text, prefixed with the abbreviation '*LDP*'.
7. Carlyle, *Chartism*, 151.
8. Ibid..
9. Jacques Derrida, *Of Grammatology*, trans. Gayatri Chakravorty Spivak (Baltimore and London: Johns Hopkins University Press, 1976), 22.
10. Christine Persak, 'Rhetoric in Praise of Silence: The Ideology of Carlyle's Paradox', *Rhetoric Society Quarterly*, 21:1 (1991), 41.
11. Quoted in ibid., 42.
12. Carlyle, *Heroes and Hero-Worship*, 79.
13. Branwen Bailey Pratt, 'Carlyle and Dickens: Heroes and Hero-Worshippers', *Dickens Studies Annual*, 12 (1983), 238.
14. Charles Dickens, *Hard Times For These Times*, ed. David Craig (Harmondsworth: Penguin, 1985), 43. All further references to this novel in Chapter 5 appear parenthetically in the text, prefixed with the abbreviation '*HT*'.
15. Margaret Simpson, *The Companion to 'Hard Times'* (Mountfield: Helm Information, 1997), 177: my emphasis.
16. Charles Dickens, 'On Strike', in *Selected Journalism, 1850–1870*, ed. David Pascoe (Harmondsworth: Penguin, 1997), 462.
17. Carlyle, *Chartism*, 175.
18. Dickens, *Martin Chuzzlewit*, 269.
19. Winter, *Mesmerized*, 333–4.
20. Persak, 'Rhetoric in Praise of Silence', 38, 41.
21. Anthony Trollope, *The Warden* (London: The Trollope Society, 1995), 125.
22. Pratt, 'Carlyle and Dickens', 242.

23. John Schad, *The Reader in the Dickensian Mirrors: Some New Language* (New York: St. Martin's Press, 1992), 125.
24. Ibid., 1.
25. Ibid.
26. Carlyle, *Chartism*, 157, 160.
27. Borchmeyer, *Richard Wagner*, 193.
28. Cited in Jonathan Arac, *Commissioned Spirits: The Shaping of Social Motion in Dickens, Carlyle, Melville and Hawthorne* (New York: Columbia University Press, 1989), 142.
29. Carlyle, *Heroes and Hero-Worship*, 14.
30. Arac, *Commissioned Spirits*, 148.
31. Bentley, *A Century of Hero-Worship*, 63: my emphasis.
32. Carlyle, 'The Opera', 398.
33. Rosen, *Schoenberg*, 39, 36: my emphasis.
34. Dickens, 'On Strike', 462.
35. Tocqueville, *Democracy in America*, 199.
36. Carlyle, *Chartism*, 158.
37. Winter, *Mesmerized*, 319.
38. Ibid., 310.
39. Ibid., 318, 331–2.
40. Carlyle, *Chartism*, 158.
41. Ibid., 157–8.
42. Rosen, *Schoenberg*, 37–41.
43. Arnold Schoenberg, 'Opinion or Insight?', 258–9.
44. Rosen, *Schoenberg*, 41: my emphasis.
45. Schoenberg, 'Opinion or Insight?', 258.
46. Ibid., 260–1.
47. Rosen, *Schoenberg*, 15: my emphasis.
48. Arnold Schoenberg, 'Heart and Brain in Music', in *Style and Idea: Selected Writings of Arnold Schoenberg*, ed. Leonard Stein, trans. Leo Black (London: Faber and Faber, 1984), 69.
49. Persak, 'Rhetoric in Praise of Silence', 40.
50. Dickens, *Martin Chuzzlewit*, 531–2.
51. Clark, 'Dickens Through Blanchot', 22, 29: my emphasis.
52. Blanchot, *The Space of Literature*, 258.
53. Ibid., 258.
54. Marx, *The Eighteenth Brumaire of Louis Bonaparte*, 301.
55. Sigmund Freud, 'The Uncanny', in *Art and Literature: 'Jensen's "Gradiva,"' 'Leonardo da Vinci', and Other Works*, in *The Penguin Freud Library*, 15 vols, ed. Albert Dickson and Angela Richards, trans. James Strachey (Harmondsworth: Penguin, 1985), XIV. 369, 347.
56. Ibid., 363.
57. Carlyle, *Past and Present*, 21: my emphasis.
58. Carlyle, *Chartism*, 157.
59. Carlyle, *Heroes and Hero-Worship*, 202–3.
60. Carlyle, *Chartism*, 156, 167.
61. David Craig, 'Introduction', in Charles Dickens, *Hard Times For These Times*, ed. David Craig (Harmondsworth: Penguin, 1985), 21.
62. Carlyle, *Chartism*, 158, 142.

63. Marx and Engels, *The Communist Manifesto*, 78. The connection between
    atonality and communism has been pointed out by various critics; as Ben
    Watson notes, 'for proletarian modernists, the end of tonality was not
    tragedy but joy' (Ben Watson, 'Backwoods Musicology: Roger Scruton's
    Aesthetics of Music', *Radical Philosophy*, 99 (2000), 5).
64. As Walter Houghton points out, for many Victorians, 'democracy ... carried
    connotations much like those of communism today' (Walter E. Houghton,
    The Victorian Frame of Mind, 1830–1870 (New Haven and London: Yale
    University Press, 1957), 55.
65. Marx and Engels, *The Communist Manifesto*, 89.
66. Ibid., 93–4.
67. Gilmour, *The Victorian Period*, 188.
68. Carlyle, 'Signs of the Times', 61–3.
69. Marx and Engels, *The Communist Manifesto*, 92.
70. Carlyle, *Chartism*, 146: my emphasis.
71. Carlyle, *Heroes and Hero-Worship*, 202.
72. Elizabeth Gaskell, *Mary Barton*, ed. Alan Shelston (London: J.M. Dent,
    1996), 170–1. Gaskell, of course, confounds Frankenstein with the monster
    he creates.
73. Marx and Engels, *The Communist Manifesto*, 121, 87.
74. Gilmour, *The Victorian Period*, 186–8.
75. Peter Scheckner notes that Jones's 'views made him popular for a time with
    Marx and Engels' (Ernest Jones, 'We Are Silent', and Peter Scheckner,
    'Notes', in *An Anthology of Chartist Poetry: Poetry of the British Working Class,
    1830s–1850s*, ed. Peter Scheckner (London and Toronto: Associated
    University Presses, 1989), 199, 335).

Afterword

1. Charles Dickens, *Martin Chuzzlewit*, 284.
2. Thomas, *The Slave Trade*, 492.
3. Hegel, *Phenomenology of Spirit*, 112.
4. Hegel, *Elements of the Philosophy of Right*, 87.
5. Norman, *Hegel's Phenomenology*, 51.
6. Carlyle, *Chartism*, 160.
7. Hegel, *Elements of the Philosophy of Right*, 87.
8. Slavery was not abolished in Cuba until 1886.
9. Carlyle, 'The Nigger Question', 364, 356, 364.
10. Brantlinger, *Rule of Darkness*, 176; Nancy Stepan quoted in ibid., 175.
11. Robert C. Young, *Colonial Desire: Hybridity in Theory, Culture and Race*
    (London: Routledge, 1995), 92.
12. Chaudhuri, 'Dickens and the Question of Slavery', 8. For an example of
    Dickens' response to the Indian Mutiny, see his letter to Angela Burdett
    Coutts, 4 October 1857, in *The Letters of Charles Dickens*, 12 vols, ed.
    Madeline House, Graham Storey and Kathleen Tillotson (Oxford:
    Clarendon Press, 1995), VIII. 459.
13. Dickens, *Martin Chuzzlewit*, 271.

14. Charles Dickens, Letter to W.W.F. De Cerjat, 30 November 1865, in *The Letters of Charles Dickens*, 12 vols, ed. Madeline House, Graham Storey and Kathleen Tillotson (Oxford: Clarendon Press, 1999), XI. 11–16.
15. Hegel, *Phenomenology of Spirit*, 117.
16. Eliot, *Daniel Deronda*, 279.
17. See, for instance, *The Tempest*, I.ii. where Prospero declares to Miranda, 'We'll visit Caliban, my *slave*' (William Shakespeare, *The Tempest*, ed. Stephen Orgel (Oxford: Oxford University Press, 1998), 118: my emphasis).
18. Eliot, *Daniel Deronda*, 279.
19. Brantlinger, *Rule of Darkness*, 179.
20. Terry Eagleton, 'Power and Knowledge in *The Lifted Veil*', *Literature and History*, 9:1 (1983), 54. I am indebted to Dr Andrew Dix for this reference.
21. Charles Dickens, 'The Niger Expedition', in *Miscellaneous Papers*, 2 vols (Geneva: Edito-Service, 1970), I. 133.
22. Susan Meyer, *Imperialism at Home: Race and Victorian Women's Fiction* (Ithaca: Cornell University Press, 1996), 160.
23. Ibid., 127.
24. Carlyle, 'Shooting Niagara', 12.
25. Carlyle, 'The Nigger Question', 362–3.
26. Frantz Fanon, *The Wretched of the Earth*, trans. Constance Farrington (Harmondsworth: Penguin, 1967), 27–8.

Bibliography

Adorno, Theodor W., *In Search of Wagner*, trans. Rodney Livingstone (London: NLB, 1981)

Adrian, Arthur A., 'Dickens on American Slavery: A Carlylean Slant', *PMLA*, 67:4 (1952), 315–29

Agacinski, Sylviane, 'We are not Sublime: Love and Sacrifice, Abraham and Ourselves', in *Kierkegaard: A Critical Reader*, ed. Jonathan Rée and Jane Chamberlain (Oxford: Blackwell, 1997), 129–50

Allingham, Philip V., 'The Names of Dickens's American Originals in *Martin Chuzzlewit*', *Dickens Quarterly*, 7:3 (1990), 329–37

Arac, Jonathan, *Commissioned Spirits: The Shaping of Social Motion in Dickens, Carlyle, Melville and Hawthorne* (New York: Columbia University Press, 1989)

Beckett, Walter, *Liszt* (London: J. M. Dent and Sons, 1963)

Bentley, Eric, *A Century of Hero-Worship* (Boston: Beacon Hill, 1957)

Bernstein, Basil, 'Social Class, Language, and Socialization', in *Language and Social Context*, ed. Pier Paolo Giglioli (Harmondsworth: Penguin, 1972), 157–78

Blanchot, Maurice, *The Space of Literature*, trans. Ann Smock (Lincoln and London: University of Nebraska Press, 1982)

Blassingame, John W., *The Slave Community: Plantation Life in the Antebellum South* (New York and Oxford: Oxford University Press, 1979)

Borchmeyer, Dieter, *Richard Wagner: Theory and Theatre*, trans. Stewart Spencer (Oxford: Clarendon Press, 1991)

Brantlinger, Patrick, *Rule of Darkness: British Literature and Imperialism, 1830–1914* (Ithaca and London: Cornell University Press, 1988)

Buckingham, James Silk, *Autobiography*, 2 vols (London: Longman, 1855), I

Bull, Malcolm, 'Mastery and Slavery in *The Lifted Veil*', *Essays in Criticism*, 48:3 (1998), 244–61

Butler, Judith, *Subjects of Desire: Hegelian Reflections in Twentieth-Century France* (New York: Columbia University Press, 1999)

Byerly, Alison, '"The Language of the Soul": George Eliot and Music', *Nineteenth-Century Literature*, 44:1 (1989), 1–17

Carlyle, Thomas, 'Characteristics', in *Critical and Miscellaneous Essays, III*, in *The Works of Thomas Carlyle*, 30 vols (London: Chapman and Hall, 1899), XXVIII. 1–43

Carlyle, Thomas, *Chartism*, 'The Nigger Question', 'The Opera', in *Critical and Miscellaneous Essays, IV*, in *The Works of Thomas Carlyle*, 30 vols (London: Chapman and Hall, 1899), XXIX. 118–204, 348–83, 397–403

Carlyle, Thomas, 'Last Words of Thomas Carlyle: On Trades-Unions, Promoterism and the Signs of the Times', in D. J. Trela, 'Thomas Carlyle "On Trades-Unions, Promoterism and the Signs of the Times": An Unknown and Nearly Unpublished Manuscript', *Victorian Institute Journal*, 25 (1997), 230–50

Carlyle, Thomas, *Latter-Day Pamphlets*, in *The Works of Thomas Carlyle*, 30 vols (London: Chapman and Hall, 1898), XX

Carlyle, Thomas, *On Heroes, Hero-Worship and the Heroic in History*, in *The Works of Thomas Carlyle*, 30 vols (London: Chapman and Hall, 1904), V

Carlyle, Thomas, *Past and Present*, in *The Works of Thomas Carlyle*, 30 vols (London: Chapman and Hall, 1899), X

Carlyle, Thomas, *Sartor Resartus*, in *The Works of Thomas Carlyle*, 30 vols (London: Chapman and Hall, 1899), I

Carlyle, Thomas, 'Shooting Niagara: And After?', in *Critical and Miscellaneous Essays, V*, in *The Works of Thomas Carlyle*, 30 vols (London: Chapman and Hall, 1899), XXX. 1–48

Carlyle, Thomas, 'Signs of the Times', and 'The Nibelungen Lied', in *Critical and Miscellaneous Essays, II*, in *The Works of Thomas Carlyle*, 30 vols (London: Chapman and Hall, 1899), XXVII. 56–82, 216–73

Carlyle, Thomas, *The Collected Letters of Thomas and Jane Welsh Carlyle*, 24 vols – in progress, ed. Charles Richard Sanders, Clyde de L. Ryals, Kenneth J. Fielding et al. (Durham, NC: Duke University Press, 1970–95), XIV

Chaudhuri, Brahma, 'Dickens and the Question of Slavery', *Dickens Quarterly*, 6:1 (1989), 3–10

Chesterton, G. K., *Criticisms and Appreciations of the Works of Charles Dickens* (London: J. M. Dent and Sons, 1992)

Cheyette, Bryan, *Constructions of 'the Jew' in English Literature and Society: Racial Representations, 1875–1945* (Cambridge: Cambridge University Press, 1993)

Cheyette, Bryan, 'White Skin, Black Masks: Jews and Jewishness in the Writings of George Eliot and Frantz Fanon', in *Cultural Readings of Imperialism: Edward Said and the Gravity of History*, ed. Keith Ansell-Pearson, Benita Parry and Judith Squires (London: Lawrence and Wishart, 1997), 106–26

Cixous, Hélène, 'Sorties: Out and Out: Attacks/Ways Out/Forays', trans. Betsy Wing, in *The Hélène Cixous Reader*, ed. Susan Sellers (London: Routledge, 1994), 35–46

Clark, Timothy, 'Dickens Through Blanchot: The Nightmare Fascination of a World Without Interiority', in *Dickens Refigured: Bodies, Desires and Other Histories*, ed. John Schad (Manchester: Manchester University Press, 1996), 22–38

Collins, Wilkie, *My Miscellanies* (Farnborough: Gregg International, 1971)

Collins, Wilkie, *The Woman in White*, ed. John Sutherland (Oxford: Oxford University Press, 1996)

Cooke, Deryck, *Gustav Mahler: An Introduction to his Music* (London: Faber and Faber, 1988)

Cotsell, Michael, *The Companion to 'Our Mutual Friend'* (London: Allen and Unwin, 1986)

Craig, David, 'Introduction', in Charles Dickens, *Hard Times For These Times*, ed. David Craig (Harmondsworth: Penguin, 1985), 11–36

Darwin, Charles, *The Origin of Species By Means of Natural Selection*, ed. J.W. Burrow (Harmondsworth: Penguin, 1968)

Dent, Edward J., *Opera* (Harmondsworth: Penguin, 1949)

Derrida, Jacques, *Glas*, trans. John P. Leavey Jr. and Richard Rand (Lincoln and London: University of Nebraska Press, 1986)

Derrida, Jacques, *Of Grammatology*, trans. Gayatri Chakravorty Spivak (Baltimore and London: Johns Hopkins University Press, 1976)

Dickens, Charles, *American Notes for General Circulation* and *Pictures From Italy*, ed. F. S. Schwarzbach and Leonée Ormond (London: J. M. Dent, 1997)

Dickens, Charles, *Dickens on America and the Americans*, ed. Michael Slater (Hassocks: Harvester Press, 1979)

Dickens, Charles, *Dombey and Son*, ed. Peter Fairclough (Harmondsworth: Penguin, 1985)

Dickens, Charles, *Hard Times For These Times*, ed. David Craig (Harmondsworth: Penguin, 1985)

Dickens, Charles, *Martin Chuzzlewit*, ed. Margaret Cardwell (Oxford: Clarendon Press, 1982)

Dickens, Charles and Henry Morley, 'North American Slavery', in *The Uncollected Writings of Charles Dickens: Household Words 1850–1859*, 2 vols, ed. Harry Stone (London: Allen Lane The Penguin Press, 1969), II. 433–42

Dickens, Charles, 'Old and New Servants', in *All the Year Round: A Weekly Journal*, ed. Charles Dickens (London: Chapman and Hall, 1867), XVIII. 79–83

Dickens, Charles, 'On Strike', in *Selected Journalism, 1850–1870*, ed. David Pascoe (Harmondsworth: Penguin, 1997), 359–63

Dickens, Charles, *Our Mutual Friend*, ed. Stephen Gill (Harmondsworth: Penguin, 1985)

Dickens, Charles, *The Letters of Charles Dickens*, 12 vols, ed. Madeline House, Graham Storey and Kathleen Tillotson (Oxford: Clarendon Press, 1974–2002), III, VIII, XI

Dickens, Charles, 'The Niger Expedition', in *Miscellaneous Papers*, 2 vols (Geneva: Edito-Service, 1970), I. 133

Douglass, Frederick, *Narrative of the Life of Frederick Douglass, an American Slave, Written By Himself*, ed. William L. Andrews and William S. McFeely (New York and London: W. W. Norton, 1997)

Duffy, Charles Gavan, *Conversations with Carlyle* (New York: Scribner, 1892)

Du Maurier, George, *Trilby*, ed. Elaine Showalter (Oxford: Oxford University Press, 1998)

Eagleton, Terry, 'Power and Knowledge in *The Lifted Veil*', *Literature and History*, 9:1 (1983), 52–61

Eliot, George, *Daniel Deronda*, ed. Graham Handley (Oxford: Oxford University Press, 1998)

Eliot, George, 'Liszt, Wagner, and Weimar', 'The Future of German Philosophy', 'The Natural History of German Life', 'A Word for the Germans', 'Servants' Logic', 'The Influence of Rationalism', in *Essays of George Eliot*, ed. Thomas Pinney (London: Routledge and Kegan Paul, 1963), 96–122, 148–53, 266–99, 386–90, 391–6, 397–414

Eliot, George, 'The Modern Hep! Hep! Hep!', in *Impressions of Theophrastus Such* (Edinburgh and London: Blackwood, 1879), 257–93

Elkins, Stanley M., *Slavery: A Problem in American Institutional and Intellectual Life* (Chicago: University of Chicago Press, 1968)

Encyclopaedia Judaica, 16 vols (Jerusalem: Keter Publishing, 1971), XVI

Fanon, Frantz, *The Wretched of the Earth*, trans. Constance Farrington (Harmondsworth: Penguin, 1967)

Feltes, N.N., '"The Greatest Plague of Life": Dickens, Masters and Servants', *Literature and History*, 8 (1978), 197–213

Findlay, J. N., 'Foreword', in Georg Wilhelm Friedrich Hegel, *Phenomenology of Spirit*, trans. A. V. Miller (Oxford: Oxford University Press, 1977), v–xxx

Flint, M.K. and E. J. Dobson, 'Weak Masters', *Review of English Studies*, 10 (1959), 58–60

Foucault, Michel, *Discipline and Punish: The Birth of the Prison*, trans. Alan Sheridan (Harmondsworth: Penguin, 1991)

Franklin, H. Bruce, 'Animal Farm Unbound', in *Modern Critical Interpretations: Frederick Douglass's 'Narrative of the Life of Frederick Douglass'*, ed. Harold Bloom (New York: Chelsea House, 1988), 29–43

Franklin, John Hope and Alfred A. Moss Jr., *From Slavery to Freedom: A History of Negro Americans* (New York: McGraw–Hill, 1988)

Freud, Sigmund, 'The Uncanny', in *Art and Literature: 'Jensen's "Gradiva"', 'Leonardo da Vinci', and Other Works*, in *The Penguin Freud Library*, 15 vols, ed. Albert Dickson and Angela Richards, trans. James Strachey (Harmondsworth: Penguin, 1985), XIV. 336–76

Froude, James Anthony, 'Party Politics', in *Short Studies on Great Subjects*, 4 vols (London: Longmans, Green and Co., 1891), III. 439–76

Fukayama, Francis, *The End of History and the Last Man* (Harmondsworth: Penguin, 1992)

Furness, Raymond, *Wagner and Literature* (Manchester: Manchester University Press, 1982)

Gallagher, Catherine, 'George Eliot and Daniel Deronda: The Prostitute and the Jewish Question', in *Sex, Politics and Science in the Nineteenth-Century Novel*, ed. Ruth Bernard Yeazell (Baltimore: Johns Hopkins University Press, 1986), 39–62

Garrison, William Lloyd, 'Preface', in Frederick Douglass, *Narrative of the Life of Frederick Douglass, An American Slave, Written by Himself*, ed. William L. Andrews and William S. McFeely (New York and London: W. W. Norton, 1997), 3–9

Gaskell, Elizabeth, *Mary Barton*, ed. Alan Shelston (London: J. M. Dent, 1996)

Gates Jr., Henry-Louis, 'Binary Oppositions in Chapter One of *Narrative of the Life of Frederick Douglass an America Slave Written by Himself'*, in *Afro-American Literature: The Reconstruction of Instruction*, ed. Dexter Fisher and Robert B. Stepto (New York: The Modern Language Association of America, 1979), 212–32

Genovese, Eugene D., *The Political Economy of Slavery: Studies in the Economy and Society of the Slave South* (London: MacGibbon and Kee, 1966)

Genovese, Eugene D., *The World the Slaveholders Made: Two Essays in Interpretation* (London: Allen Lane The Penguin Press, 1970)

Gibson, William and Bruce Sterling, *The Difference Engine* (New York: Bantam, 1991)

Gilchrist, Marianne McLeod, 'The Shaw Family of Staten Island: Elizabeth Gaskell's American Friends', *The Gaskell Society Journal*, 9 (1995), 1–12

Gilmour, Robin, *The Victorian Period: The Intellectual and Cultural Context of English Literature, 1830–1890* (Harlow: Longman, 1993)

Gilroy, Paul, *The Black Atlantic: Modernity and Double Consciousness* (London: Verso, 1993)

Goldman, Albert, and Evert Sprinchorn, 'Introduction', in *Wagner on Music and Drama: A Selection from Richard Wagner's Prose Works*, ed. Albert Goldman and Evert Sprinchorn, trans. William Ashton Ellis (London: Victor Gollancz, 1977), 11–33

Gray, Beryl, *George Eliot and Music* (Basingstoke: Macmillan, 1989)

Harris, Wendell V., *The Omnipresent Debate: Empiricism and Transcendentalism in Nineteenth-Century English Prose* (DeKalb: Northern Illinois University, 1981)

Hedley, Arthur, *Chopin*, ed. Maurice J. E. Brown (London: J. M. Dent and Sons, 1974)

Hegel, Georg Wilhelm Friedrich, *Elements of the Philosophy of Right*, ed. Allen W. Wood, trans. H. B. Nisbet (Cambridge: Cambridge University Press, 1991)

Hegel, Georg Wilhelm Friedrich, *Hegel: The Letters*, ed. and trans. C. Butler and C. Seiler (Indianapolis: University of Indiana Press, 1984)

Hegel, Georg Wilhelm Friedrich, *Lectures on the History of Philosophy*, trans. E.S. Haldane and Frances H. Simson, 3 vols (London: Routledge and Kegan Paul, 1968), I

Hegel, Georg Wilhelm Friedrich, *Phenomenology of Spirit*, trans. A. V. Miller (Oxford: Oxford University Press, 1977)

Hegel, Georg Wilhelm Friedrich, *Phenomenology of Spirit: A Selection*, ed. and trans. Howard P. Kainz (Pennsylvania: Pennsylvania State University Press, 1994)

Hegel, Georg Wilhelm Friedrich, *Philosophy of Mind*, trans. William Wallace and A.V. Miller (Oxford: Clarendon Press, 1971)

Hegel, Georg Wilhelm Friedrich, *System of Ethical Life* and *First Philosophy of Spirit*, ed. and trans. H.S. Harris and T.M. Knox (Albany: University of New York Press, 1979)

Hegel, Georg Wilhelm Friedrich, *The Philosophical Propaedeutic*, ed. Michael George and Andrew Vincent, trans. A.V. Miller (Oxford: Basil Blackwell, 1986)

Hegel, Georg Wilhelm Friedrich, *The Philosophy of History*, trans. J. Sibree (New York: Dover, 1956)

Heller, Tamar, *Dead Secrets: Wilkie Collins and the Female Gothic* (New Haven and London: Yale University Press, 1992)

Hendershot, Cyndy, 'A Sensation Novel's Appropriation of the Terror-Gothic: Wilkie Collins' The Woman in White', *Clues*, 13 (1992), 127–33

Horn, Pamela, *The Rise and Fall of the Victorian Servant* (Stroud: Sutton, 1995)

Houghton, Walter E., *The Victorian Frame of Mind, 1830–1870* (New Haven and London: Yale University Press, 1957)

Jacobs, Robert L., 'The Role of Music in George Eliot's Novels', *Music Review*, 45 (1984), 277–82

Jones, Ernest, 'We Are Silent', in *An Anthology of Chartist Poetry: Poetry of the British Working Class, 1830s–1850s*, ed. Peter Scheckner (London and Toronto: Associated University Presses, 1989), 199–201

Kant, Immanuel, *Critique of Pure Reason*, ed. Vasilis Politis, trans. J.M.D. Meiklejohn (London: J. M. Dent, 1993)

Kant, Immanuel, *Religion Within the Limits of Reason Alone*, trans. Theodore M. Greene and Hoyt H. Hudson (New York: Harper and Row, 1960)

Kojève, Alexandre, *Introduction to the Reading of Hegel: Lectures on the 'Phenomenology of Spirit'*, ed. Raymond Queneau and Alan Bloom, trans. James H. Nichols (New York and London: Basic Books, 1969)

Lacan, Jacques, *Écrits: A Selection*, trans. Alan Sheridan (London: Tavistock, 1977)

Le Quesne, A.L., *Carlyle* (Oxford: Oxford University Press, 1982)

Levenson, Shirley Frank, 'The Use of Music in Daniel Deronda', *Nineteenth-Century Fiction*, 24 (1969), 317–34

Levine, Lawrence W., *Black Culture and Black Consciousness: Afro-American Folk Thought From Slavery to Freedom* (New York: Oxford University Press, 1977)

Lewes, George Henry, *The Biographical History of Philosophy: From Its Origin in Greece Down to the Present Day* (London: John W. Parker and Son, 1857)

Lincoln, Abraham, 'Address to the Young Men's Lyceum of Springfield, Illinois: The Perpetuation of Our Political Institutions', 'Final Emancipation

Proclamation', in *The Portable Abraham Lincoln*, ed. Andrew Delbanco (Harmondsworth: Penguin, 1993), 17–26, 271–3

Lindsay, A. D., 'Introduction', in Immanuel Kant, *Critique of Pure Reason*, trans. J.M.D. Meiklejohn (London: J. M. Dent and Sons, 1934), vii–xx

Lodge, Oliver, 'Science in the "Sixties"', in *The Eighteen-Sixties: Essays by Fellows of the Royal Society of Literature*, ed. John Drinkwater (Cambridge: Cambridge University Press, 1932), 245–69

MacDonald, Susan Peck, '*Middlemarch, Daniel Deronda*, and Hegel's Master–Slave Relationship', in *Courage and Tools: The Florence Howe Award for Feminist Scholarship, 1974–1989*, ed. Joanne Glasgow and Angela Ingram (New York: Modern Language Association of America, 1990), 52–69

MacKethan, Lucinda H., 'Metaphors of Mastery in the Slave Narratives', in *The Art of Slave Narrative: Original Essays in Criticism and Theory*, ed. John Sekora and Darwin T. Turner (Illinois: Western Illinois University Press, 1982), 55–69

Magee, Bryan, *Aspects of Wagner* (St. Albans: Granada, 1972)

Mahler, Gustav, *Symphony No.1 in D Major* (London: Ernst Eulenberg, 1964)

Marshall, Dorothy, *The English Domestic Servant in History* (London: The Historical Association, 1949)

Marx, Karl *Capital: A Critique of Political Economy*, trans. Ben Fowkes (Harmondsworth: Penguin, 1976), I

Marx, Karl, *The Eighteenth Brumaire of Louis Bonaparte*, in *Selected Writings*, ed. David McLellan (Oxford: Oxford University Press, 1977), 300–25

Marx, Karl and Friedrich Engels, *The Communist Manifesto*, ed. A.J.P. Taylor (Harmondsworth: Penguin, 1967, 1985)

McBride, Theresa, *The Domestic Revolution: The Modernisation of Household Service in England and France, 1820–1920* (London: Croom Helm, 1976)

McGrady, Richard, *Music and Musicians in Nineteenth Century Cornwall: The World of Joseph Emidy – Slave, Violinist and Composer* (Exeter: University of Exeter Press, 1991)

Meckier, Jerome, *Innocent Abroad: Charles Dickens's American Engagements* (Lexington: University Press of Kentucky, 1990)

Meyer, Susan, *Imperialism at Home: Race and Victorian Women's Fiction* (Ithaca: Cornell University Press, 1996)

Michaelides, Solon, *The Ancient Music of Greece: An Encyclopaedia* (London: Faber and Faber, 1978)

Mill, John Stuart, *On Liberty*, and *Considerations on Representative Government*, in *On Liberty and Other Essays*, ed. John Gray (Oxford: Oxford University Press, 1998), 1–128, 203–467

Miller, D. A., *The Novel and the Police* (Berkeley: University of California Press, 1988)

Mills, C. Wright, *The Marxists* (Harmondsworth: Penguin, 1963)

Musgrave, Marian E., 'Patterns of Violence and Non-Violence in Pro-Slavery and Anti-Slavery Fiction', *CLA*, 16 (1973), 426–37

Naman, Anne Aresty, *The Jew in the Victorian Novel: Some Relationships Between Prejudice and Art* (New York: AMS Press, 1980)

Nietzsche, Friedrich, *Nietzsche Contra Wagner*, in *The Portable Nietzsche*, ed. and trans. Walter Kaufmann (London: Chatto and Windus, 1971)

Nietzsche, Friedrich, *On the Genealogy of Morals: A Polemic*, trans. Douglas Smith (Oxford: Oxford University Press, 1998)

Norman, Richard, *Hegel's Phenomenology: A Philosophical Introduction* (New Jersey: Humanities Press, 1976)

Osborne, Charles, *The Complete Operas of Wagner: A Critical Guide* (London: Grange Books, 1995)

Parish, Peter J., *Slavery: The Many Faces of a Southern Institution* (Durham: British Association for American Studies, 1979)

Park, T. Peter, 'Thomas Carlyle and the Jews', *Journal of European Studies*, 20:1 (1990), 1–21

Patton, Cynthia Ellen, '"For Moments a God Man": Thomas Carlyle and Musical Morality', *Carlyle Studies Annual*, 17 (1997), 51–9

Persak, Christine, 'Rhetoric in Praise of Silence: The Ideology of Carlyle's Paradox', *Rhetoric Society Quarterly*, 21:1 (1991), 38–52

Pick, Daniel, *Svengali's Web: The Alien Enchanter in Modern Culture* (New Haven and London: Yale University Press, 2000)

Plant, Raymond, *Hegel*, (London: George Allen and Unwin, 1972)

Plato, *Republic*, trans. Robin Waterfield (Oxford: Oxford University Press, 1998)

Pratt, Branwen Bailey, 'Carlyle and Dickens: Heroes and Hero-Worshippers', *Dickens Studies Annual*, 12 (1983), 233–46

Reichen, Charles-Albert, *A History of Chemistry* (London: Leisure Arts, 1964)

Robbins, Bruce, *The Servant's Hand: English Fiction From Below* (Durham, NC and London: Duke University Press, 1993)

Roper, Jon, *Democracy and Its Critics: Anglo-American Democratic Thought in the Nineteenth Century* (London: Unwin Hyman, 1989)

Rose, Paul Lawrence, *Wagner: Race and Revolution* (London: Faber and Faber, 1992)

Rosen, Charles, *Schoenberg* (Glasgow: Fontana, 1976)

Sachar, Howard M., *A History of the Jews in America* (New York: Alfred A. Knopf, 1992)

Sartre, Jean-Paul, *Being and Nothingness: An Essay on Phenomenological Ontology*, trans. Hazel E. Barnes (London: Methuen, 1957)

Saussure, Ferdinand de, *Course in General Linguistics*, ed. Charles Bally and Albert Sechehaye, trans. Roy Harris (London: Duckworth, 1983)

Schad, John, *The Reader in the Dickensian Mirrors: Some New Language* (New York: St. Martin's Press, 1992)

Schad, John, *Victorians in Theory: From Derrida to Browning* (Manchester: Manchester University Press, 1999)

Scheckner, Peter, 'Notes', in *An Anthology of Chartist Poetry: Poetry of the British Working Class, 1830s–1850s*, ed. Peter Scheckner (London and Toronto: Associated University Presses, 1989), 326–45

Schoenberg, Arnold, 'Heart and Brain in Music', 'Is it Fair?', 'Opinion or Insight?', in *Style and Idea: Selected Writings of Arnold Schoenberg*, ed. Leonard Stein, trans. Leo Black (London: Faber and Faber, 1984), 53–76, 249–50, 258–64

Schopenhauer, Arthur, *The World as Will and Idea*, ed. David Berman, trans. Jill Berman (London: J. M. Dent, 1995)

Schwarzbach, F. S., 'Appendix A: Historical Background', in Charles Dickens, *American Notes for General Circulation* and *Pictures From Italy*, ed. F.S. Schwarzbach and Leonée Ormond (London: J.M. Dent, 1997), 271–3

Shakespeare, William, *The Tempest*, ed. Stephen Orgel (Oxford: Oxford University Press, 1998)

Shapiro, Ian, 'Three Fallacies Concerning Majorities, Minorities, and Democratic Politics', in *Majorities and Minorities*, ed. John W. Chapman and Alan Wertheimer (New York and London: New York University Press, 1990), 79–125

Shklar, Judith N., *Freedom and Independence: A Study of the Political Ideas of Hegel's 'Phenomenology of Mind'* (Cambridge: Cambridge University Press, 1976)

Shuttleworth, Sally, *George Eliot and Nineteenth-Century Science: The Make-Believe of a Beginning* (Cambridge: Cambridge University Press, 1984)

Simpson, Margaret, *The Companion to 'Hard Times'* (Mountfield: Helm Information, 1997)

Singer, Peter, *Hegel* (Oxford: Oxford University Press, 1983)

Stobart, J.C., *The Glory That Was Greece*, ed. R.J. Hopper (London: Book Club Associates, 1972)

Stowe, Harriet Beecher, *Uncle Tom's Cabin; or, Life Among the Lowly*, ed. Ann Douglas (Harmondsworth: Penguin, 1986)

Sussman, Herbert, 'Cyberpunk Meets Charles Babbage: The Difference Engine as Alternative Victorian History', *Victorian Studies*, 38:1 (1995), 1–23

Tanner, Michael, *Wagner* (London: HarperCollins, 1996)

Taylor, Jenny Bourne, *In the Secret Theatre of Home: Wilkie Collins, Sensation Narrative and Nineteenth-Century Psychology* (London: Routledge, 1988)

Thomas, Deborah A., 'Dickens and Indigestion: The Deadly Dinners of the Rich', *Dickens Studies Newsletter*, 14:1 (1983), 7–12

Thomas, Hugh, *The Slave Trade: The History of the Atlantic Slave Trade, 1440–1870* (London: Picador, 1997)

Thomson, Thomas, *The History of Chemistry* (New York: Arno Press, 1975)

Tillotson, Kathleen, 'Introduction: The Lighter Reading of the Eighteen-Sixties', in Wilkie Collins, *The Woman in White*, ed. Anthea Trodd (Boston: Houghton Mifflin, 1969), ix–xxvi

Tocqueville, Alexis de, *Democracy in America*, ed. Henry Steele Commager, trans. Henry Reeve (London: Oxford University Press, 1946)

Tolstoy, Leo, *War and Peace*, trans. Rosemary Edmonds (Harmondsworth: Penguin, 1982)

Trollope, Anthony, *The Warden* (London: The Trollope Society, 1995)

Turner, E.S., *What the Butler Saw: Two Hundred and Fifty Years of the Servant Problem* (London: Michael Joseph, 1962)

Wagner, Richard, *A Communication to My Friends*, in *Richard Wagner's Prose Works*, 8 vols, trans. William Ashton Ellis (London: Kegan Paul, 1892), I. 267–392

Wagner, Richard, *Beethoven*, in *Richard Wagner's Prose Works*, 8 vols, trans. William Ashton Ellis (London: Kegan Paul, 1896), V. 57–126

Wagner, Richard, 'Judaism in Music', in *Richard Wagner: Stories and Essays*, ed. Charles Osborne (London: Peter Owen, 1973), 23–39

Wagner, Richard, *Opera and Drama*, in *Richard Wagner's Prose Works*, 8 vols, trans. William Ashton Ellis (New York: Broude Brothers, 1966), II

Wagner, Richard, *The Ring of the Nibelung*, trans. Andrew Porter (London: Faber Music, 1970)

Wagner, Richard, *Wagner on Music and Drama: A Selection from Richard Wagner's Prose Works*, ed. Albert Goldman and Evert Sprinchorn, trans. William Ashton Ellis (London: Victor Gollancz, 1977)

Walvin, James, *Questioning Slavery* (London: Routledge, 1996)

Watson, Ben, 'Backwoods Musicology: Roger Scruton's Aesthetics of Music', *Radical Philosophy*, 99 (2000), 2–5

Webb, Beatrice, *My Apprenticeship* (Cambridge: Cambridge University Press, 1979)

Weber, William, *Music and the Middle Class: The Social Structure of Concert Life in London, Paris and Vienna* (London: Croom Helm, 1975)

Weld, Theodore D., *American Slavery As It Is: Testimony of a Thousand Witnesses* (New York: Arno Press, 1968)

Wertheimer, Alan, 'Introduction', in *Majorities and Minorities*, ed. John W. Chapman and Alan Wertheimer (New York and London: New York University Press, 1990), 1–8

Winter, Alison, *Mesmerized: Powers of Mind in Victorian Britain* (Chicago and London: University of Chicago Press, 1998)

Young, Robert C., *Colonial Desire: Hybridity in Theory, Culture and Race* (London: Routledge, 1995)

Ziolowski, Thad, 'Antitheses: The Dialectic of Violence and Literacy in Frederick Douglass's *Narrative* of 1845', in *Frederick Douglass: New Literary and Historical Essays*, ed. Eric J. Sundquist (Cambridge: Cambridge University Press, 1990), 148–65

Index